A BIOGRAPHY OF LONELINESS

A BIOGRAPHY OF LONELINESS

The History of an Emotion

Fay Bound Alberti

OXFORD UNIVERSITY PRESS

OXFORD
UNIVERSITY PRESS

Great Clarendon Street, Oxford, OX2 6DP,
United Kingdom

Oxford University Press is a department of the University of Oxford.
It furthers the University's objective of excellence in research, scholarship,
and education by publishing worldwide. Oxford is a registered trade mark of
Oxford University Press in the UK and in certain other countries

First Edition published in 2019

Impression: 1

Published in the United States of America by Oxford University Press
198 Madison Avenue, New York, NY 10016, United States of America

British Library Cataloguing in Publication Data
Data available

Library of Congress Control Number: 2019947207

ISBN 978–0–19–881134–3

Printed and bound in Great Britain by
Clays Ltd, Elcograf S.p.A.

For Millie Bound and Jacob George Alberti, as ever.
For Jenny Calcoen for being my soul sister.
And for Sandra Vigon, for holding up a light.

PREFACE

No (Wo)man Is an Island

Why loneliness? That's what people asked initially, when I told them I was writing this book. Well, not everyone. Those who hadn't lived with loneliness, hadn't felt its edges in the dark. Then in the space of a year, it didn't seem so strange a topic: loneliness became ubiquitous. It was talked of in newspapers and on radio programmes; it was a national epidemic; it had its own Minister. In the early twenty-first century we find ourselves in the midst of a 'loneliness epidemic', while worry about loneliness makes it more inevitable. Talking about loneliness seems to spread, contagion-like, until it has become part of the social fabric. Certainly, it has become a convenient hook on which to hang a number of discontents. Loneliness has become an emotional hold-all: a shorthand for the absence of happiness, for a sense of disconnect, for depression and alienation, for social isolation. Except when it isn't. Sometimes loneliness is sought out and desired; not just solitude, which has its own history, but also loneliness: that painful sense of disconnect which can be physical, emotional, symbolic, sensorial, attitudinal.

So what is loneliness, and why does it seem so ubiquitous? As a cultural historian who has spent a lot of time thinking about the emotional body, I am intrigued by how quickly a perceived yet undefined emotional state can give rise to such cultural panic.

And I am interested in how loneliness, like other emotional states—anger, love, fear, sadness—might take on different meanings depending on context; how loneliness can be physical as well as mental; and how loneliness as an individual experience might be shaped by and reflect bigger social concerns that include gender, ethnicity, age, environment, religion, science, and even economics.

Why economics? Loneliness is expensive, which is arguably why it has attracted so much governmental attention. The health and social care needs related to loneliness are escalating in the West, because of an ageing demographic. Notably the West: very little attention has been paid to the rest of the world, to how loneliness changes over time, or how it looks different in different lights. Presuming that loneliness is universal and part of the human condition means that nobody is accountable, no matter how much deprivation prevails. So, loneliness is political, too.

My interest was not purely historical. I have been lonely. And the different ways I have experienced loneliness—as a child, a teenager, a writer, a mother, a wife, a divorcée—whatever the badges we give to our life stages, this is what gave me the idea for the book's title. Loneliness has a biography. It is not a static 'thing' but a protean beast that changes over time. Historically, loneliness has emerged as a 'modern' emotion. And also as a concept which gets layered with meanings. *A Biography of Loneliness* is about the idea of loneliness in history, as well as the different ways it intersects with minds, bodies, objects, and places.

And places, as well as people, matter to the experience of loneliness. I grew up on an isolated Welsh hilltop. There was no internet in the 1980s. For most of my teenage years we had no telephone. The nearest neighbour was a mile away. My family experience was impoverished, unhappy, traumatic. Our Englishness set us apart from the Welsh-speaking villagers. We were hippies and most definitely Other. I was isolated and alone. And yet I did not endure loneliness; I enjoyed it. A natural introvert, I spent my days in the woods, making up stories, plotting alternative lives. My community was populated by fictional characters. Was it enough?

When I was a child, yes. Not when I was older. Our needs change with us. And so does our experience of loneliness. Loneliness in youth can become a habit in old age, so perhaps our interventions into elderly loneliness need to start far earlier. Loneliness—especially chronic loneliness, linked to deprivation—can be terrible. When disconnected, socially or emotionally, from others, people can get ill. Deprived of touch, of meaningful human engagement, people can die. Chronic loneliness is not choosy; it often settles on the shoulders of those who have suffered enough, with mental or physical health problems, with addiction, with abuse.

Transient loneliness, by contrast, the kind you slip in and out of on life's journey—moving away to university, changing jobs, getting divorced—can be a spur to personal growth, a way of figuring out what one wants in relationships with others. And what one does not want, for loneliness in a crowd, or with a disengaged other, is the worst kind of lack. Loneliness can be a life choice and a companion, rather than a shadow. Sometimes loneliness is positive and nurturing, providing a space for us to think and grow and learn. And I do not mean merely solitude, or the state of being alone, but a profound awareness of the boundaries of the self which can, in the right contexts, be restorative. Some people step into loneliness and out again, then, like it's little more than a puddle. For others, it's an ocean without end.

Does loneliness have a cure? Or rather, does unwanted loneliness have a cure? For there's the rub: the element of choice. And there is no quick-fix treatment, no one size fits all. Loneliness as a modern social affliction has grown up in the cracks, in the formation of a society that was less inclusive and communal and more grounded in the scientific, medicalized idea of an individual mind, set against the rest. Loneliness thrives when there is a disconnect between the individual and the world, a disconnect that is so characteristic of neoliberalism, but not an inevitable part of the human condition.

As the poet John Donne put it in 1624: 'Any man's death diminishes me/Because I am involved in mankind'. By being human, we are necessarily part of a force that is greater than ourselves. It is not inevitable that old people fear getting older because they are alone, that victims of violence are emotionally unsupported, that homeless people exist and are vulnerable. These systemic forms of enforced loneliness are the product of circumstance, and ideology. Yes, wealthy people can be (and often are) lonely and isolated, money being no guarantee of 'belonging'. But it's a different kind of loneliness to the social isolation imposed by poverty. Many of the divisions and hierarchies that have developed since the eighteenth century—between self and world, individual and community, public and private—have been naturalized through the politics and philosophy of individualism. Is it any coincidence that a language of loneliness emerged at the same time?

If loneliness is an epidemic, then stemming its spread depends on rooting out the conditions that allowed it to take hold. That is not the same as saying that all loneliness is bad, or that loneliness as a sense of lack didn't exist in the pre-modern world. The counter argument to claims of its modernity is: oh, but just because the language of loneliness didn't exist before 1800, that doesn't mean people didn't feel lonely. To that I say simply this: the invention of a language for loneliness reflects the framing of a new emotional state. Yes, solitude could be negative in earlier centuries, and people talked about being alone in a negative way. But the philosophical and spiritual framework was different. The universal belief in some kind of God in pre-modern Britain—usually a paternalistic deity, certainly providing a sense of place in the world—provided a framework for belonging that, for good or ill, no longer exists. A medieval monk, reclusive and alone yet inhabiting a mental universe in which God is ever-present, will not experience the same sense of abandonment and lack as a person without this narrative framework. We are suspended in universes of our making in the twenty-first century, in which the certainty of the self and one's uniqueness matters far more than any collective sense of belonging.

This book is not exhaustive. It is merely one biography. But it seeks to open up new ways of envisaging and exploring loneliness in the modern age, and to offer insights into its physical and psychological meanings. This duality—the separating off of the mind and the body—calls for the wider lens of a longue durée approach. My academic training was in early modern cultures, where there was no division of mind and body, where emotions (or passions) were regarded holistically. Yet today we regard loneliness as a mental affliction, though tending to the body remains just as important as tending to the mind.

I became obsessed, while writing this book, with the sheer physicality of loneliness, of how a sense of lack can make the belly feel so empty. I observed the effects of loneliness on my own body. Unable to think myself out of that embodied experience, I fed the senses: I splurged on heady-smelling soaps and scented candles, I listened to music and meditation on a loop, I petted dogs, smelled babies' necks, hugged my kids, lifted weights, walked tens of thousands of steps a day, chopped vegetables, cooked, slept. Tending to my own body reminded me of its physical rootedness, of the imagined communities of which I was part. There was comfort in tending to the body, in acknowledging emotional experience as far more than a product of the mind. And I was reminded that loneliness, like any emotional state, is physical as well as mental. After all, we are embodied beings whose worlds are defined not only in isolation but also through our belief systems and our relationships with others: objects, animals, people.

Which brings me to the people who have supported me not only during the writing of *A Biography of Loneliness*, but also while I was figuring out the next steps. Thanks to those who have given me strength in many different ways: Emma and Hugh Alberti, Jenny Calcoen, Nicola Chessner, Stef Eastoe, Patricia Greene, Jo Jenkins, Mark Jenner, Bridget McDermott, Paddy Ricard, Barbara Rosenwein, Barbara Taylor, and Sandra Vigon. Thank you to Javier Moscoso for inviting me to keynote at the European Philosophical Society for the History of Emotions in 2017, which allowed me to test out some of the ideas in this book. I am grateful to Sarah Nettleton for pointing me towards her materialities of care project at just the right moment, and to those people at the University of York, and York Hospital, who offered not only welcoming discussions, but also helpful insights into loneliness—especially Holly Speight, Sally Gordon, Lydia Harris, Bhavesh Patel, Yvonne Birks, Andrew Grace, Kate Pickett, Neil Wilson, and Karen Bloor. I have enjoyed being part of this community, as well as the UCL Loneliness and Social Isolation in Mental Health network, led by Sonia Johnson and Alexandra Pitman. Thank you to Kellie Payne of the Campaign to End Loneliness for inviting discussion, to Stephanie Cacioppo for sharing her research, and to Pamela Qualter for inviting me to participate in an ESRC Think Piece. Thanks to Millie Bound and Jacob Alberti for having such strong, emotional reactions to cover ideas (combined, thankfully, with an artistic eye). Finally, a sincere debt of thanks to Peter Stearns and the anonymous reviewers at *Emotion Review*, who offered insightful and generous advice when I was working out the transition between oneliness and loneliness.

FAY BOUND ALBERTI
London, 11 May 2018

CONTENTS

LIST OF ILLUSTRATIONS

Loneliness is neither good nor bad, but a point of intense and timeless awareness of the Self, a beginning which initiates totally new sensitivities and awarenesses, and which results in bringing a person deeply in touch with his own existence and in touch with others in a fundamental sense.

Clark Moustakas, *Loneliness*

You are born alone. You die alone. The value of the space in between is trust and love. That's why geometrically speaking the circle is a one. Everything comes to you from the other. You have to be able to reach the other. If not you are alone.

Louise Bourgeois, *Destruction of the Father*

INTRODUCTION

Loneliness as a 'Modern Epidemic'

Loneliness is the leprosy of the 21st century.

The Economist on Twitter, 2018

According to Beatles legend, Paul McCartney was the originator of 'Eleanor Rigby', which appeared on the band's *Revolver* album. It was McCartney's concern for elderly people since he was a child, it is said, that sparked the image of Eleanor Rigby as a 'lonely old spinster', picking up rice after the kind of wedding that she would never enjoy.[1] On a broader level, the song tapped in to a wave of social concern about contemporary society connected to social change in the 1960s UK and US. Amid anti-establishment sentiment, including the civil rights movement and protests over the Vietnam war, changing socio-economic structures and intensified urbanization meant that more people were living alone, and outside of traditional family units.[2] There was a growing problem of homelessness and poverty in the UK, with its attendant medical and social ills. By telling the story of 'Eleanor Rigby', the Beatles drew attention to a troubling and rising trend of loneliness as a modern affliction: 'all the lonely people—where do they all come from?'

Half a century later, loneliness has become an 'epidemic', devastating for public health, and the emotional equivalent of leprosy, according to *The Economist*. Like leprosy, it is implied, loneliness is contagious and debilitating. It is something to fear and avoid at all costs. It is also apparently universal. According to British medical journals like *The Lancet*, and even that old stalwart of traditional British values, *The Daily Mail*, the UK is experiencing an epidemic of loneliness.[3] Studies suggest somewhere between 30 and 50 per cent of those surveyed in Britain and North America feel lonely. In fact, Britain has been termed the 'loneliness capital of Europe'.[4] And that is before we consider the self-imposed political loneliness of Brexit. Children are lonely, teenagers are lonely; so are young mums, divorced people, old people, and bereaved people, just some of the social groups that are periodically singled out for particular concern by the British press.[5] We are arguably in the midst of a moral panic.

Amid this rise of concern about loneliness in the UK, the government announced the creation of a Minister for Loneliness in January 2018.[6] The post, which was taken by Tracey Crouch, was created to carry on the work of the Labour Party MP Jo Cox, tragically murdered by a far right sympathizer two years earlier.[7] By the end of the year, Crouch had resigned, citing a delay to betting reforms as the reason.[8] Despite publicity around the post, there was no reference to how it might intersect with the government's austerity targets, including the social care and welfare benefit cuts that created demographic inequalities in the experience of loneliness. A vocal representative of the Remain movement, Jo Cox had worked to support minorities and refugees experiencing social isolation and economic precarity. Her work continues in the Jo Cox Loneliness Commission.[9] Cox's murder took place in the run-up to the UK EU referendum, when the UK Independence Party (UKIP) was warning that a vote to stay in the European Union would result in 'swarms' of immigrants entering the UK. 'This is for Britain', her murderer said.[10]

Cox's murderer had a long history of mental health problems, loneliness, and isolation. Newspapers referred to him as 'a loner'; a term often given to those who commit acts of terror, who don't seem to fit in with neighbours or friends.[11] In this tragic situation, then, we have two different versions of loneliness: loneliness among people in need of social contact, as identified by Jo Cox, and loneliness as symptomatic of dangerous antisocial leanings: the 'loner'. This divergence is indicative of how little we really know about loneliness, its etymology, its meanings, how it intersects with solitude, how it might be experienced by different people, and—crucially—how it might have changed over time.

This *Biography of Loneliness* will explore the history and meanings of loneliness in its societal, psychological, socio-economic, and philosophical contexts. It considers the modern rise of loneliness as an epidemic and an emotional state, and the apparent explosion of loneliness since 'Eleanor Rigby' was written. What happened between 1966 and 2018 to propel loneliness to the forefront of popular and political consciousness? And how does modern loneliness relate to the past? Have we always been lonely? Why has loneliness become such a problem?

One response relates to the framing of loneliness. Fear about loneliness creates loneliness. Certainly, this outcome has been found among elderly people who are fearful of being alone and vulnerable as they age. Yet there have also been some profound social, economic, and political shifts that have taken place since the 1960s, and that have pushed loneliness to the fore of popular and governmental consciousness. These shifts include rising living costs, inflation, immigration, and changing familial social structures, as well as the *laissez-faire* (French, literally 'let do') politics of Margaret Thatcher in the 1980s and the gradual abandonment of the idea of society and community in pursuit of the individual. Neoliberalism has been blamed for many things, including a rejection of collective values and the pursuit—whatever the cost—of individual aggrandisement.[12]

Against this backdrop of socio-economic and political transformation, there is intense political interest in the financial cost of illness. Loneliness is perceived as a national and economic burden, because it gives rise to a wide range of emotional and physical illnesses. The illnesses linked to loneliness, with a variety of explanations as to the cause and the direction of travel, range from depression and anxiety to heart attacks, strokes, cancers, and decreased immune response.[13] Links between loneliness and poor mental and physical health have been particularly closely monitored in old age. The National Health Service (NHS) website suggests that lonely people are 30 per cent more likely to die earlier than less lonely people, with loneliness being a risk factor for heart problems, strokes, dementia, depression, and anxiety among the aged.[14]

It is understandable, in light of the above, that loneliness has been described as a modern 'epidemic'. But this terminology is politically and socially powerful. It leads to knee-jerk political soundbites rather than thoughtful, historically informed discussion about what loneliness might mean, and why it might be rising. Perhaps rather than viewing loneliness as inevitable, especially in old age, and focusing on scientific reasons for its physical effects (such as hormonal shifts in the body), we would do better to consider the links between loneliness and other lifestyle factors, ranging from comfort eating, obesity, and physical inactivity (an unholy trinity that is often correlated with loneliness), to practical concerns, like an isolated person not having a companion to remind them to take their heart medication. Loneliness does not happen in a vacuum but is deeply connected with all aspects of our mental, physical, and psychological health. Loneliness is a whole-body affliction, of that there is no doubt. But as this book shows, the story of loneliness is a complex one.

How should we define loneliness, this peculiar but oft-cited condition that has no opposite? A useful modern definition is stated by Professor Lars Andersson, from the Department of Social and Welfare Studies at Linköping University in Sweden, one of the most enlightened countries when it comes to investigating the health and social condition of the aged and most vulnerable in society. Andersson's definition of loneliness is 'an enduring condition of emotional distress that arises when a person feels estranged from, misunderstood, or rejected by others and/or lacks appropriate social partners for desired activities, particularly activities that provide a sense of social integration and opportunities for emotional intimacy'.[15] Loneliness is not the state of being alone, then, though it is often mistaken as such. It is a conscious, cognitive feeling of estrangement or social separation from meaningful others; an emotional lack that concerns a person's place in the world.

Loneliness is entirely subjective. It has been measured, apparently objectively, in relation to personal statements, by use of the UCLA Loneliness Scale. This questionnaire asks individuals to describe their feelings of loneliness according to a sliding scale between 'never' and 'often'. It has been criticized for being worded negatively and has been revised several times. It has also been altered to help assess loneliness in the elderly.[16] Attempts to capture loneliness *as* a subjective experience are necessarily problematic, partly because loneliness is shrouded in shame in the West, for reasons that relate to historical connections between loneliness and personal failing. The interventions recommended tend to include increased contact with other people, without necessarily considering the difference between social contact and *meaningful* social contact, or the limitations that can be placed upon someone who wants to interact with others but is unable to due to health challenges, or personality traits like shyness.

Another reason why loneliness is difficult to capture subjectively and objectively is that it is not a single emotional state. In this book, I describe loneliness as an emotion 'cluster', a blend of different emotions that might range from anger, resentment, and sorrow to jealousy, shame, and self-pity. The composition of loneliness varies according to the perception and experience of the individual, their circumstances and environment. Conflicting emotions can be felt at the same time, and loneliness can change over time depending on a range of cultural factors, expectations, and desires.

Describing loneliness in this way helps to traverse the complex, often contradictory history of emotion concepts. It also helps to explain why the history of loneliness is entirely missing in the rapidly expanding field of emotion history. Its history is crucial in understanding what loneliness is today, as well as how it has emerged in different places, times, and cultures. And it's crucial if we want loneliness to be less prevalent. What happens when we essentialize loneliness *as* a human universal, along with other emotions, is that we disregard significant beliefs that help shape emotional experience—these include the relationship of the individual to others, to God, the relevance of human agency and desires, and the societal expectations in which individual experience takes place. Loneliness becomes a hazard of being human, rather than a fundamental disconnect between the individual and the social structures and expectations through which she or he lives and engages with the world.

I was drawn to study the history of loneliness when I was working on facial disfigurement and face transplants. I realized how common social isolation and loneliness were to the experience of physical difference and disability, and yet how difficult it was to access: there have not been histories of loneliness in the same way that there have been histories of love, anger, or fear. There have been studies of living alone and changes in socio-economic structures that suggest growing loneliness as a result of the shift from collective, face-to-face agrarian communities to urbanized, anonymized ones.[17] There have been important studies of solitude in relation to religion, focusing for instance on monasticism and the ideal of solitude as a means of being closer to God.[18] More recently, the writer Olivia Laing has explored the differences between solitude and loneliness, identifying the creative and positive aspects of both, and the tendency in the modern West to elide the two quite different states.[19]

So, why hasn't loneliness featured in the history of emotions? One reason is language. Another is the historical construction of emotion categories. Loneliness does not feature in the 'big six' list of emotions that are still regarded popularly as basic emotions, and that tend to be linked to facial expressions. Those emotions, seen in the work of the American psychologist Paul Ekman, are: disgust, sadness, happiness, fear, anger, and surprise.[20] Other scholars have argued that there are eight basic emotions that form polar opposites: joy–sadness; anger–fear; trust–distrust; surprise–anticipation.[21]

Since the 1990s, more nuanced approaches to emotion have criticized this biologically reductionist model, including from the discipline of history.[22] These approaches recognize that rather than being universal, emotions are developed within complex power relations, and through the lenses of historically specific disciplines.[23] Indeed, recent work within one of those disciplines, neuroscience, suggests that the very notion of individually boundaried emotions, like 'anger, or sadness, or fear', is incorrect.[24]

We do not have to view emotions as 'natural kinds', to use Barrett's (2017) phrase, to distinguish between socially recognizable forms of emotion as an event (an angry outburst, or a sad event) and a feeling state that mutates and shifts and has been difficult to pin down. Loneliness is not alone in being such a state—other states (or concepts) like 'nostalgia' and 'pity' have been similarly neglected. Interestingly, ancient theorists were more nuanced than many modern writers. Aristotle, for instance, did not describe emotions purely as single states, but as 'feelings accompanied by pleasure or pain' that might include not only 'anger, fear, joy and love' but also 'confidence, hatred, longing, emulation and pity'.[25] Classical ideas about emotion were more expansive than those we use today. Influenced by humoral philosophy, they were also based on viewing the mind and body differently than we do today.[26]

Given the complexity of the subject, I contend that we need a better understanding of what loneliness is as both historical concept and experience, as well as how it affects different people (differently) during their lifespan. We need to read loneliness, like obesity, as a perceived 'disease of civilization', a condition that is chronic, pathological, and associated with the way we live in the modern, industrial West.[27] Certainly, there are many parallels between loneliness and obesity. Both are seen to put excessive demands on the health services, both are linked to mental and physical illnesses, and both are associated with an inability of the individual to conform to prevailing social expectations. In both 'conditions', moreover, the person is pathologically locked within their own boundaries—in the body in the case of morbid obesity, and the mind in the case of loneliness.

A Biography of Loneliness

Have people always been lonely? Is loneliness a state that can afflict us all, regardless of our time in place and history? I don't believe so, though that claim for universalism is, well, universal. 'Man's inevitable and infinite loneliness is not solely an awful condition of human existence', wrote the American psychologist Clark Moustakas, in a 1960s treatise born from personal experience, 'it is also the instrument through which man experiences new compassion and new beauty'.[28] This statement is more complex than it might at first appear. On the one hand, it argues that loneliness is an integral part of the human condition, which this book refutes. On the other, it acknowledges that loneliness can be positive as well as negative; that it can give rise to previously unexplored depths of emotional experience, a subject that is explored in this book.

Viewing loneliness in the West through a wide historical lens, *A Biography of Loneliness* argues that loneliness in its modern sense emerged as both a term and a recognizable experience around 1800, soon after ideas about sociability, and secularism, became important to the social and political fabric. It was reinforced by the emergence of an all-encompassing ideology of the individual: in the mind and physical sciences, in economic structures, in philosophy and politics. The evolution of language provides clues to the gradual development of loneliness since the birth of modernity. This process involved many different influences, from the decline of religion to the industrial revolution, of which neoliberalism is just the latest, toxic iteration.[29] Each of the chapters contained here point not only to the complexities of loneliness as an experience, but also its links to relationships between the individual and society and the connections between emotional and physical need.

Since loneliness is an emotion cluster that mutates across an individual's lifespan, especially in the 'pinch-points' that are personally defining, it needs to be studied at particular moments. *A Biography of Loneliness* examines loneliness not only in relation to its historical emergence, but also how loneliness might impact people according to life stage. For some chronically lonely individuals, loneliness takes hold in childhood and adolescence, as it did for the American writer Sylvia Plath. For Plath, an unending loneliness seems to have accompanied her in an emotionally uncertain childhood through an allegedly abusive marriage, alongside chronic mental health problems that resulted in suicide. Crucially, loneliness forged in childhood and adolescence seems to set a pattern for loneliness in later life, which is a subject that requires much more investigation.[30] Loneliness in the young is no less a problem than loneliness in the aged, but it will necessarily manifest itself differently according to expectations, abilities, and environment.

In the twenty-first century, discussions of young people and loneliness tend to focus on digital culture and social media. Loneliness was undoubtedly a problem for the youth in Victorian Britain, as for Charles Dickens' orphans. Yet the image of the lonely adolescent has ramped up since the onset of the digital revolution. There is a lack of clarity in health and policy research about the implications of this form of technology across the lifespan and in relation to a broader pattern of digital emotions. For elderly people in the UK, for instance, there has been discussion of 'pet robots' to offer companionship when the human touch is missing. In other cultures, notably Japan, sex robots have been available for some time to assuage the loneliness of isolated men, though the market is expanding.[31]

Patterns of social engagement among British millennials in particular have been altered by the diffusion of social media.[32] New apps and platforms are constantly being developed, and it is difficult for parents to keep up, let alone stay on top of threats and benefits. Parents are not alone in this; around the globe, social and legal infrastructure is playing catch-up to a form of knowledge creation, exchange, and dissemination that has no established rules and does not follow traditional values and conventions. Young and old people alike are struggling to engage with and use digital media in ways that are consistent with the presentation of the self in everyday life; the difference is that digital selves may be multiple and conflicting, and the satisfaction derived from them not necessarily sustainable or as fulfilling as that acquired in real-life situations.

One key reason why loneliness has become such a problem in the twenty-first century is the way it connects to broader social, economic, and political crises. Concern about loneliness among the aged, for instance, is a manifestation of broader concerns about an ageing population in the West, and considerable anxiety over how that population will be supported in an individualistic age when families are often dispersed. Most policy interventions are focused on the aged because of the significant impact of elderly loneliness on social and medical care. Particularly vulnerable are society's 'oldest old': over eighty years old and living alone.

The theme of living alone is an important one. There is a difference between solitude and loneliness. Yet wanting a special someone and not finding them can be a lonely process, for all ages.[33] The language and history of the romantic ideal are important here, for an inability to find 'the one' can generate loneliness through a sense of lack. The trope of a 'soulmate' in Western culture emerged in the Romantic period and is associated with tremendous emotional struggle and the need of separation from the rest of society—as in the Byronic hero motif.

Older people crave soulmates through the Internet,[34] just as much as the young, though this image is considered less attractive to readers. The sexuality of old people is a decidedly niche market that is seldom considered in health and policy terms.[35] The loneliness of loss is another significant life stage confronted by older people. Widow(er)hood or the death of a loved one creates a loneliness that sets one emotionally apart, and physically if one is socially isolated. This kind of loneliness is also a great leveller of experience; there is a depth of social and familial isolation linked to widow(er)hood, whether one is princess or pauper.

Nostalgia for what is lost is central to the loneliness of widow(er) hood. Nostalgia as an emotional state shares many characteristics of, and can influence, loneliness. So, too, can homesickness, which compounds a sense of not belonging, which is so key to the perception of loneliness.[36] The lack of belonging is most profound in those who are homeless and refugees, who have no place to call home. There is a particular kind of loneliness found among the 'roofless and rootless', whose homeless or refugee status brings in feelings of isolation linked to the symbolism of home, food, and the tokens of domesticity. Yet homeless people are among the most socially and politically neglected when it comes to understanding loneliness. Ethnicity provides another important variable, and again there has been insufficient research into the connecting variables of ethnicity, poverty, and loneliness.[37] Nor has there been much research into the enforced impact of social exclusion through homophobia or prejudice against those leading traditionally unconventional lives.[38]

Class and gender differences are important in the experience of loneliness, and I have tried to articulate that throughout this book. Men tend to have higher loneliness scores than women; arguably because of single-sex or homosocial socializing and the fact that women are typically encouraged to talk about their feelings.[39] Yet these statistics will be influenced by class, gender, sex identity, and other variables. The highest levels of loneliness seem to be found among the poorest groups in society, reflecting an increased breakdown in support networks in proportion to the levels of deprivation experienced.[40] For every stereotypical image of a hermit-like Howard Hughes, there are ten thousand impoverished lonely people whose suffering is similarly invisible.

Embodied Loneliness

Loneliness, as I have outlined above, is about the body as much as the mind. That is a theme that will be taken up extensively in this book, through a consideration of the bodily and material cultures of loneliness. We tend, in the West, to regard loneliness as a mental affliction and to offer remedies that engage the mind—talking therapies, book groups, interventions based on combatting depression and anxiety through connectedness to others. Yet that connectedness needs to be more than rational. This focus says more about the history of the mind and body in scientific medicine than it does about the lived experience of loneliness.[41] The physicality of loneliness was tended to from the time of the ancients to the eighteenth century. Today it is largely ignored, and yet loneliness is manifest in the language of the body—through the metaphors of 'cold' people that are indifferent or 'warm' people who offer companionship, as well as the hot baths and warm clothes that are instinctively used by those who feel most lonely. The physicality of loneliness and connectedness is also apparent in the ways we structure our material worlds, finding in objects a way to communicate emotions as well as to avoid loneliness. Excessive materialism, however, makes people lonelier, creating a wider sense of lack.

Loneliness is not always bad. Indeed, there is an extensive literature on the luxury of solitude as well as loneliness, especially when linked to creativity and art. As the work of artists like William Wordsworth, Virginia Woolf, and May Sarton show, loneliness can be a gift as well as a burden. Does this recognition help in the management of loneliness in the twenty-first century? Is there a way to create great art without being lonely? And does the joy of loneliness have relevance to those who have little and who do not produce great works of art?

My hope in writing this book is to help shape answers to these and related questions. And to open up the topic of loneliness more generally as a complex and historically situated emotional state. I hope, also, to encourage more comparative analysis across history, anthropology, and geography. *A Biography of Loneliness* focuses on the West in general and in the UK in particular; different responses and experiences of loneliness might be indicated in cultures that do not prioritize so highly the status of the individual. There are hints that societies which are collectivist may actually report *more* loneliness than individualistic societies, though it is unclear whether this simply reflects more ease in discussing loneliness; it might be less shameful in countries that recognize the value of the collective. There might also be a comparison between familial and friendship lack. Loneliness in collectivist cultures, for instance, has been associated with a lack of family support, whereas loneliness in individualistic cultures speaks to a lack of extra-familial connection.[42] This raises the broader question of whether 'loneliness' means the same thing in collectivist cultures as it does in individualistic communities. To give just one example, 'lonely' in Arabic translates as *wahid*, which means 'one' or 'single' in English. This provides an interesting spin on my claim that loneliness emerged in the UK as a result of greater focus on the individual. 'Family' in the Arab world means more than the individual; connectedness between people is central to a common and individual identity.[43]

It may be that the embeddedness of the individual in those social contexts means that that the language of loneliness does not exist, as was the case in eighteenth-century Britain. But it is impossible to make authoritative claims about loneliness in the Arab world based on the lack of evidence (and I am wary of the implied presumption that the Arab world is therefore less 'developed' than the West, which is far from what I am saying). Most health, policy, and social science work focuses on those industrialized areas where loneliness has been identified as a problem, including North-West Europe and North America. The research samples often tend to be homogenous, so that it is difficult to address cultural diversity; there is a lack of comparative work even into diverse communities within the UK.[44] There are clearly some crucial connections needed among diverse but rapidly changing cultures.

First, though, I want to turn to the history of loneliness in Britain, and the specific claim that is being made in this book: that modern loneliness is a product of the nineteenth century, of an increasingly scientific, philosophical, and industrial focus on the individual over the collective, on the self against the world. In this, there is only one question that matters. How did the unemotional, physical state of being alone, conceived for centuries simply as 'oneliness', become transformed into a modern, pathologized epidemic?

CHAPTER 1

WHEN 'ONELINESS' BECAME LONELINESS

The birth of a modern emotion

The history of loneliness is fundamental to understanding its prevalence and meanings in the twenty-first century. And yet that history has been virtually neglected. Of course, there have been books about loneliness—as well as programmes on the radio and television and self-help guides—that lament its rise as a twenty-first-century challenge to health and wellbeing, and panic about loneliness as a modern 'epidemic'. But what of its history, its meanings, and its longevity? What can we learn about the way loneliness has evolved over time, or its British context?

'Loneliness' is a relatively modern phenomenon, both as a word, and perhaps more controversially, as an experience. Let us begin with language. To some degree, language is a challenge in the history of emotion, for there is always a lack of clarity in how feelings of emotion (the quickened heartbeat when spying a loved one) can be articulated through an available and appropriate emotion register (in this case, desire), and its expression, which can be verbal, textual, bodily, or material.[1] Some emotional traces are more recoverable than others; a plaintive love letter lasts longer than a handkerchief wet with tears. There is often a space, too, between an emotional experience and the act of talking about that experience—as a result of shame, self-denial, or lack of self-awareness. Recorders of the past, including diarists, are not transparent, but tend to write for a future audience, real or imagined, and shape their stories accordingly.[2]

Even if we uncover the traces of emotions in the past, then, they may be expressed in ways that are unfamiliar to us. The exchange of furniture or household objects has been read in the past as indicative of a utilitarian approach to marriage formation, for instance, rather than the expression of profound feelings of love and commitment.[3] Loneliness is no exception to the changeability of emotional language. Yet I am nevertheless staking a claim that loneliness in its current manifestation is a recent phenomenon, at least in the UK and arguably in the post-industrial West.

The Invention of Lonelivness

There was little mention of 'loneliness' in published texts in English prior to the end of the eighteenth century. Indeed, its appearance is almost negligible. Yet from around 1800, the term began to be used with increasing frequency, rising to a peak at the end of the twentieth century (see Appendix, Figure 10).

The meanings of loneliness also changed. In the sixteenth and seventeenth centuries, loneliness did not have the ideological and psychological weight that it does today. Loneliness meant simply 'oneliness', which was less a psychological or emotional experience than a physical one. Deriving from the term 'lonely', oneliness meant simply the condition of being alone. Oneliness was often contextualized as a religious experience, for it allowed communion with an ever-present God.

In 1656, Thomas Blount, an antiquarian and lexicographer, published his *Glossographia; or, a dictionary interpreting the hard words of whatsoever language, now used in our refined English tongue*. The book went through several editions and was the largest of the early dictionaries. In the 1661 edition, Blount described loneliness as 'an [*sic*] *one*; an oneliness, or loneliness, a single or singleness'. The English lexicographer and stenographer Elisha Coles published his own *English Dictionary* in 1676. In it, he defined 'loneliness' as 'solitude' or 'wandering alone', with none of its modern, negative emotional connotations.

Although loneliness features little in printed texts prior to the 1800s, the term 'lonely' does. Again, however, it is less a description of an emotional state than an indicator of the physical state of being alone. This is fundamentally important in critiquing the universal, inevitable nature of loneliness in the present day. And it also challenges the idea that 'lonely' in the past meant the same as it does in the present. Such ideas are problematic because they imply that emotions are static and unchanging over time. Yet they are commonplace in Shakespeare studies, for instance, and in accounts of Hamlet's soliloquies that are presumed to show the eternal effects of human isolation.[4]

If we move beyond usage to etymology, The *Oxford English Dictionary* gives two definitions of lonely, a word that itself originated as late as the sixteenth century. These include: '1. Sad because one has no friends or company. Without companions; solitary... 2. (of a place) unfrequented and remote'. Only the *second* of these meanings—a place 'unfrequented and remote'—was used frequently before around 1800. Accounts of being lonely prior to this are filled with religious revelations and moral accounts of human folly, as well as physical descriptions of isolated places where remarkable events occurred. For example, the use of loneliness in the Bible typically denotes the physical separation of the Messiah from others, as Jesus 'withdrew to lonely places and prayed' (Luke 5:16). Even Samuel Johnson's *A Dictionary of the English Language* (1755) described the adjective 'lonely' purely in terms of the state of being alone (the 'lonely fox'), or a deserted place ('lonely rocks'). The term did not necessarily carry any emotional import.

The Importance of Solitude

The deliberate act of choosing to be lonely—as in being physically alone—might be to commune with God, in the early modern period, and increasingly by the eighteenth century, with nature. There is an extensive body of literature linked to the discovery of new lands, and the 'primitive', in which solitude is inherent, but not necessarily problematized. Indeed, in Daniel Defoe's *The Life and Adventures of Robinson Crusoe* (1719), the story of a shipwrecked man who spent twenty-eight years alone on a remote tropical island, loneliness does not feature, and not only because Crusoe forms a master/slave relationship with Friday. There is not a single reference to the main protagonist feeling 'lonely' or experiencing 'loneliness' in the novel. Crusoe is alone, but he never defines himself as lonely, a phenomenon or experience incomprehensible to modern readers.

Consider, by contrast, the Twentieth-Century Fox drama *Castaway* (Zemeckis 2000), which borrows from *Robinson Crusoe*, and concerns a FedEx employee Chuck (Tom Hanks) being stranded on a desert island. Since he has nobody to talk to, Chuck marks a face on a volleyball and calls the ball 'Wilson'. (Wilson is an American sporting equipment manufacturer, and the company now sells the replica balls on its website.) For modern viewers, this plot development makes far more sense: it connects to some innate human need for companionship and the belief that isolation has a devastating impact on one's mental health.[5]

In Defoe's time, however, solitude was not necessarily problematic. Let us turn again to Johnson's *Dictionary*, which also defined 'solitude' as meaning a 'lonely life; state of being alone'.[6] Solitude had a similar and sporadic pattern of incidence to 'lonely' between 1550 and 1800. Solitude has fallen out of favour as a term in the twenty-first century but was once widely used. The term 'solitude' comes from the Latin *solitudo*, and means simply: '1. the state or situation of being alone' and '2. a lonely or uninhabited place'. As with 'lonely', there was no emotional experience necessarily attached to solitude; both referred merely to the physical experience of 'oneliness' (see Appendix, Figures 11 and 12).

The term 'solitude' was used less in printed works from the mid-nineteenth century. I believe that this decline corresponds with the increasing use of 'loneliness' as a shorthand for both the state of being alone and the experience of being lonely. Thus, the use of 'solitude' dipped at the same time the language of loneliness and being lonely became more common. Now, because loneliness and being lonely were not discussed prior to the late eighteenth century, these terms do not appear in the medical literature. The present-day pathologization of 'loneliness' as a mental and physical affliction was non-existent. What medical writers and others *did* talk about before the late eighteenth century was solitude, which had a number of negative and positive connotations.

Like loneliness, solitude has a neglected history. Yet it is also an important aspect of the history of emotion. Again, solitude did not necessarily invoke any negative emotional response. Rather, solitude could be enjoyed and savoured. The historian Barbara Taylor has written of the enjoyment of solitude by the Genevan philosopher Jean-Jacques Rousseau and the English philosopher and writer Mary Wollstonecraft, especially when linked to eighteenth-century passions of nature and the natural world. The 'retreat' to nature as a means to find individual happiness links to the psychological root of pastoral literature, and to deistic ideas of God-in-nature.[7]

Solitude was not incompatible with sociability, then, as it could be mentally and physically invigorating, and enable the individual to fare better in society. In *The Pleasures of Solitude*, P.L. Courtier justifies its value, not as the desire of a 'surly misanthrope', but rather to 'escape the throng's turmoil, To breathe the cooling freshness of the grove!... For, all we fondly cherish, dearly prize, All that the fancy or the heart can move; full oft the busy scene of life denies'. Similarly, in J.G. Zimmerman and J.B. Mercier's *Solitude Considered, in Regard to its Influence upon the Mind and the Heart*, the authors claimed that:

> The rudiments of a great character can only be formed in Solitude. It is there alone that the solidity of thought, the fondness for activity, the abhorrence of indolence, which constitute the characters of a HERO and a SAGE are first acquired.

This reinforcement of the value of solitude is reminiscent of the ancient hermit ideal, with isolation as a spiritual path.[8] Oneliness in the presence of God could be, for the deliberately isolated (as for Christ in the wilderness), a subject of intense creative and spiritual

Figure 1. 'John Bigg, an eccentric hermit'. Line engraving by Wilkes.

reflection. For the creative, too, there has always been a power in solitude, which seems to echo and reflect that connection to a higher spiritual power.[9] Of course, hermits might also reject society for non-religious reasons. One example is John Bigg, the 'Dinton Hermit' (1629–96) (Figure 1).

Once clerk to Simon Mayne, one of the judges responsible for sentencing King Charles I to death in 1649, Bigg withdrew from society at the Restoration, when Mayne was executed as a Regicide. The reasons for his social withdrawal are unclear; some claimed it was remorse at his hand in the King's death; others that he feared retribution. Living in a cave, he became dependent on the charity of others, begging for food and asking for strips of leather, which he attached to his clothes.[10]

Solitude, Gender, and Class

Choosing to be alone for artistic purposes, by contrast, was an educated middle-class activity, requiring physical space as well as time away from economic activities. It was also traditionally white, male, and privileged; the same conventions have not been applied to black writers and women have long been identified through family structures rather than in terms of their own individual accomplishments.

All emotional states and representations are gendered, now as in the past. One of the important aspects of that gendering is how social performances of an emotion served to justify and uphold traditional social relationships. In the sixteenth century, women's tears proved that women were wetter than men; that they lacked the heat of men's bodies. In the nineteenth century, those tears marked women's femininity and lack of suitability for public life, meaning that they were deemed inferior in a whole different (but nonetheless influential) way.[11]

The lonely woman is a similarly recurring trope in literature that reflects the passivity expected of women, especially middle-class women from the late eighteenth century onwards, whose place was increasingly restricted to the home. In early modern literature the lone woman—usually an ungoverned spinster or widow—plays a different and subversive figure as she moves between the private and public spheres and threatens the patriarchal order. Solitary women, then, could be a threat.[12]

There were gendered roles for men too, linked to solitude. One convention was that men, through reasons of religiosity or intellect, spent their days in isolation as either hermits or scholars. Indeed, Rousseau gladly took up that self-description when he went in search of solitude.[13] Women *could* be alone for religious reasons, and later for creative reasons, but in Western literature, they were far more likely to have solitude imposed upon them, a common literary trope including the abandonment or neglect of a lover. Forbearance and patience became a woman's lot, which was rather different from the self-imposed ideal of solitude, and a caricature of the female part became that of the imaginary sister of Viola in *Twelfth Night*: 'She pined in thought/And with a green and yellow melancholy/She sat like patience on a monument/ Smiling at grief. Was not this love indeed?' (Shakespeare, *Twelfth Night*, 2, 4, 110–13). The 'abandoned woman' was in some ways then the poetic counterpart of the 'solitary man', and part of a much longer literary tradition that found its way into personal letters and correspondence in the seventeenth century and beyond.[14]

Solitude and Health

Excessive solitude could be potentially damaging to health—as indicated by the 'green and yellow melancholy', which simultaneously invoked the lovesickness of an abandoned virgin. Solitude was particularly problematic when it was imposed from the outside rather than sought from within. And in the pre-modern, humoral tradition which dominated Western medicine from the second to the late eighteenth centuries, solitude could impact on the balance of one's psychological and physical health.

Good health concerned the internal balance of the four humours, and an imbalance in the fluids of the body, brought about by the passions or the 'non-naturals' or the habits of the body, which included sleep and movement, food and drink, and bodily excretions, produced a variety of mental and physical ailments, from depression to obesity.[15] Too little solitude, like too much exercise, could deplete the spirits; too much made them sluggish and prone to melancholia. This is why excessive solitude in the 1700s was linked by medical writers to mental afflictions, worry, and self-doubt.

In Robert Burton's *Anatomy of Melancholy* (1621), the Oxford cleric enumerated all the different causes of melancholia and depression, from which he had long suffered. There is no reference to 'loneliness' or even 'solitude' in the book, but there are multiple references to the state of being 'alone', which often led him to over-thinking. Scholars were thought to be particularly prone to melancholia through excess rumination in humoral medicine, and Burton acknowledged this in his introductory 'Abstract of Melancholy':

When I go musing all alone
Thinking of divers things fore-known.
When I build castles in the air,
Void of sorrow and void of fear,
Pleasing myself with phantasms sweet,
Methinks the time runs very fleet.
All my joys to this are folly,
Naught so sweet as melancholy...
When I lie waking all alone,
Recounting what I have ill done,
My thoughts on me then tyrannise,
Fear and sorrow me surprise,
Whether I tarry still or go,
Methinks the time moves very slow.
All my griefs to this are jolly,
Naught so mad as melancholy...
Friends and companions get you gone,
'Tis my desire to be alone;
Ne'er well but when my thoughts and I
Do domineer in privacy.[16]

The letters of consultation by the eighteenth-century Scottish physician William Cullen similarly provide a wealth of information about the impact of loneliness on interpersonal relationships, as well as health.[17] It was not uncommon by the eighteenth century for men and women with sufficient recourse to money, literacy, and status to write to physicians to discuss their health concerns and to pursue healing.[18] Mental and physical health was still a collaborative exercise between physicians and their patients, with the latter picking up ideas from conversations with others and advice manuals like William Buchan's *Domestic Medicine*, which went through at least eighty editions.[19] Patients and physicians drew on a shared understanding about the role of the humours in generating ill health as well as, by the eighteenth century, the nerves. Although it was the physical structures of the body (its nerves and fibres) that became the source of illness, rather than the humours, 'nervous debility' told the same story: too much time alone had a negative physical and emotional impact.

In a letter regarding one Mrs Rae (1779), for instance, Cullen suggested that his patient suffered from 'nervous weakness, often tedious but never dangerous'. He recommended exercise—specifically horse riding—in order to physically invigorate her fibres and spirits. In this context, Rousseau's and Wollstonecraft's brisk walks in pursuit of solitude ironically became the very means through which its negative excesses could be avoided.[20] In Cullen's view, tea and coffee were to be avoided as they were stimulants, but it was most important that Mrs Rae's mind be occupied. As Cullen explained, 'her mind requires as much attention as her body. However averse she should see her friends both at home & abroad, every amusement & easy occupation are to be sought for while Silence & Solitude are to be avoided'. Mrs Allan, a 'hysteric melancholic', was similarly urged to seek companionship and engage in conversation (1777), though Cullen 'never knew reasoning' to have much effect with hysterical women.[21]

In the nineteenth century, Western medicine found new ways of classifying mental and physical health and developed a series of specialisms around emotional and psychological wellbeing on the one hand, and physical organs, systems, and parts on the other. What is profoundly different in modern medical, as opposed to humoral, interpretations of solitude, moreover, is that its positive characteristics are usually absent. We are so committed to the ideal of sociability as a model for mental health that we do not always tend to the positive aspects of being alone, nor to its impact on the body as well as the mind. Yet the benefits of loneliness (*Einsamkeit*) were stressed in German philosophy and literature until as late as 1945.[22] Reminiscent of the pursuit of solitude in earlier centuries, the term relates to the voluntary withdrawal from life's hectic progress, so that individuals could reflect, meditate, and commune with God or a higher creative force.

It may well be that solitude was considered more problematic in physiology and medicine in the latter part of the eighteenth century, corresponding to a philosophical and political context in which sociability—in some ways the antonym of solitude—was increasingly important in learned British culture. The literary critic and English professor John Mullan has explored the ways in which the rise of the novel from the mid-eighteenth century was entangled with the rise of a particular kind of 'public sphere' sentimentalism, and the emergence of literary sensitivity and empathy as part of the development of civil society.[23] In some ways, this is reminiscent of the historian William Reddy's claims about the emergence of a particular kind of 'affect' in French post-Revolutionary society, in which one form of emotional regime was replaced by another.[24] Performing sociability through public gatherings and collective participation in some kind of shared consensus of value was one of the ways through which civil society was manifested and reinforced. And this meant a prevalence of emotional language linked to gender, empathy, and moral and ethical responsibility towards others.[25]

Sociability was linked to politeness, and to attentiveness to form, worldliness, and gentility. These characteristics of polite eighteenth-century society also concerned symbolic, bodily, gestural, and verbal display codes through which sociability could be enacted.[26] In the *Spectator*, a daily publication founded by Joseph

Addison and Richard Steele, philosophy and manners were taught to aspiring middle-class men and women, with accounts by such characters as Sir Roger de Coverley reminding readers of the 'benevolence' that, in an ideal state, 'flows out towards everyone' one meets.[27] Such sentiment was expressed in stoic philosophy, which emphasized the value of 'sensus communus' (the idea that common sense connected the individual and society), and by poets like Alexander Pope, for whom 'Self-love and Social be the Same'.[28]

To a great extent, these philosophical imperatives were realized in the metaphors of the physical body. The emotions that forged connections between people were echoed in the nerves and fibres that symbolically linked one person to another, and to the body of the state, or the body politic.[29] I would suggest that this meta-narrative of change in which sociability and connections were fundamentally important to the social fabric might help to explain why it was that solitude became more frequently referenced in publications between 1750 and 1850, whether as an antagonistic force to the production of civil, sociable society, or as a personal quest for peace in a hectic world. The latter perspective, in which the search for the individual was an absolute necessity in the mechanized industrial age, became central to the work of the Romantic poets, who privileged solitary wandering in pursuit of literary and emotional fulfilment.[30]

The Making of Modern Loneliness

How has loneliness, as a distinct emotion cluster, taken over from solitude and oneliness as a symbol of social separateness and a sign of social disconnect? What are the pathways by which loneliness became so ubiquitous as a social and emotional condition and a modern-day 'problem'? Demographic historians explain this as a result of structural change; loneliness becomes a direct and inevitable consequence of late modernity, when a large proportion of the world live in highly developed, globalized, secular societies. Historian Keith Snell argues that the most significant historical cause of loneliness is living alone, which often stems from bereavement.[31] Sole living was also caused by the transition from a traditionally agrarian, face-to-face society (in which multiple generations lived within the same household, social mobility was low, and few people moved outside the boundaries of their village) to an urban, socially mobile workforce, in which new, independent households were created.[32]

Social and demographic shifts certainly played a factor. But they are not the only explanation. Loneliness is not an inevitable correlation of space. The writer Olivia Laing's much-acclaimed book *The Lonely City* similarly identifies single dwelling as exacerbating loneliness.[33] Yet she also notes how being with other people in a shared physical space is not the same as being together in a shared *emotional* space. The idea that environmental changes necessarily brought emotional changes presumes an unchanging picture of the self and emotion. So, we have to ask: what other factors were at play?

The emergence of 'loneliness' as a coherent emotional state was a product of demographic change and urbanization *accompanied by* a number of other significant factors in creating an increasingly individualized, secular, and potentially alienated existence. These factors include modern scientific beliefs about the body and the mind and the decline of the soul as a source of explanation. After the early neurological work of the French philosopher René Descartes (best known for his dictum: 'I think therefore I am'), it became possible to view the human body as an automaton, and physical movement, including the heartbeat, as reflecting physiological impulse, rather than a spiritual presence. Mind and body were separable states and the body was under the control of the mind (*qua* brain).

Following these scientific and spiritual changes were mass industrialization and urbanization, with traditional domestic manufacture being replaced by factory-scale piecework. Underpinning economic and social change was the work of Charles Darwin and the rise of evolutionary biology, which was manifested and communicated through a range of fictional plots and social metaphors.[34] The philosophy of the individual predominated; the individual was more important than, and opposed to, society.

Little wonder then that Victorian novels were full of lonely characters, in search of psychological growth and freedom while pitted against a hostile and uncaring world. Yes, there are many lone figures in the world's literature, from the exile of Rama in the ancient Indian epic poem *Ramayana*, through the seventeenth-century French abduction tales of Mademoiselle de Scudéry.[35] And at the heart of many of these stories is the individual pitted against society, or on some transformative quest. But what is characteristic of the depiction of aloneness, and subsequently loneliness in the nineteenth-century novel, is a growing emphasis on psychological realism since the publication of Samuel Richardson's *Pamela; or, Virtue Rewarded* in 1740, a backdrop of industrialization (with its accompanying social imagery and metaphors), and a growing public/private divide, which required women to receive emotional satisfaction and companionship from the domestic sphere.[36]

With an expansion of bourgeois literary forms from the eighteenth century, aimed at a readership with significant levels of leisure and literacy, and well versed in the literary tropes of romance and individualism, loneliness began to be used in novels and poems to mark not only the battle for belonging on the part of the protagonist, but also the absence of this emotional satisfaction. In many cases the lack of social acceptance and the desirability of a romantic mate are blended, as in I.D. Hardy's *Love, Honour and Obey* (1881):

> Zeb is standing by the companion-way, *looking on at the sociable groups around, and feeling rather lonely*, when a gentleman—the same whose attention had been attracted to her before dinner, at which meal, however, his place had been far from her—approaches, gazes at the veiled face searchingly in the dim light to make sure that it *is* 'the handsome girl with the black eyes'. (p. 233, emphases added)

Lonely female protagonists move through Victorian fiction, from Charlotte Brontë's *Villette* (1853) to Anne Brontë's *Tenant of Wildfell Hall* (1848), from George Eliot's *The Mill on the Floss* (1860) to Thomas Hardy's *Tess of the d'Urbervilles* (1892). In many cases, these characters, with their themes of emotional resistance or martyrdom, played with earlier variations of women as 'Patience on a monument, smiling at grief'. Of course, heroines could overcome their loneliness, but it was typically through a 'Reader, I married him' acquiescence to the status quo and the ideal of the romantic love fulfilled—or lost in the case of *Great Expectations*' Miss Havisham (Dickens 1861).

Charles Dickens' works also depicted a variety of models of loneliness, especially in children, in the context of an unfeeling, mechanistic industrial society. Thus, the heroes and heroines of

Dickens' novels—Pip in *Great Expectations*, for instance, or Oliver in the eponymous *Oliver Twist* (1837)—found themselves alone, abandoned, and friendless in a bleak and hostile world. Such characters drew attention, often deliberately, to a psychological paradox in nineteenth-century industrial metaphors: on the one hand, it was necessary for the working classes to operate like cogs in a machine, but on the other hand, that was a potentially dehumanizing process, even for those whose life was nasty, brutish, and short.[37] In the late industrial age, moreover, the themes of sociability and social connectedness took on new metaphors, as the nervous system of Britain and its people were connected by electricity and the telegraph.[38] Incidentally, the digital age has bodily metaphors of its own, with the brain *qua* mind as a kind of Google, endlessly connecting and disconnecting from one idea, event, and person to another. Metaphors for loneliness are overwhelmingly embodied too; they tend to involve images and degrees of warmth, which is suggestive of the physicality of contact with another. Thus, lonely people are 'left out in the cold'.

The poetic depiction of the lonely individual outside of society, whether through error, weakness, unfeeling social structures, or bad luck, was compatible not only with the principles of evolutionary biology, but also with the emergence of the individual as an object of early psychiatry: a monadic, delimited self, set against the world. With the mind sciences, neurological and biological principles started to explain the kinds of nervous disorders seen in the eighteenth century (and manifested by excessive solitude), with considerable influence from psychoanalytic theory and the work of theorists like the Austrian neurologist Sigmund Freud. Freud did not write specifically about loneliness, but he did write about the fear of being alone. He uses the anecdote of a child, who is frightened of the dark unless his aunt speaks to him, at which point 'it gets lighter'. Darkness and light, like cold and warmth, may be seen as embodied experiences of loneliness. More importantly, perhaps, Freud's subject Dora is a diagnosed hysteric, who is described as unsociable and locked into an incommensurate longing for a distant woman, who would become, perhaps, the mother figure in Freud's other writings.[39] Loneliness, it was implied, marked a sort of neuroticism, an inadequate development of the self that cannot adapt and thrive in adverse circumstance.

For other writers, including the psychiatrist Carl Gustav Jung, loneliness manifested the modern dilemma of humankind. For Jung, the lifelong journey of the human being is the differentiation of the self from others. This process of individuation meant separating out the conscious and unconscious elements of existence, with the individual engaging with the overriding themes of the collective unconscious, as well as with the language and symbols that were available. Jung differentiated between 'introverted' and 'extroverted' types, based on how those individuals engaged with the external world, and there was a degree of neuroticism associated with introversion and the desire for solitude.

Modern loneliness became, by the early twentieth century, a mental problem linked to the operation of mind. Philosophies of social alienation, which stressed low common values and a high degree of isolation between individuals, reinforced the idea that loneliness was a dysfunctional and negative part of the human psyche, caused by the onset of modernization and a profound individual disconnect from others. Karl Marx, Émile Durkheim, and others predicted the five prominent features of alienation:

powerlessness, meaninglessness, normlessness, isolation, and self-estrangement.[40]

For the founder of German sociology Frederick Tönnies, there were two types of social groupings: *Gemeinschaft*, usually translated as 'community' based on togetherness and mutual bonds, and *Gesellschaft*, or groups sustained for the benefit of the individual. Emotional connections are seldom so rigidly defined, yet the nostalgic idea of the 'lost Gemeinschaft' is still used in the twenty-first century to explain loneliness among the elderly.[41]

Alienation, like the philosophies of existentialism and phenomenology, identified the helplessness of the individual in relation to the world, as well as the complex inevitability (at least for existentialists) of loneliness. Yet intellectual truth and freedom for the German philosopher Martin Heidegger, for instance, was found not only in solitude but also in loneliness, since that is the path towards true self-knowledge. There is a reminder, here, of the intellectual isolationism of the early monastic hermits, in the quest for meaning lying within (though Heidegger refuses a theological voice).[42] Others, including the so-called first existentialist Søren Kierkegaard (whose work particularly influenced Heidegger), similarly invoked the idea that—as Sartre put it in the play *No Exit*—'hell is other people'.[43]

While Freud had not expressed specifically this concept of social alienation, his notion of a subconscious versus a conscious mind, and the ego-super-ego and id, created a space between the individual and society, and affirmed the idea that there was a disconnect between self and world. It is not my aim to rehearse all the different philosophical perspectives that emerged during the twentieth century, including Max Weber's recognition that it was the individualism of Protestantism that underpinned the tenets of economic capitalism.[44] What is most significant is the twentieth-century emergence of 'self versus world' and 'individual versus society' which were naturalized in economic and political structures and beliefs that still govern intellectual discussion in the twenty-first-century West. At that extreme, loneliness is not merely an inevitable part of the fragmented human condition, but also a distinctly psychological state linked to one's ability to interact with others.

I have intimated above, with reference to Taylor's argument about the modern self, and the impossibility of being alone in a world filled by God, that with the decline of religion, or more specifically the emergence of rational humanism, secularity was crucial to the modern formation of loneliness as an emotion cluster. Freud acknowledged that 'devout, intrinsic religion' provided something of a buffer for loneliness. It is an interesting, though underexplored, question whether the pursuit of religion in the twenty-first century is triggered by loneliness, or whether God provides a comfort to people today.[45] I am not, of course, suggesting that religion has disappeared, or that modern life is irredeemably secular, though there has been a distinct shift from the seventeenth century to the present in terms of the performance of religious catechisms and homilies in everyday life. But that does not mean that people are less spiritual; merely that their spirituality becomes expressed in different ways, and in pockets of culture that aren't necessarily connected to everyday practice. Rather, I am identifying a philosophical and civic trend by which loneliness as a social phenomenon depends on a version of the self that need not be developed in relation to a paternalistic God or an internalized belief system, but via external, secular identification with peer groups and communities that share, and outwardly perform, rituals of belonging.[46]

All societies have rituals. In the early modern period, these might have included compulsory attendance at church and the ceremonials of worship including the catechism; in the early twenty-first century rituals of belonging might include YouTube shopping 'mall haul' videos, where people share the unpacking of their bags. Whether a religious or secular activity is taking place, the repetition and reassertion of these rituals are a way for members of a society to find meaning and belonging, however temporarily.[47] We might argue that some performances of identity and belonging in a fragmented climate of digital postmodernity, characterized by instability, competition, and increased consumerism, reinforce the idea of loneliness as a chronic, destabilizing force.

In any case, the demands of twenty-first-century selfhood have connected new ways of putting the individual at the centre of myriad networks by which emotional performances are created and reproduced. The paradox of social media is that it produces the same isolation and loneliness that it seeks to overcome. In the same way that suicide could spread from person to person through a social contagion (as expressed in 1912 by the French sociologist Émile Durkheim, who used the term 'anomie' to explain how individual and social instability was caused by a breakdown of ideals), loneliness has been imagined as a product of the social forces of late modernity. In this context, social ties can unravel across an entire network of people, causing the societal fabric to disintegrate. In the words of the neuroscientist

John Cacioppo, social networks begin to 'fray at the edges, like a yarn that comes loose at the end of a crocheted sweater'.[48]

Loneliness as a Product of Historical Forces

Viewing loneliness as a product of historical forces helps to explain how it has become so profound in the twenty-first century. There will always be 'pinch-points' of loneliness; those moments when the individual in the modern age will be aware that she or he is experiencing a rite of passage: adolescent love, the birth of a child, marriage, life-threatening illness or death, divorce, or any number of significant moments that can be experienced alongside others or alone. Amid a backdrop of collective change, individual lives are lived.

The first such life that I want to explore is that of the American poet and writer Sylvia Plath. While much has been written about the work of Plath, her mental illness, and her marriage to the Yorkshire poet laureate Ted Hughes, little has been said about her loneliness, which seems to have dogged her entire life. Many themes related to loneliness—chronic versus transient emotional states, the impact of gender, and the significant moments at which loneliness might occur, including childhood and adolescence, romance, marriage, parenthood, and single parenthood—emerge through a study of Plath's journals and letters. It is to those writings I will now turn.

CHAPTER 2

A 'DISEASE OF THE BLOOD'?

The chronic loneliness of Sylvia Plath

God, but life is loneliness.

Sylvia Plath, *Journal*[1]

Between 2017 and 2018 two volumes of the letters of the American author Sylvia Plath were published.[2] They offer unique insights into her mental health, her relationships with others—including, notably, her husband and fellow writer Ted Hughes (Figure 2)—and her state of mind when she died by suicide on 11 February 1963. While the first volume focused on Plath's childhood and adolescence, her college years, and her meeting Hughes, the second garnered even more media attention, for it includes a dozen letters Plath sent to her psychiatrist before her death. In them, she accused Hughes of beating her and causing a miscarriage, as well as wishing her dead. Plath's relationship with Hughes has attracted much media attention, from the defacement of Plath's headstone to remove his name, to their surviving daughter Frieda's impassioned defence of her father.[3]

It is understandable that the daughter of Plath and Hughes might feel torn by the allegations against her father, and that she might also seek ways to understand and excuse his violence

Figure 2. Sylvia Plath and Ted Hughes, pictured in 1956. Creative Commons.

by reference to the life the couple lived: chaotic, artistic, and impassioned. Frieda recognizes that these letters overshadow everything else included in the volume; that the scandal attached to Plath and Hughes is all that is discussed, save for the art. And it was the art that mattered in the end, Frieda suggests, which was throughout Plath's letters her recurring refrain: Hughes was a 'genius' and she was grateful to have known him, even when she resented how much it cost her—financially, physically, emotionally.

Disentangling the artist from the life is never an easy task, and it is not my intention to debate Plath's marriage and Hughes' violence, or to weigh in on the considerable inequalities recognized by Plath: that Hughes had intellectual and practical freedom, while she juggled childcare, domesticity, and art. I am interested in the way loneliness shadowed her recorded life. For it was not only there at the end, when she died. It dogged her from childhood, through adolescence and early adulthood; it accompanied her during her marriage to, and struggles with, Hughes, and it lingered when he left her. Loneliness was not only evident in Plath's fictional writings, but also in the related themes of identity and psychological health that she addressed openly in her journals and letters. The chronic loneliness catalogued in her writing was different in quality and timbre to episodic loneliness (which is shorter-term and linked to life events), reminding us that time intersects with loneliness in important yet neglected ways.

Emotional distress and loneliness intersect in Plath's work, mental illness and loneliness feeding off one another, and producing profound social isolation. In reading Plath's writing and considering her attempts at self-fashioning—how she presented herself to the world, as well as how she wished to appear—it is apparent that her experience of loneliness evolved and changed through her life, according to circumstance, the social and political demands of society, and her literary ambitions. Plath's attempts to find a real companion—first a friend, and later a lover; someone who understood her completely and with whom she could truly be herself—were manifest in her letters to her mother, her friends, and her husband.

It is also possible that Plath's own self-fashioning as a tormented artist, with deliberate parallels with Virginia Woolf, meant that the literary loneliness that was expressed provided Plath with a much-needed sense of identity. I am not suggesting that Plath's death was directly the result of Woolf's suicide, though she was interested in the suicides of a number of tormented and creative women including Marilyn Monroe, whose blonde hair Plath copied, and who also died by suicide in 1962, the year before Plath.[4]

Most scholars who have focused on the life and works of Plath have talked about her passionate affair with Hughes and her ultimate mental illness and suicide as though this end was somehow inevitable.[5] This narrative is symptomatic of the cultural need to view Plath and Hughes as star-crossed and tempestuous lovers: from Orpheus and Eurydice to Elizabeth Taylor and Richard Burton, this is a trope that has captured the public imagination. The need for a soulmate and its loss, or lack, has traditionally been one of the key themes in the articulation of loneliness among young women. It was also, sadly, apparent in Plath's work.

Plath's letters reveal a lonely child, who struggled to make friends, and who felt something of a misfit. Born in Boston, USA in 1932, she was introverted and literary from a young age, writing poetry and publishing in magazines and newspapers. She was also an avid journal keeper and letter writer. Her father, Otto Emil Plath, was an entomologist and Professor of Biology at Boston University, who died of complications linked to diabetes when she was just eight years old. Plath's mother, Aurelia Frances Schober, had been one of Otto's students.[6]

After Otto's death, Sylvia and her brother Warren were raised by Aurelia, who worked as a teaching substitute at a local high school. Plath studied at Smith College, a women's liberal arts college in Northampton, Massachusetts. During those studies, Plath drove herself to excess, constantly in search of perfection, and worrying about wasting her time with friends (that she nevertheless was desperate to have). After Smith she won a scholarship to attend Newnham College, Cambridge. It was there that Plath met, and married, the poet Ted Hughes in 1956. The couple lived together first in the United States and then in England. They had two children, Frieda and Nicholas, before they separated in 1962. In 1963, Plath died by suicide after gassing herself in the oven.

Much is hidden in the bare bones of this familiar biography, including the ways loneliness fleshed out Plath's existence. Particular moments of crisis included the death of Plath's father when she was a young child, Plath's intense and problematic relationship with her mother, her college experiences and thwarted attempts to feel as though she belonged, her romantic relationships and the search for that significant 'other', her career challenges, and the relatively short time frame in which she experienced marriage, motherhood, and separation.

The gendered language that Plath used to describe her emotional experiences is also important: the metaphors of miscarried, aborted, and mutated foetuses that depict lost creativity, the trope of suicide and its links to mental health and social pressures; the 'bell jar' that is placed over society and through which everything becomes distorted (the metaphor, indeed, that became synonymous with Plath's only published novel), and the natural imagery—of water, corruption, power—that runs through Plath's poetry. Through all of this language, and the viscerality of passion and desire, loneliness stood separate and fixed, a spectre that she could not escape.

The Loneliness of Childhood

The BBC Loneliness Survey of 2018 found that loneliness among the young was common.[7] It was certainly central to Plath's early existence. As a child, she felt 'different' from others, and she often felt excluded.[8] Plath's complex, unresolved feelings towards her late father were expressed in her poem 'Daddy', written soon before her death. The poem, composed of sixteen five-line stanzas, is brutal and visceral, referring to him as a 'black shoe' in which she can no longer fit. If Plath's father was a 'brute' and 'Marble-heavy', then he was also a mould for the romantic and sexual relationships that Plath would experience, the love and yearning Plath felt for her father being transplanted onto other lovers, including Ted Hughes.

Otto Plath seemed something of a tyrant in the home and yet someone she desperately admired; her paternal adoration led to conflict with Hughes. Plath also had a complex emotional attitude towards her mother, which she would discuss in her relationship with her therapist as an adult, and which she also explored through reading books on psychiatry and psychology, including the work of Sigmund Freud and Carl Jung. Intellectualizing her feelings for her parents did not prevent her from needing them as an adult just as she had in childhood. While she lacked friends her own age, she yearned for her mother's contact, her mother's companionship, as well as feeling responsible for her mother's emotional state. On 18 July 1943, when Plath was just eleven years old and away at camp, she wrote to her mother, Aurelia, telling her that she felt 'left out' as many of the girls were going home. She hadn't heard from her mother and wanted to know she was alright, as she worried when there was no news.[9]

Plath wrote her mother letters daily and practised signing off differently—from 'Sylvia' to 'Siv', 'Sivvy', 'your Sylvy', 'your very own Sylvia-girl', and 'me'. What is clear in these early letters is the evolution of a child's maternal attachment, and the conscious self-fashioning that is common to adolescent development. What is also apparent, however, is that Plath worked hard at her studies, valuing herself in relation to her academic achievements, yet lacking a special friend with whom she might share childhood experiences. In 'Missing Mother' she wrote about the sense of abandonment she felt when her mother was away.[10] Plath continued to write to her mother with a child-like dependency, especially when she went to college and her loneliness became more acute.

'I AM A SMITH GIRL NOW'

In 1950, Plath started at Smith College, a private, independent women's liberal arts college in Northampton, Massachusetts.[11] Plath was thrilled, and excited about the possibility of making friends, as well as excelling in her studies. The importance of her material world was paramount in emotionally grounding her during those first days and weeks away from home. She wrote to Aurelia to describe the physicality of her room and surroundings, noting that 'tangible things' could be 'friendly': the maple-top desk that felt like 'velvet', the clock that ticked like the beat of a heart.[12] For lonely people, material objects are often anthropomorphized, taking on human characteristics and providing a particular kind of comfort.

Plath wrote to her mother, often more than once a day, about every single aspect of her life at Smith: her studies, romantic entanglements, clothes, friendships, mental health, weight, emotional wellbeing, and money worries (Plath was supported by a 'promising young writers' scholarship courtesy of the Smith alumna and writer Olive Higgins Prouty). She fretted about her ability to keep up with her academic studies, to achieve the highest grades, and to balance that achievement with a social life, a romantic life, and the ability to be creative. On 2 October 1950, when she had been at Smith for less than a month, she described herself as utterly 'exhausted'.[13]

Plath's rigorous application to her studies, and her constant worrying about whether she was performing well enough, getting enough sleep, and going to be able to publish, exacerbated her existing mental health problems. And in turn those mental health problems proved to be socially isolating; more than half of all people with diagnosed emotional problems describe themselves as lonely.[14] Losing sense of what was proportionate study, or how much was enough, it was difficult for Plath to get support from other students, or to feel less lonely, since she envisaged them as competition, or obstacles in her path. Nevertheless, she wanted to be desired, and was anxious that she would never find fulfilment with a friend, or a lover.

In November 1950, Plath went to see a presentation by the Professor of Philosophy Peter Bertocci on 'The Question of Sex before Marriage'. Reporting to her mother the large turnout, and the fact that Plath was not currently infatuated with a boy (and therefore, in her view, able to regard the talk entirely logically), she saw she was compartmentalizing her life in an unsustainable way. She had thrown all her energies into her studies, but was without either boyfriend or female friends; no one to 'pour myself into', as she lamented.[15] Pouring herself into someone, giving her all, was characteristic of Plath's attitude towards her life. But these desires were also expected of women in the 1950s; questions of marriage, domesticity, and entertaining bumped up repeatedly against her desires to write, to be alone, to become famous.

Plath's growing awareness, and sadness, that Aurelia could no longer provide the emotional security and companionship she once had was difficult to bear. Growing up was a wrench; she wanted to remain a child, free from the responsibilities of womanhood, and even taking care of herself.[16] It was only during visits home, when she was physically and emotionally cared for by her mother, that Plath seemed able to relax; this isn't unusual for a woman her age (she was only eighteen years old when she went away to college), but it is apparent that Plath needed regular bouts of convalescence, of feeling utterly and completely cared for, in order to maintain her life at Smith. Thus, she wrote to her mother after one such episode, calling her 'mummy', notably, rather than her usual 'mother' or 'mum', thanking her for feeding her, buying her perfume and stockings, letting her lie in, and pampering her for a few days.[17]

During her time at Smith, Plath wrote letters to connect herself to the world outside, and the writing of those letters was just as important as the sending of them. In writing, one reinforces one's connections with others through a physical act. Receiving letters is an affirmation that those relationships exist. It helps to assuage loneliness because letters are physical objects that can be read again and again. In her final correspondence, Plath would recall how letters were the only things tethering her to an external reality, though the occasional telephone call with her mother had always brought her joy.[18]

Besides her mother, Plath wrote to Hans Joachim-Neuport, a German pen-pal with whom she discussed the possibility of a nuclear holocaust, and Eddie Cohen, a man who began writing to her after one of her poems was published in the magazine *Seventeen*. In both cases she was consciously trying out identities, which offered an alternative to her day-to-day isolation at Smith. Occasionally, Plath experienced moments when she was 'very collegiate', when she connected with other girls and felt a sense of belonging.[19] But most of the time, Plath's experience was a lonely one, in which she worked as hard as possible and punctuated a gruelling routine with the occasional date. Her only friend at that time was Ann Davidow, with whom she discussed the pressures of study and the difficulties of depression and anxiety. Bonding with Davidow was therapeutic and made her feel less isolated. No wonder, then, that when Davidow left Smith, she felt betrayed and alone.[20] Davidow left because of her worsening mental health. Plath had observed her friend's changing mood and noticed that Davidow's jollity seemed 'more artificial' than before.

Plath reported to her mother that the girls had discussed depression and suicidal urges. This is one of the first times Plath raises the idea of suicide; throughout her subsequent journal entries and letters there is a recurring image of suicide—of others, particularly friends and writers—framed as a way out, an escape from the cloyingly depressing nature of existence. There was also a sense of companionship in sharing suicidal thoughts and mental illness, of bonding: like Plath, Davidow felt that the other girls were 'very cliquey'.[21] Davidow stored up razor blades and talked endlessly about suicide, according to Plath; if Aurelia were *her* mother, Plath wrote, she would be alright.

Without the friendship of Davidow, college life became bleaker for Plath. There was nobody to confide in, and Plath was unable to skate or play bridge or do any of the things that the popular girls did.[22] The spectre of being lonely while not alone is related to the fundamental difference between solitude and loneliness; it is not whether or not people are *around*, but the recognition that one has nothing in common with others that is so challenging. It is meaningful connections that matter. When Plath tried to connect with other girls, she wrote to Davidow, she was 'looked at oddly'. Having thrown all her energies into her relationship with Davidow, she was now completely alone.[23] Sitting in her room alone, she cried for her loss: 'I am so lonely…this single room is so lonely'.[24]

Plath wrote to her mother to complain about Davidow leaving, lamenting she had been Plath's only friend. There was nobody to 'wash socks with' besides her, a charming and, predictably, given Plath's emotional embeddedness in the material world of her surroundings, physical reference to the everyday intimacy of friendship. These day-to-day moments of connectedness were what Plath missed most of all. She had been excited to get a single room, imagining herself studying the entire time, but actually found the lack of companionship hard to bear.[25]

Plath did write to, and of, other girls at Smith besides Davidow, including Marcia (Marty) Stern.[26] Yet she consistently viewed herself as separate from her peers and as unable to connect. In her journals, Plath noted the visceral physicality of this feeling; loneliness disrupting the whole body as well as the mind. Loneliness, she wrote, came from a 'vague core of the self—like a disease of the blood' that was dispersed so fully through the self that it was impossible to know where it originated. Loneliness was like an infection, or a 'contagion', a term that has become popular in conceptualizing loneliness as an epidemic.[27] Loneliness and homesickness for Plath went hand in hand; homesickness became a language that was acceptable to explain to others the 'sick feeling' which dominated her core; homesickness did not have the negative connotations of loneliness, after all, and it was far more likely to invite a sympathetic response.[28]

The material culture of one's environment could cease, in moments of loneliness, to be comforting. Being alone, and conscious of one's loneliness, can overwhelm the senses and the mind. Hypersensitivity, or links between physical sensitivity and emotional fragility, means that ordinary objects can take on new meanings.[29] Plath complained about the relentless ticking of the clock that had once comforted her, and the 'false cheerful resilience of the electric light'.[30] There was also, in these observations, an implicit presumption of the natural world as a healthier and less lonely space, just as it had been for the Romantic poets. Certainly, when Plath wrote about her summers on the beach, or out in nature, she seems to have been happier, healthier, and less melancholy.

There was a marked disjuncture between the bright and breezy letters that Plath wrote to her mother and the fearful, isolated self that was described in her journal. She recounted how day after day she sat in the library, with the fans whirring and the lights glaring, seeing girls having fun and being together while she felt remote and isolated. Her sense of alienation and loneliness was so profound that she felt lacking in identity: 'faceless'.[31]

Loneliness and the Suicidal Urge

For a young woman like Plath, desperate to have friends and yet conscious of the gulf between herself and others, worrying that she never really got to know people but merely passed by them in the corridors, writing fulfilled an emotional function. She could receive an emotional echo in her letters and her journals, figuratively by connecting with others and metaphorically by marking a blank page: I am here.[32] Yet, unable to secure a sense of belonging with girls at Smith, Plath continued to seek identification with a romantic other, a man who would complete her and make her feel special. This desire, she recognized, was antithetical to her desire for fame and success as a writer in the 1950s, when women were supposed to focus their creative energies in the home. Her romantic life had been largely disappointing; the men she met failed, in the main, to interest and engage her.

Plath was split, then, between the woman that she wanted to be—successful, published, independent, surrounded by friends and lovers—and the lonely, homesick girl she retreated to in her own room, and her own mind. In November 1951 she began to write of her deteriorating mental health, and her desperate need for something, someone to make her feel complete. She felt too old to go home and 'blubber' into her mother's skirts, and ill-equipped to deal with men because she lacked any 'parental directive' or a father's guidance.[33] She longed to abdicate responsibility for herself and to follow other women she admired, like the writers Virginia Woolf and Sara Teasdale, into the ambivalent escape of suicide.

The historian Chris Millard has written about suicide and self-harm as ways of drawing attention to one's internal turmoil in post-war Britain and this seems pertinent here.[34] Ideational behaviour, including talking and thinking about suicide, as Plath seems to have done, has been associated with loneliness in twenty-first-century studies.[35] A constant refrain through Plath's writing is the ideal of suicide, and she self-harmed and enacted suicide attempts on a number of occasions.[36] The image of drowning was particularly prominent in Plath's writing. Soon after a discussion of Virginia Woolf's own fate, for instance, she declared her desire for a 'colossal wave, sweeping tidal over me, drowning'. Loneliness was at the heart of this yearning for oblivion, for how could she ever find 'that communication with other human beings' that she so desperately wanted?[37]

On one occasion, Plath made cuts into her legs, testing whether she was brave enough to end her own life. The theatrical element is clear—these marks would be visible, they would announce to the world (and certainly to her mother) that she was suffering—though that did not make her suffering any less genuine.[38] Plath was treated for depression by a (unbeknownst to her and her mother) scandal-embroiled psychiatrist, who prescribed a course of sleeping pills and a badly administered course of electroconvulsive therapy, or ECT.[39] Plath's sponsor at Smith, Olive Higgins Prouty, paid for much of her hospital care, just as she had supported her through college. Prouty and others had similarly experienced depression and 'hysterical symptoms' in addition to a love of writing.[40] Between the 1920s and the 1950s, then, self-harm and suicide became a well-trodden possibility for women who experienced profound, painful feelings of social and psychological exclusion.[41]

On 24 August 1952, Plath actually did attempt to end her life by taking her mother's sleeping tablets. In a letter to her friend Eddie Cohen some months later, she narrated what had happened. She didn't mention the generalized sense of loneliness and ostracization that were long-standing but reported the most recent disappointments: she was taking the wrong subjects at Smith, she was turned down for a writing course at Harvard, she felt unable to become a writer.[42] Metaphors of fertility were scattered throughout Plath's writing, particularly linked to sexuality and the feminine. She wrote of bearing misshapen children, of monster children, of being raped, being violated; violent images that populated the landscape of her creativity as well as her personal correspondence. In the midst of other happy and content women, either married or busy or creative, Plath felt like an aberration, a non-woman 'incapable of loving or feeling'.[43] Imagined comparisons with others are telling, and common in lonely people. Self-evaluated social skills tend to be lower among the lonely than among those with strong social networks. The belief that others are more popular, better at social engagement, or happier is characteristic of lonely 'self-talk'.[44]

Plath described to Cohen how she had waited until her mother and brother were out and swallowed handfuls of her mother's sleeping tablets, before concealing herself in her mother's basement. She left a note for her mother telling her she had gone on a long walk and would not be back for a day or so. The police were called, but no trace was found of Plath until two days later, when her brother heard her cries for help as the family sat down to dinner. Plath had woken up in the crawl space, hitting her face against the wall (which resulted in a permanent scar). Two weeks of incarceration in the hospital followed and Plath started seeing a psychiatrist, Dr Ruth Beuscher, to whom those letters would later emerge concerning her marriage breakdown and Hughes' violence and adultery.

There was an artificial breeziness about Plath's letters after the suicide attempt; commentators have attributed this quality to Plath's desperation to be well, to get on with living; even a competitive urge against her friend Jane Anderson, who was similarly experiencing a 'nervous breakdown' but took far longer to recover.[45] I suspect this is doing Plath a disservice. What seems clear from her letters is her keen awareness of what she needs to get well—articulated in a letter to her boyfriend Gordon Latymer: time in the coffee-shop, being social, and companionship with other girls.[46] As it was, she confided in Cohen (perhaps shielding from Latymer the full extent of her mental illness) that she woke up in horror in the night, dreaming of the 'shock room'. What she really needed at those moments was what she never seemed to have: 'someone to love' and be with her at those times of crisis.[47]

Re-entering Smith in January 1954 and having to repeat the second semester of her junior year was especially challenging. If the other girls rejected her before, they seemed to do so doubly now, as Plath was set apart not only by her intense working habits but also her earmarked insanity. Housemates regarded her as something of an oddity, according to Plath's biographer Adrian Wilson, and a 'talking point' who was subject to 'speculative gossip'.[48] Plath's behaviour after her suicide attempt was also perceived as strange. She had a 'split personality', said one of the friends who Plath visited in New York, and was something of a phoney.[49] Plath's belief that she was socially excluded, then, and looked at strangely by the other girls, seems to have had some basis in reality.

In 1954, Plath submitted her thesis, *The Magic Mirror: A Study of the Double in Two of Dostoyevsky's Novels,* which explores the theme of the dual personality. Plath's own writing, as well as her musings in her journal, similarly addressed questions of personality, suicide, identity attachment, and mental health.[50] In *The Magic Mirror,* Plath wrote of the motifs that recurred in the character of Golyadkin, in the novel *The Double,* particularly his recurring identification with 'low forms of animal life' and his 'wishes for oblivion or death'.[51] She contemplates 'the seductiveness of suicide as a release from prolonged torment', which was a motif in Plath's autobiographical musings.[52] Her vision of suicidal ideation—as 'the bird flies itself to the hunter'—is also reminiscent of the avian images and visions that arise, especially in relation to Plath's relationship with Ted Hughes: he was the hunter, she the hunted, each locked in a struggle to survive.

The lonelier and more depressed Plath felt, the harder it was for her to integrate into the social world, so that loneliness became part of a destructive psychological cycle. For Plath, the desire to be 'extrovert'—which in Western society has been so much more celebrated than introversion—was also key. If she could transform her personality, she figured, she might find it easier to enter the social fray, and to be one of the girls rather than feeling cut off and remote. Why could she not be one of those who could simply join in with others and 'seek comfort in numbers'?[53] Why did she have to be alone?

Plath worked hard to be *seen* as an extrovert, having internalized negative associations between introversion and neuroticism. What she perceived as her own 'inferiority complex' she also understood to be linked to cultural expectations of women in the 1950s.[54] She was conscious that she was expected to choose a partner for life, and that everything rode upon that decision, and that responsibility (along with men's inability to provide fulfilment) made her feel stifled, uncertain, and out of kilter with the cultural climate. How could she be content as a mother, and a wife, when she was so desperate to write? A particular kind of loneliness, then, concerns the disparity between social expectation and self-identification. The feeling of being different, of not fitting in, applies to adulthood and later life, just as it does to childhood.[55]

In May 1953, Plath won a prize to be a guest editor at *Mademoiselle* magazine and travelled to New York to take it up.[56] She would draw on those experiences in her subsequent novel, *The Bell Jar*. Plath was exhausted and overworked; her journal entries for July show that she was in a precarious emotional state, needing the comfort of others and yet isolated and alone. She was feeling, particularly, the lack of parental guidance and support.[57] Acquaintances were unsympathetic, especially when Plath's need for attention led her to 'steal' another girl's boyfriend.[58] Plath complained to her mother that she was tired and lonely and jealous and just wanted to be looked after: after all, 'human beings need each other so'.[59]

The Need for a Romantic Other

Much of Plath's journals is concerned with restricted choices: what it meant to be a woman, when one had to be so careful of one's sexual conduct and choices, and the need to reconcile the desire for security (she constantly worried about money) with sexual and intellectual stimulation.[60] Plath yearned for a special relationship, just as she had craved a special friend who understood her: another person to entrust with her feelings and dreams; 'someone to pour myself into'.[61]

In February 1956 Plath attended a party thrown for the poet Ted Hughes.[62] Plath's relationship with Hughes has been talked about elsewhere, and it is not the explicit subject of this chapter. Nor is the extent to which marital discord and violence can produce its own, unique pattern of loneliness, physical and emotional abuse being linked to shame, isolation, and secrecy. One might imagine that meeting Hughes, whom Plath fell desperately in love with, could mark the end of her unfulfilled loneliness. But that was not the case—initially because she lacked a network of friends with whom to share her happiness. As she explained to her mother, it was like finding a 'diamond mine' and having nobody to tell.[63] The rites of passage that make up a person's life—those socially and emotionally important transitions like becoming an adult, falling in love, finding a job, getting married—need to be affirmed and celebrated by others. The lack of affirmation produces a disparity, again, between what is expected and what is experienced.[64] Once she had attached herself to Hughes, moreover, Plath missed him terribly when they were apart, and became increasingly isolated as 'loneliness serves only to shut me up more'.[65] The physicality of her love for Hughes numbed everything else; she wanted to devour him, to gorge herself on him until she felt emotionally sated.

In June 1957, Plath and Hughes moved to the United States. She taught at Smith College, her alma mater, though it was always Ted's career that would come first. Plath found it difficult to teach and have enough time and energy to write, and much of her journals reveal that adjustment; to finding space to write at the same time as putting her man's needs first. Plath's relationship with Hughes was intense and passionate, but it was also violent. On 11 June 1958, Plath wrote of the aftermath of a fight in which she 'got hit and saw stars'. This was not the first time, or the last, that Plath recorded being physically or emotionally hurt by a partner.

The couple returned to England in 1959 and their daughter Frieda was born the following year. Plath also published her first collection of poetry, *The Colossus*. They moved to Devon and rented out their London flat to Assia and David Wevill. In June 1962, Plath had a car accident—she drove the car into a river—that she later described as a suicide attempt. In July the same year, Plath discovered Hughes and Assia were having an affair, and she separated from Hughes.

As a single parent, worried about money and the future, resentful of Hughes' success, though also proud of him, Plath's loneliness and emotional isolation seems to have peaked. The winter of 1963 was bitterly cold, the pipes in Plath's flat froze, and the children were constantly unwell. Plath spoke to her friend and GP John Horder, who arranged both antidepressants and for a live-in nurse to help out, but she was unable to prevent the spectre of suicidal ideation returning. Plath was dead by the time the nurse arrived, having gassed herself in the oven in the early morning of 11 February 1963. Professionally disappointed by the lack of critical interest in her book *The Bell Jar*, romantically rejected, and emotionally overwhelmed, Plath chose death over a life that had become intolerably difficult.

The Isolating Nature of Mental Illness

The experience of mental illness produces its own, particular quality of loneliness, as though a glass window has been placed between oneself and the world. It becomes impossible to relate to the everyday; to other people; and all too possible to be absorbed by one's own pain. What tortured, middle-of-the-night thoughts may have been running through Plath's head just before her death it is impossible to know. But her final letters are tormented, agitated, relentlessly rehashing all that had happened between her and Hughes, as well as her desperate, fragile attempts to begin a new life in London. A recurring theme remained that of social isolation and emotional lack: how would she ever find the connection with another that she craved?[66]

Some of the most important themes throughout Plath's journals and letters were her frantic attempts to secure this continuity and community, to resist abandonment, real or imagined (by her mother, her father, her partners, her friends). The idea that mental illness and creativity were linked has become something of a cultural trope, but for Plath the heightened sensitivity that allowed her to feel so deeply was also that which left her prone to loneliness.[67]

Plath's endless questions about self-identity, the lack of friendships, and one's role in the world were not, of course, restricted to artists. Nor was the desire for a special someone, a soulmate, with whom one might feel complete. Indeed, this trope has been common in British literature and culture since at least the Romantic period. It also had significant implications for the sense of loss that accompanies one of the most profound indicators of loneliness in the twenty-first century: lonely hearts and the search for love.

CHAPTER 3

LONELINESS AND LACK

Romantic love, from Wuthering Heights to Twilight

> Each of us when separated, having one side only, like a flat fish, is but the indenture of a man, and he is always looking for his other half.
>
> Aristophanes, in Plato's *Symposium* (285–370 BCE)

> I cannot live without my life! I cannot live without my soul!
>
> Cathy, in *Wuthering Heights* (1847)

In the modern West, the idea of the significant other has become synonymous with that of the 'soulmate' or the 'one'; a belief that there is one special person we are each supposed to be with, to 'complete' us, or 'make us whole'. This romantic image of the significant other dominates: in Valentine's Day celebrations, in supermarket 'meals for two', in the language of 'soulmates'; in novels, films, and songs in which love is all you need. Which translates as a particular kind of love, that—as the language of romance has it—'knocks you off your feet' and 'bowls you over', yet keeps you 'hungry for more'. Romantic love is physically and emotionally intense, highly idealized, and threatening to the stability of the individual self; yet the obliteration of the self *into* another person is all that is desired. Around this single, passionate vision, all else is ordered in the idealized world of traditionally heterosexual relationships: courtship, marriage, a home, children; growing old together and expecting that passion to persevere, even in the face of rising divorce rates. There is a gulf between emotional expectation and the realities of long-term relationships, in other words, in which each idealized version of a union is seen as different from all others.[1]

We might argue that the ideal of an 'other', without whom one is destined to always be incomplete, creates an inevitable sense of loneliness through lack; if loneliness represents a gulf between the emotional and social connections that are desired and those that are achieved, and the cultural ideal is for a soulmate, then how can a person be truly fulfilled without one? Within heterosexual relationships, moreover, the ideal of a soulmate also fosters a sense of co-dependency in which women, in particular, have been expected historically to prioritize that relationship over everything else, as seen in the case of Sylvia Plath. There is often in the case of the many romantic visions of 'the one', a sense of danger, of instability, of domination and control, that presents an emotionally unhealthy version of romantic relationships.

The case studies used for this discussion are two novels in which the soulmate is central—*Wuthering Heights* and the *Twilight series*. Each shares the image of the romantic hero as dangerous, close to nature, a threat to the stability of the self, and yet the only alternative to desolation and loneliness on the part of the suffering heroine. Firstly, however, I want to explore the philosophical basis of much romantic love in the twenty-first century, and the quest for wholeness on which the pursuit of love depends: the idea of the soulmate. Where does the image of the soulmate come from? And how does its existence impact on ideas of loneliness, real or imagined?

The concept of a soulmate is an ancient one, though not in its modern guise. The idea of another person who 'completes us' derives from the writings of the classical Greek philosopher Plato. In *The Symposium*, written around 385 BCE, Plato depicts a dialogue between a group of notable men attending a banquet.[2] The men included the philosopher Socrates (Plato's teacher), the General Alcibiades, the Athenian aristocrat Phaedrus, and the comic playwright Aristophanes. Each of the men were charged by the host to speak in praise of Eros, the god of love and desire, associated not only with erotic love, but also with the heady emotional connotations linked to love, including what Phaedrus termed 'that courage which, as Homer says, the god breathes into the souls of some heroes'. Love was figured here as an entity that was both earthly and spiritual, mixed with the sacred and the profane, in this—partly tongue-in-cheek, wine-fuelled—discussion of the merits of Love.

When it was his turn to speak, Aristophanes stated that humans were once different physical and emotional beings. Rather than being mere man or woman, there was man, woman, and a 'union of the two' which was called Androgynous. There were therefore three distinct beings. And these creatures moved differently to their classical antecedents:

> The Primeval man was round, his back and sides forming a circle; and he had four hands and feet, one head with two faces, looking opposite ways, set on a round neck; also four ears, two privy members [male and female genitalia] and the remainder to correspond.[3]

Now, because of this tripartite state of the human, there were not two sexes but three that corresponded to the sun (man), the earth (woman), and the man-woman of the moon. The number three has long had symbolic meaning, from the Holy Trinity to Macbeth's three witches. These terrible creatures attacked the gods, leaving them with a conundrum. Was it better to kill and annihilate the entire species with a thunderbolt (in which case the gods would lose out on future sacrifices), or to punish them in some other way? Zeus came up with the answer: he would 'cut them in two, and then they will be diminished in strength and increased in numbers'. This he did, halving humans like an 'egg' and turning each face in so that each individual might contemplate themselves. He pulled the skin from the sides towards the navel, 'like the purses which draw in, and he made one mouth at the centre, which he fastened in a knot (the same which is called the navel)'.[4] No sooner had they been separated than:

> The two parts of man, each desiring his other half, came together, and throwing their arms about one another, entwined in mutual embraces, longing to grow into one...and when one of the halves died and the other survived, the survivor sought another mate, man or woman as we call them...and clung to that.

In recognition of this apparently innate need for the 'other', Zeus turned the genitalia to the front, and changed the reproduction of humans from sowing of the seed 'like grasshoppers in the ground' to penetrative sex, 'in order that by the mutual embraces of man and woman they might breed, and the race might continue...so ancient is the desire of one another which is implanted in us, reuniting our original nature, making one of two, and healing the state of man'.

The problem raised by Aristophanes' story is one which is immediately recognizable within modern definitions of an 'other' by which we might become whole. 'Each of us when separated', Aristophanes continued, has 'one side only, like a flat fish...and he is always looking for his other half'. There was not, however, the association in classical Greece with the idea of the perfect heterosexual match that is so dominant in the twenty-first-century West; the sexual and emotional desires of individuals depended, quite literally, on how they were cut: 'the women who are a section of the woman do not care for men, but have female attachments...they who are a section of the male follow the male, and while they are young, being slices of the original man, they hang about men and embrace them...and these when they grow up become our statesmen'. Nevertheless, a profound transformation takes place 'when one of them meets with his other half, *the actual half of himself*, whether he be a lover of youth or a lover of another sort':

> The pair are lost in an amazement of love and friendship and intimacy, and would not be out of the other's sight, as I may say, even for a moment: these are the people who pass their whole lives together; yet they could not explain what they desire of one another. For the intense yearning which each of them has towards the other does not appear to be the desire of lover's intercourse, but of something else which the soul of either evidently desires and cannot tell, and of which she has only a dark and doubtful presentiment...This meeting and melting into one another, this becoming one instead of two, was the very expression of [an] ancient need.

In this view, it is only by discovering the special 'other' whom one is destined to be with, and who can complete the self, that happiness is possible. Indeed, this very merging of the souls and the body of those destined couples is the opposite of loneliness, for it is impossible to feel lonely, in a modern sense, if one is emotionally, physically, and spiritually connected to a significant other.

A similar argument is made in modern psychology, in signifying the birth of the self, formed in oneness with a loving and engaged parent, rather than in the formation of a romantic relationship.

The pitfalls of the soulmate, which has since become the prototype or yardstick for 'true romance' in the West, are clear. The idea that there is a special someone for everyone, and that wholeness is dependent on finding that person, is incredibly limiting. It also creates a gap between perception and reality, and a sense of failure for those who do not find 'the one'. Nor is it a vision conducive to community thinking. If there is only one 'other' to be found, then romantic love is an individualist experience.[5] Especially in evolutionary biology and the quest for a mate.

The 'survival of the fittest' concept was only introduced in the fifth edition of Charles Darwin's *Origin of Species*, and intended to mean simply that those who produce the most offspring were likely to pass their characteristics to the next generation. Yet it has been used by Social Darwinists to justify imperialism, racism, genetics, and social inequality.[6] The militaristic language of romance, as a conquest that has clear winners and losers, has a longer tradition, for instance the proverb: 'all is fair in love and war' (John Lyly's *Euphues: The anatomy of wit*, 1578).[7]

This rhetoric of sexual conquest finds its way into the language of the soulmate, not only in terms of how one is ideally presented for the gaze of the other, but also because it pits women against other women, men against men. And it prioritizes emotional and sexual satisfaction over other qualities, such as economic support or companionship. To explore this further, let's look at the original, eighteenth-century formulation of the 'soulmate', which borrowed from the ideas of Plato in a far more domesticated guise.

The 'Soulmate' as a Romantic Ideal

The first recorded usage of the term 'soul mate' (as two separate words: soul + mate) was by the Romantic poet Samuel Taylor Coleridge. In a *Letter to a Young Lady* (1822), Coleridge acknowledged the absorption of marriage for women, for whom 'it is an act tantamount to Suicide—for it is a state which, once entered into, fills the *whole* sphere of a Woman's moral and personal Being, her Enjoyment and her Duties'. In marriage, he continued, the extremes of happiness and misery can be felt, and most people choose a match that is somewhere between 'indifference' and 'liking'. Yet 'in order not to be miserable', Coleridge advised, it was necessary to have 'a *Soul*-mate as well as a *House* or a *Yoke*-mate'. For who would 'blend your whole personality, as far as God has put it in your power to do so—all that you call "I"—soul, body and estate—with one, the contagion of whose habits and conversations you would have to guard against in behalf of your own soul; and the insidious influence of which on the tone and spirit of your thoughts, feelings, objects, and unconscious tendencies and manners would be as the atmosphere in which you lived!'[8] Throughout the letter, Coleridge uses gardening imagery—identifying the 'soil, climate', and 'aspect' in which one's happiness might 'bloom'—and here he invokes the atmosphere, in each case envisaging the growth and development of human character and experience (and soul) as natural phenomena that needed only the right conditions in which to thrive. These conditions were not only ideal for social and psychological development; they were also ordained by God: 'God said that it was not well for the human Being to be alone; to be what *we* ought to be we need support, help, communion in good'.[9]

By the time this letter was written, the theme of loneliness as a distinct emotional state was increasingly commonplace. So, too, was the literary idea that a marriage could mark some kind of spiritual union; a similar expression, 'partner of my soul', was recorded in the diary of a well-read eighteenth-century shopkeeper, Thomas Turner, in 1761.[10] That such sentiment gathered momentum by the time of the Romantics is unsurprising. So, too, is that this concept could be read in secular and classical as well as religious terms. For in the Romantic period, secular humanism, literary self-consciousness, a love of the natural, and a pursuit of individual health, wealth, and happiness were physical as well as emotional obligations, on which mental and physical health depended.

Thus, Coleridge moves from agricultural language to pathological medical imagery, imagining the health of the physical body as paralleling that of the mind. 'Do not marry a man suffering from "*inveterate Gout* or consumption" or experiencing "Palsy on one side"', he wrote, using the ailments 'figuratively': 'under the names of bodily complaints [I] am really thinking, and meaning you to think, of moral and intellectual Defects and Diseases'.[11] Why? Because it is this 'more precious Half' of a person, and not their manners, appearance, or outward bearing, that mattered most.

When Coleridge used the term soulmate, therefore, it was in the context of understanding the 'I' of a person to be composed of three interrelated but distinct states: 'soul, body and estate'.[12] In this reference to the individual as a social as well as a spiritual and physical being, Coleridge recognized the conventions of marriage must embrace the emotional and religious as well as the material needs of women and men. It was not so much that Coleridge was subscribing to the idea of 'the one' in any modern sense, but that the concept of a soulmate was a neat linguistic and philosophical device to use alongside the more conventional contemporary terms: 'House' or 'Yoke' mate. Historians have traditionally focused on marriage as a voyage of love *or* financial gain, an approach which is unhelpful and overly simplistic.[13]

What is important about Coleridge's statement is that a soulmate needed both material and emotional fulfilment. Significantly, that person need not be a spouse; an important part of Romantic culture was the quest for human connection, and the need for lasting bonds between individuals. What is often overlooked in the story of sociability and the growth of affect is the increasing importance, in Romantic ideology, that one's spiritual, sexual, and emotional needs could be fulfilled through a particular kind of human rather than spiritual relationship.

In the wake of Coleridge's writings, there was an increasing trend, in British literature, for the term 'soulmate' to mean an individual who was intended to complete the self (as it meant in Plato's time), with the added thrill of romance. This redefinition of love, from the companionship and duty of a friend to a sexual ideal that was characterized by individual desire, seems to have been characteristic of the pursuit of individualism. The term 'soulmate' picked up traction particularly in early twentieth-century English publications, first from the late 1930s, and with a steady climb during the 1960s, before a dramatic spike from around 1980. The increasingly common use of the term 'soulmate' from the 1980s may be linked to its appearance in personal ads and media discussions about the search for the 'one'.

'Lonely hearts' also peaked as a literary term in the late nineteenth century, linked as it was to emotional sentiment around the heart as an affective and symbolic organ of romance.[14] In the early twentieth century, the idea of a 'lonely heart' as a social identity, especially a woman who struggles to find a mate, was prevalent in fiction and newspapers, suggesting the commercialization of the quest for love. *The Guardian* newspaper still has a 'soulmate' dating page that fulfils the same function, though it has gone online, along with other, digital dating technologies to make the search for love more user-friendly and 'scientific'.

The modern ideal of the soulmate may have been fully realized by the early twentieth century. Yet its roots belong in the nineteenth, with the Romantic association of love, longing, and the natural world with the passionate desire for individual fulfilment through a union that was both otherworldly and physical. In both *Wuthering Heights* and the *Eclipse* series, a woman is set in pursuit of a 'soulmate' or significant other, without whom she is lonely (yet with whom she is unable to enter the 'normal' realms of the social). Both novels involve dangerous sexuality, and a brooding and menacing male protagonist who is part of, but also separate from, the natural landscape. Both female protagonists, Cathy and Bella, are pitted against social convention and individual desire. Their choices lie between implied sexual and emotional fulfilment or a sterile but conforming life; those choices also revolve around the promise of being seen or not being seen and being endangered or being safe. In both we find the internalization and perpetuation of the idea of the intense romantic ideal as a desirable—and indeed the *only*—form of love worth fighting for. Lack of fulfilment, or the loss of that ideal, brings emotional desolation and loneliness.

Love and the Soul in Fiction: The Case of *Wuthering Heights*

Let us consider first *Wuthering Heights*, published in 1847 under the pseudonym Ellis Bell, and Emily Brontë's only published novel. It is now regarded as a literary classic, but at the time was controversial, in its depiction of cruelty, hypocrisy, and unsympathetic characterization. Much has been written about the imagining of the wild moors of Haworth as a counterpart to gentile, yet artificial sensitivities, and about the conflict between established country folk and newcomers, unaccustomed to the stark realities of rural life. The romantic relationship between its key protagonists has been widely discussed—and popularized through a wide range of artefacts, including a number one hit in the form of *Wuthering Heights* by Kate Bush in 1978. The love between Catherine and Heathcliff, and between Catherine and Edgar, is a subject that has stimulated much literary discussion. I want to look at the novel here through the combined lenses of loneliness and romantic love, as the depiction of romantic love as an ideal in *Wuthering Heights* creates a tormented vision in which the individual whose love is unrequited must be cast adrift in the lonely moors.

Wuthering Heights was heavily criticized on its first publication.[15] Commentators were shocked at the brutal characters, entirely lacking in any moral purpose or influence. There are suggestions of the Gothic in the novel: the sinister, castle-like buildings, the hint of demonic behaviours, the passion-driven hero or anti-hero, and the fainting and fragile heroine; the promise of the supernatural, such as a ghost; the terrifying spectacle of nature; winding paths and secret places; moonlight and darkness. Of course, *Wuthering*

Heights contains all these elements, and many more, which were increasingly commonplace in English literature since the late eighteenth century.[16] But *Wuthering Heights* is also a novel of intense 'romantic sensibilities': 'the novel is replete with the effusion of tumultuous passion and high-pitched emotions', says one critic—'in fact, the romantically poetic rendering of elemental passions, particularly of Heathcliff and Catherine, makes the novel almost akin to a lyrical poem'.[17] The story also taps into a series of conventional, post-Romantic narratives about the indivisibility and inescapability of love, as a spiritual and earthly quest.

In a series of gendered tropes about illness, sensibility, nature, and civilization, Catherine and Heathcliff are depicted as antithetically different, but absolutely necessary for the completeness of one with the other. Heathcliff represents the wildness of unspoiled nature, paralleled by the moors that cannot be tamed by the gentile, ineffectual, attempts of the Lintons (Figure 3).

The character of Catherine, by contrast, must be punished for conforming to conventional expectations of gender and class, rather than allowing herself to be free, uninhibited, and passionate. The cult of the delicate and sensitive woman, idealizing fragility, was dominant in early nineteenth-century Britain, when women's 'complaints' dominated literary and medical discussions of female abilities and susceptibilities.[18] Edgar, cultured and refined, is set against the restless, violent Heathcliff, who pays no heed to social conventions, or the requirements of civilized behaviour. Yet Heathcliff is also a shadow of Catherine and a glimpse into what she could become. Thus, she announces that Heathcliff is 'more myself than I am', and 'whatever our souls are made of, his and mine are the same'. 'I *am* Heathcliff—he's always, always in my mind…as my own being'. Heathcliff, in turn, calls Catherine

Figure 3. Laurence Olivier as Heathcliff in *Wuthering Heights* (1939), Samuel Goldwyn Pictures.

his 'life' and his 'soul'. Catherine acts against her 'soul' and her 'heart' when she marries Edgar, and the outcome can only be dire for Catherine's mental and physical health. And Heathcliff cannot survive without Catherine. When she dies, he rails against the world, declaring that 'I cannot live without my life! I cannot live without my soul!'

Although the characters in *Wuthering Heights* are extreme caricatures of the prevailing gender and social in the nineteenth century, the image of the suffering and abandoned lover was all too familiar, especially for women. In one analysis of the cause of death in some 250 Victorian novels, more female characters died from unrequited or lost love than any other cause combined.[19]

Such was the power of love in inciting a breakdown due to the extremes of passion; and the power of failed domesticity in damning a woman to oblivion.

The characterization of Heathcliff in many ways appears to follow the model of a 'Byronic hero', so-called after the poet George Gordon Byron or Lord Byron (1788–1824); such heroes were characterized by a gruffly handsome appearance, a defiance of convention, a charismatic pursuit of desire and individual fulfilment, and a transgressive sexual appeal or danger that pitted desire against duty.[20] Byron's semi-autobiographical epic narrative poem *Childe Harold's Pilgrimage* (1812–18) depicted a defiant, moody hero that skirted outside social convention and yet was capable of deep feelings and affection. Since Byron was widely regarded as something of a sexually voracious and moody individual in his own right, handsome yet dangerous, passionate yet committed, the man and the myth became blurred in public consciousness. And when he was fatally wounded in the Greek War of Independence, the theme of the Byronic hero became fixed. It is an image that would have been well known to contemporary readers of *Wuthering Heights*.[21]

Appropriately, then, Heathcliff remarks to Nelly that Isabelle had pictured him 'a hero of romance and expecting unlimited indulgences from my chivalrous devotion'.[22] The passionate romance is revealed to be a fantasy, rather than a reality, but it was nevertheless influential in constructing the image of the desirable yet dastardly romantic hero and the enthralled, abandoned heroine. The theme of the 'soulmate' is a tormenting one, for it sets the bar on heterosexual intimacy, at the same time as it promises only passionate destruction. It also allows for a high level of abuse to be carried out in relationships, in the belief that to be passionately desired by a soulmate produces a level of passion that supersedes any social convention or normative codes of conduct.[23] Alarmingly, these threads also run through twenty-first-century fiction aimed at teenage girls and young women.

Love Conquers All, Even Werewolves and Vampires

The invocation of the Gothic has resurfaced in a plethora of mainstream novels aimed at women and girls that feature the same tropes of danger, passion, death and decay, a curse, insanity, the supernatural, and—persistently—vampires. Between 2005 and 2008, four books were published that compose the series *Twilight*. These would later be made into the *Twilight Saga* film series by Summit Entertainment. Written by American author Stephenie Meyer, the books chart the life of teenager Isabella (Bella) Swan, who moves to her father's house in Forks, Washington, when her mother leaves their home in Phoenix, Arizona with her new husband. In Forks she meets and falls in love with Edward Cullen, a 104-year-old vampire, and also with Jacob, who is a werewolf. Heralding the beginning of a new era in vampire fiction, the series sold over 120 million copies worldwide by 2011 and had been translated into forty different languages. From a feminist perspective, these books are problematic, for they valorise unhealthy romantic relationships.[24] They also suggest that nothing is quite so lonely as unrequited love.

The plot of the *Twilight* books revolves around Bella's decision to be with Edward (and sometimes Jacob), and the intensity of the passion she has for Edward in particular; a passion that means she has to forgo her humanity, be socially ostracized, and be closer to nature in a brutal sense; eventually hunting in the forest with the other vampires, whose way of life was once repulsive to her. These novels—and more especially the films that followed—have been hugely successful and spurred significant literary debate as to their literary and social value. There are critics that suggest Bella's relationship with Edward represents Christian abstinence as a goal for girls (if they have sex, he will kill her. He desires her blood, yet he cannot control himself if he bites her). The books also sensationalize what is an essentially abusive relationship: Edward controls what Bella can and can't do, who she can and can't see; and there is an ever-present fear of violent death.

The plot of the series is remarkably similar to *Wuthering Heights* in that it involves a young woman who is drawn to a handsome yet dangerous man, and the ultimate fulfilment or rejection of that relationship is the pivot on which the books hinge. Bella is persistently exposed to danger through her dealings with Edward; from the sadistic vampire who seeks to consume her, to her own sense of disconnect from her family and friends since she cannot inhabit both worlds. A love-triangle is produced by the inclusion of the shape-shifting wolf Jacob, who identifies that being with Edward is killing Bella. He tells her that they could be together without her having to change or adapt at all. She could keep her family and friends; she could keep her life. By contrast, absorption into Edward's world is only possible by her literal consumption and her transformation into an impossibly beautiful vampire. Along the way, Edward has to prove his love for Bella by exposing himself to danger (with the Volturi, the coven that rules on vampire codes of conduct). Bella gets pregnant and almost dies as this hitherto unknown birth between a vampire and a human produces a child that is both immortal and possesses special vampire and human qualities.

There is, in the end, some wrapping up of disagreements and an equilibrium that is at odds with the dramatic unfolding of the protagonists' relationship and the blissfully unaware human world in which they will continue to live—separately but together, unified by their extraordinary bond. Unlike *Wuthering Heights,* love conquers all; unlike the Gothic originals, modern novels are rose-tinted for a Hollywood audience in which the death of the protagonists would not be remotely satisfying. Interestingly, in the film version, the story is played out as though the characters had died, which the shocked audience discovers later is merely a glimpse into a possible but vanquished future. Normal service is resumed after that teasing subversion of convention, and viewers get their happy ending.

What I want to focus on more fully here are the connections between *Twilight* and *Wuthering Heights,* and the ways in which the relationship between Edward and Bella, like that between Heathcliff and Cathy, explores and reinforces key themes: about the conflict between self and society (or desire and convention), the meaning of belonging and loneliness, the nature of love, and the nature/civilization divide. Both works explore the limits and expectation of female desire and the extent to which the self can ever actually thrive without that significant 'other'. Or rather, whether women can thrive. Edward was miserable and spied on Bella from a distance, but he managed to stay away. Bella pushed herself into more and more dangerous situations, including sexual danger, in pursuit of a response from Edward. The overall message seems to be that the relationship is inevitable, and for all its pain, worth pursuing.

The term 'soulmate' is used repeatedly by characters justifying this outwardly unhealthy union in *Eclipse*, which is the third novel in the *Twilight* series.[25] To have a soulmate is the ideal situation that is projected in Bella's life (by her mother, by her female friends), and a pattern she sees in other members of Edward's family, the members of whom will literally live forever as they are immortal. This is a considerable contrast to Bella's own life, as her parents had split up when she was young, her father seems lonely, and her high-school classmates are trying, and failing, to secure 'the one'. Edward becomes Bella's saviour; he will take her away from a life that is ordinary, and he will transform her into someone brighter and better in every way. Except one—she may lose her soul. Bella believes it's worth the risk. Edward rapidly becomes the logic of Bella's existence. She has no hobbies or interests, as manifested when they separate, and she spends months in her own room pining and becoming so unwell that her father worries for her health. She only eventually becomes active when she realizes she can put herself physically in danger because that draws Edward towards her and he can 'save' her all over again.

As if the resonances between the stories weren't enough, Meyer explicitly references the plot of *Wuthering Heights*. This is to crank up the sense that the story of Bella and Edward is tapping into universal truths about love. In *Eclipse*, there are several scenes where Bella is wandering around with a dog-eared copy of *Wuthering Heights*, and she even enters into a conversation with Edward about its merits. He is initially dismissive of the book, but eventually expresses surprise that he is able, at last, to comprehend Heathcliff, a man who seems to suffer as Edward does. 'The more time I spend with you', he says to Bella, 'the more human emotions seem comprehensible to me. I'm discovering that I can sympathize with Heathcliff in ways I didn't think possible before'.[26]

The comparison runs both ways, as Heathcliff—in a quote from the book read by Bella—is roused by passion and jealousy towards a potential love rival (much as Edward had expressed his antipathy towards the 'dog' Jacob): 'The moment her regard ceased, I would have torn his heart out and drank his blood!'.[27] Heathcliff is equally vampiric, then, and equally bloodthirsty. Bella also compares herself to Cathy, 'only my options were so much better than hers, neither one evil, neither one weak. And here I sat, crying about it, not doing anything productive to make it right. Just like Cathy'.[28] It is Edward who will whisper in her ear, channelling Heathcliff, the infamous phrase from *Wuthering Heights*: 'I cannot live without my life! I cannot live without my soul!'

The cultural success of the *Twilight Saga* in this context reasserts the idea that a soulmate is crucial for an individual's development, and particularly for a woman. A woman's value is defined by absorption into another, and in a relationship that can be abusive as long as he is 'the one'. It also suggests that women who do not find this kind of love are 'unlucky' or failed. Even 'desperate' women like Bridget Jones eventually find their soulmates (like the *Twilight* series, *Bridget Jones' Diary* has tapped in to a range of cultural archetypes about romantic relationships, with the eponymous and unlikely heroine becoming shorthand for a lack of success in love).[29]

Today there are thousands of self-help books, like *The Soulmate Secret*, that promise to help readers find their special one; there are also numerous books and guides and programmes set up to support lonely people in their search for love, and even suicide-pacts arranged by those who do not succeed.[30] Clearly, the idea of a soulmate or a perfect romantic partner (and the parallel loss associated with its absence) continues to flourish. The reasons *why* seem related to the quest for individual identity and belonging that is being described in this book as linked to modernity. The decline of an overarching narrative of religion, in which one is cared for unconditionally, and the corresponding rise of individualistic ideas about the development of the individual, as well as the onset of mass consumerism and globalization, which focus on the perfection of that individual self and a prevailing psychological discourse that sets the individual against the world from birth, has identified romantic love as the prime source through which spiritual, mental, psychological, and physical satisfaction can be achieved.

What, then, of those who never find 'true love', who do not experience close connections in their families of origin, and/or spend their lives looking for 'the one'? If we accept that emotional experiences tend to be patterned according to cultural archetypes—teenage girls dreaming of being loved the way Bella is loved by Edward (or Jacob), and older people searching online for their soulmate even when multiple marriages have failed—then it becomes entirely possible that the influence of the soulmate myth helps to fuel loneliness. And being lonely in a crowd takes on new and powerful meanings. If we are only complete with a partner who fulfils us (in whatever sense that is taken), how can we ever be whole, without 'the one'? The social psychologist Valerie Walkerdine's work is instructive here, especially in understanding how young girls, positioned as passive recipients of men's desire from a young age, can be particularly moulded, from youth, to expect their individual fulfilment to be dependent on a (usually youthful and vital) male other.[31]

This creation of a model of *yearning* for fulfilment can follow individuals throughout their lives. Young single people and recently divorced people seem especially likely to report feeling lonely because unattached, while longing for 'one special person'.[32] In studies of single, divorced, married, and widowed adults, those who were married tended to show less loneliness, though of course loneliness within marriage—compounding feelings of not being understood, not being 'seen'—is a separate social problem.[33] The presumptions made about single people continue to be overwhelmingly gendered: consider the 1970s image of a 'swinging bachelor' against that of a 'lonely spinster'.[34]

And for single women, often accused of being 'too selective' in their pursuit of a mate, the ideal of passive, feminine acquiescence to a romantic ideal is apparent as a cultural norm.[35] In the early twentieth century, a cultural presumption in Britain, no matter that women had been making their own living in the world for centuries, was that single women were simply 'waiting for marriage'.[36] There was also a strong body of criticism advising that women should not wait too long to secure a match in case they lost their erotic allure and/or ability to reproduce, both of which have been historically depicted as women's (particularly white women's) key assets. Today, that theme has been reawakened in the concept of 'erotic capital', which young women are supposed to possess in relation to their aesthetic appearance, and which depreciates as an asset over time.[37] At its most repugnant, this institutionalized patriarchal and biological reduction of women is found in the INCEL movement, a self-defining group of men who describe themselves as 'involuntarily celibate' as a result of women's freedom over their bodies (and legitimize violent actions and terrorism as a result).[38]

Although most studies into loneliness among single people focus on the elderly and alone, then, usually as a result of widow(er) hood and the disparate geography of families in the twenty-first century, there is clearly more work needed into loneliness and romantic aspirations and delusions; in particular the cultural role of the soulmate in generating a sense of lack. In terms of behaviours associated with loneliness and the search for a romantic 'other', there is a considerable body of work into the negative, often self-defeating search for love on the Internet, where presumed intimacy is often gratified immediately without being deep or long-lasting or meaningful.[39] (I am making a distinction here between the search for long-term relationships and casual encounters, though the motivations of people using dating apps can be diverse.)[40]

The search for romance, and the belief in a soulmate, impacts on our experience of loneliness as individuals and a society. If the sentiment of two people together against the world is an ideal (regardless of how individuals behave through the legitimacy of 'passion'), then there are clear social and emotional impacts, both in terms of how people experience love, and how they feel about its lack. Without that significant other, the threat of lack suggests, we will be forever 'separated, having one side only, like a flat fish, always looking for [our] other half'. Another question, of course, is what happens to those who find their soulmates, who live out the dream of a lifetime together, until one of them dies. Widowhood, or widowerhood, can also bring a distinct and culturally laden form of loneliness, as the next chapter shows.

CHAPTER 4

WIDOW(ER)HOOD AND LOSS

From Thomas Turner to the Widow of Windsor

> I looked over to his chair and when I saw it, that was the first time I really, really cried after he died.
>
> June Bernicoff, star of UK's Channel 4 reality show, *Gogglebox*

In December 2017 the British tabloids announced the death of Leon Bernicoff, one of the stars of the reality television show *Gogglebox*, shown on Channel 4. June and Leon had starred in ten series of the programme since it began in 2013. The popular couple also appeared in an Age UK advert aimed at preventing loneliness among the elderly at Christmastime.[1] When Leon's death was announced at the age of eighty-three, his widow June reported that it was not until she watched their last episode together, when she realized he was not in his chair, that she was hit by the full extent of her grief. It took a material reminder of absence in the form of Leon's empty chair, for the 'sense of loss' she experienced to became clear.[2]

It is common for all those grieving a loved one to report profound grief attached to the 'empty chair': the dinner place seated for someone who will never arrive; the armchair that is no longer used.[3] It has become an everyday, physical reminder of a tear in one's emotional fabric. One that is fixed, permanent, and cannot be healed. Psychotherapeutic interventions sometimes use that image of the chair, figurate or literal, as a tool to promote healing in bereaved patients. By speaking to the imagined inhabitant of that chair, it is felt, a person might unburden themselves of some of the grief, anger, and anxiety that might attach itself to loss.[4]

The empty chair can take on the character and the presence of its user. I remember my Grandad Sidney's chair, with the special lever that lifted him from his seat, the shape of his skull permanently indented into the headrest. Sidney didn't use Brylcreem so it didn't leave a smear behind, like Grandad Ron's head did, causing my grandmother to rearrange the antimacassar with a glare. But Sidney's chair held his presence in every stitch. It was turned to the window of his sheltered accommodation so that he could watch the comings and goings of my cousins' house, and poke fun at the neighbours, cackling away with a cigarette in one hand and a ventilator in the other. Whenever I slept on the couch, I would wake to the sound of his hacking cough and his silhouette, pressed in that chair and outlined against the dawn.

When Sidney died, that chair became a memorial. It was and always would be 'Sidney's Chair'. My Grandma Rose sat in the other corner of the room, watching this empty chair, gazing past it at the window and waiting for the doorbell to ring. She never quite recovered from Sidney's death; each time I saw her, she was smaller, frailer, and lonelier.

Loneliness and Nostalgia

The pain of loss is most problematic among the old—particularly the 'oldest old', those over eighty, for whom bereavement becomes all too frequent. The material culture of loneliness—not just chairs but slippers and sideboards, photographs and plates—takes on a particular kind of significance in old age, as the objects associated with one's family and loved ones become mementoes of a lost or painfully mourned social identity. There are links, then, between loneliness and nostalgia, as well as loneliness and homesickness. Nostalgia can include a mourning for what has been lost; a sense of lack compared to what were once the key elements of a life: friends, children, a spouse. Yet nostalgia is not just a negative experience when connected to loneliness; it can also be a powerful and positive force.

Nostalgia, or a 'sentimental longing for the past', as defined by one group of psychological researchers, can help to combat loneliness. The most persistent subjects of nostalgia, including memories of holidays, birthdays, family events, and weddings, are reminders of social attachments and connectedness. Those events might be remembered with sadness as well as happiness (sadness that they are in the past; happiness that they occurred); but in the main, higher levels of happiness than sadness have been reported.[5] Thus, 'nostalgic reverie' can 'reignite meaningful relational bonds and re-establish a symbolic connection with significant others'.[6]

The set of relationships that one carries in one's head, in other words, can protect against perceptions of social disconnect in the present, even if those relationships no longer exist. This recognition raises key questions about the role of memory in understanding loneliness, as well as the significance of time. One of the problems of chronic loneliness, loneliness that exists for many years, is that these imagined networks do not hold the same restorative function, perhaps because the meaningful bonds they invoke were never present. Time and memory are key areas where loneliness needs more research and exploration, in the case of old age and dementia, as well as through the potentially enduring loneliness initiated by a difficult childhood.

In this chapter, and in keeping with the priorities of loneliness research in the UK and its focus on end of life, I want to turn to the loneliness of widow(er)hood, which brings particular *forms* of loneliness (the plural is important, since loneliness is not always experienced in the same way). That does not, mean, however, that the meanings of loneliness in widow(er)hood universally recur at the same time and in the same ways. Rather, its manifestations depend on individual circumstance and experience as well as historically situated belief systems that include the role of marriage, religion, social networks, and even fate.

Widow(er)hood as a Particular Form of Loss

Modern accounts of widow(er)hood that focus on the specific emotional qualities of losing a spouse recount the overwhelming pain of bereavement, along with the practicalities of mourning and the silence that follows.[7] We tend not, as a society, to talk about the positive elements of widow(er)hood, as considered in *The Widowed Self*, by the Canadian Professor of Gerontology Deborah van der Hoonaard.[8] In her book, van der Hoonaard described the joyful rediscovery of new experiences and new connections despite the loss of her partner. Importantly, the author deals with the experience of loneliness among older women, many of whom express uncertainty, grief, and resentment at the reductionist term 'widow', which reinforces the cultural assumptions connected to the term—frail, elderly, needing care—while ignoring complex lived experiences that might range from relief to unfulfilled sexual longing. Moreover, the nostalgia or loneliness of loss might continue for many years, even when new relationships are forged, and old connections rediscovered.

The language of widow(er)hood, while reductionist, reminds us of traditional cultural assumptions of marriage and the emotional, intellectual, sexual, and practical bonds that are severed by death. The term 'widow' comes from the Old English *widewe*, from an Indo-European root meaning 'be empty'; which compares with the Sanskrit *vidh*, meaning 'be destitute', and the Latin *viduus*, 'bereft'. Widows have been viewed with particular suspicion in history; as figures of ridicule in sixteenth- and seventeenth-century literature as well as rampant sexual predators preying on younger, unmarried men.[9] The term continues to have negative associations, as acknowledged by van der Hoonaard's interviewees.[10]

The French dramatist (of Italian origin) Pierre de Larivey (1549–1619)—widely credited with bringing the Italian 'comedy of intrigue' into France—published a farcical comedy in Paris in 1579 called *La veuve (The Widow)* that played with social conventions around widows and remarriage, and its pursuit as a way to avoid solitude.[11] The complexities and contradictions around widows' experience—including the desire for companionship and the fear of losing autonomy—were closely revealed in private writing. Alongside these emotional expressions were the complex social relationships brought by widow(er)hood.

On the one hand, widows reinforced the biblical image of the suffering and the destitute, widowhood being 'a plague of God upon the ungodly'.[12] Widows were to be pitied, and yet posed a threat to the hierarchical, patriarchal order in which marriage was the ideal. Widows, especially widows with property, subverted the idea that women were the property of men, and legally dependent on them; widowhood is likely to have brought some women autonomy and freedom.[13] Yet widowhood was equally expected to bring grief and sorrow. Religious writers urged for restrained sorrow in dealing with the experience of widowhood. The English churchman Thomas Fuller (1608–61) depicted 'the good widow' as 'a woman whose head hath been quite cut off and yet she liveth':

> Her grief for her husband, though real, is moderate. Excessive was the sorrow of King Richard the Second, beseeming him neither as a king, man or Christian…But our widow's sorrow is no storm, but a still rain. Indeed, some foolishly discharge a surplusage of their passions on themselves tearing their hair, so that their friends coming to the funeral know not which most to bemoan, the dead husband or the dying widow. Yet commonly it comes to pass, that such widow's grief is quickly emptied, which streameth out at so large a rent; whilst their tears that drop will hold running a long time.[14]

Such patriarchal conventions stemmed from an understanding that women were to be ruled by men, a legal and social presumption that meant widowhood could be potentially liberating as well as emotionally challenging. These contradictions were explored in relation to the 'Book of M', the memoirs of Katherine Austen. Katherine Austen described her six years of widowhood as the 'Most saddest Yeares'; 'The world may think I tread upon Roses', she said, 'but they know not the sack cloth I have walkt on, not the heauines and bitternes of my minde'.[15] Though Austen had three children when her thirty-six-year-old husband died, she possessed a legacy from her mother and a number of London properties, so was well-off by seventeenth-century standards.

Though she found widowhood a struggle, largely because of the efforts needed to maintain her financial security and protect her children's inheritance, Austen recognized that remarrying would bring its own challenges. As in descriptions of the passions, through the metaphor of sailing on the seas of life (or the 'sea of griefe' and the 'waters of peril'), Austen steered her way through a sometimes tumultuous journey in which she sought solace and help from God.[16]

Sources for studying widow(er)hood in history are few and far between, at least for the poorer levels of society. There is more extant material for the upper levels of society, and for men, who were more likely to leave their trace on the world. Here I would like to consider the writings of two people from contrasting backgrounds, class, and sex, in order to consider how widow(er)hood was expressed in language, symbols, and materiality. I will focus, too, on the different conventions used in order to explore change and continuity in understandings of widowed loneliness and the impact of gender, wealth, and changing patterns of consumerism. The first case study will be the eighteenth-century English shopkeeper Thomas Turner, and the second, Queen Victoria.

The Case of Thomas Turner

Thomas Turner was the son of a yeoman, born in Kent.[17] The first editors of his diary defined Turner as 'grocer, draper, haberdasher, hatter, clothier, druggist, ironmonger, stationer, glover, undertaker, and what not', as Turner was involved in a wide range of activities in East Hoathly, Sussex, where he kept his shop.[18] We can learn much about Turner's lifestyle and relationships through his diary, which he kept for eleven years. He wrote about his desires and expectations for his business and (to a limited degree) his emotional life in the context of the conventions of the time. And that covered a lot of ground; Turner was not only a shopkeeper but also an undertaker, schoolmaster, surveyor, and overseer of the poor; he wrote wills and helped with taxes. He played cricket and read widely, including the work of William Shakespeare, Joseph Addison, and Samuel Richardson; he enjoyed summarizing their books in his diaries, and reading alone with his wife and friends, which was a common custom in the sociable, bourgeois world of the eighteenth century.

Turner married his first wife Margaret ('Peggy') Slater in 1753 and they had one child, a son named Peter. Sadly, the child did not survive. On 16 January 1755, Turner wrote in his diary that 'this morning about 1 o'clock I had the misfortune to lose my little boy Peter, aged 21 weeks, 3 days'. The sadness of losing a child was noted; that Turner did not go on to lament the child over the following weeks was not a sign that he cared for his son any more or less than his descendants might, but that the languages of grief were different. Eighteenth-century society was outwardly religious, and the literary conventions of the time, not only in relation to parenting styles, but also marriage, tended to extol the Protestant virtues of hard work and emotional discipline in dealing with one's lot.

In marriage, a companionable ideal predominated, as discussed in conduct manuals of the time, and in the writings of the English essayist Joseph Addison; civility and restraint mattered. Turner did not always enjoy a harmonious relationship with his wife Peggy, and when they fell out, which seems to have been often, he would set out in his diary his disappointment about their situation, as well as what he had hoped and expected from the union. Those hopes and expectations used the conventions of religious and civil discourse and implicitly referred back to the codes of behaviour that were advised in marriage guides and conduct manuals. When he and his wife 'had words', for instance, Turner would lament the gap between his experience of marriage and what he had anticipated when he entered the union:

> Oh! What a happiness there must be in a married state when there is a sincere regard on both sides and each party truly satisfied with the other's merit; but it is impossible for tongue or pen to express the uneasiness that attends the contrary.[19]

> Let me recall the resolution of a man and proceed. A man, did I say? Oh! How the sound of that word makes me start. I know not scarce what I am. All that I know is I am happy in having that person, who of all the sex I ever had the greatest respect for, for my wife. But again, how unhappy to have that only one in whom all my earthly facility was centred to be of such an unhappy temper as not only to make me, but herself also, miserable.[20]

When he was not getting along with his wife, Turner sought friendship and companionship among his friendship networks. Unfortunately, he was not as blessed with support there as he would have liked, and he frequently lamented the same in his diary, feeling as though others were 'cold' and indifferent. On 22 February 1756, Turner noted that he visited his mother's house and his brother was there:

> Whether just imaginary I cannot, no, I will not, say but I think I was received very coldly, not only by my mother, but all the family... My mother and I had a great many words, or at least my mother had with me. What my friends would have with me I know not; I have always done to the utmost of my power to serve them. I can with justice to myself and all mankind say I have their interest entirely at

> heart and never think myself more happy than in serving them; and were I assured I was to blame, I should even despise myself, and even think myself not worthy to be ranked among the rest of mankind was I to be cruel and undutiful to a mother, and one who is a widow, though doubtless I am not exempt from faults. No, I am moral, but still how happy could I be, would my friends let but a free and sincere communication of friendship once more be opened between us, and which has of late been shut up, but upon what account I cannot tell.[21]

On other occasions, Turner felt 'deserted by all my friends... But, however, what to attribute the coldness and indifference with which I am treated by my friends and relations I am at a loss to guess. Sometimes I think I must be a prodigy that all my relations in general seem to be so indifferent to me'. In the end, there was 'nought to trust except the Divine Providence and my own industry'.[22] When Thomas' mother died on 1 April 1759, he was melancholy; she was sixty-two years of age, and though there was clearly friction between them, her death compounded this sense of isolation. On 5 April he had lunch with his siblings and extended relations, afterwards attending his mother's burial service:

> We are now left as it were without any head, quite mother and fatherless, and it seems just as if we was now a-going to turn out in a wild world without any friends. Oh, may the God of all mercy pour His holy spirit into our hearts that we may grow in grace and unite together with brotherly love and kindness and always think of our high calling through our blessed saviour and redeemer Jesus Christ.[23]

Conscious of his temporality, grieving his mother as well as his own lack of friends, Thomas nevertheless was able to reach out to the ideal and the comfort of God, and to structure his emotional responses in accordance with religious philosophy. Christ suffered too; Christ had been alone on the cross. And how could one ever be truly alone when God was there?

When Turner's wife became 'very ill' in 1759 (of 'a violent colic, the gravel and an obstruction of the catamenia', or menstrual flow), Turner's thoughts immediately turned to the further breakdown of family ties:

> Oh, how melancholy a time it is [when I,] quite destitute of father or mother, am in all probability to lose my wife, the only friend I believe I have now in the world, and the alone centre of my worldly happiness! When I indulge the serious thought, what imagery can paint the gloomy scene that seems just ready to open itself as it were for a theatre for my future troubles to be acted upon.[24]

Turner's self-conscious description of the 'theatre' of his grief should not be read as artifice; this mode of expression was in keeping with eighteenth-century civil discourse and emotional sensibility. In between worrying about his wife and predicting her impending death, he entertained visitors and carried out his usual business. Through his own sickness, when he injured his side and was convinced it would turn 'cancerous', Turner had prayed to God that he would 'pour into my heart the graces of his Holy Spirit'.[25] While illness could be an isolating time, Turner's belief in the protection and the will of God provided succour, as well as a framework for his emotional experiences and expression. Similarly, anxiety about the ill health of a spouse could be framed according to God's mercy and will. On 25 October 1760, Turner spent the day at home, where his wife seemed slightly recovered:

> In the even read Gibson on lukewarmness in religion, and a sermon of his entitled *Trust in God, the best remedy against fears of all kinds,* both of which I look upon as extreme good things.[26]

Turner was referring to a hugely influential treatise by Edmund Gibson (1669–1748), a British divine who served as Bishop of Lincoln and Bishop of London, Gibson's *Trust in God, the best remedy against fears of all kinds: a sermon.*[27] Gibson's *Trust in God* assured readers that:

> God has the sole Disposal of the Blessings of this Life; it is he alone that maketh Poor and maketh Rich: Or whether our Minds are disturbed at the *general* Vicissitude and Uncertainty of human Affairs; all these, however unsteady they appear to us, are directed to their proper Ends by the infinite Power and Wisdom of God.[28]

Peggy died on 23 June 1761. 'It pleased Almighty God to take from me my beloved wife', Turner recorded in his diary, 'who, poor creature has laboured under a severe though lingering illness for these 38 weeks past, which she bore with the greatest resignation to the Divine will'.[29] 'I am now destitute', Turner wrote, using a phrase he relied on often when speaking of his social isolation, 'of a friend to converse with or even a sincere friend on whom I could rely for advice now that I have lost the dear, dear partner of my soul'.[30]

The terminology and concept of the term 'soulmate' is one which has become secular, despite its religious origins, and commonplace to describe a specific kind of connectedness between people—usually romantic. Turner's particular formulation 'partner of my soul' seems to have figured as a shorthand for happiness in marriage after the English dramatist and later poet laureate Nicholas Rowe's *The Royal Convert* (1707), dealing with the persecutions endured by Aribert, son of Hengist and the Christian maiden Ethelinda: 'I trust thee with the Partner of my Soul/My wife, the kindest, dearest, and the truest/That ever wore the Name'.[31]

Turner's use of the term is important, for it shows how often emotional expression borrows from terminology used within one's social circles and cultural reference points; it is one of the ways by which emotions themselves become internalized and reproduced.[32]

When Peggy was on her deathbed, Turner was resentful that his friends and relatives did not seem to offer him companionship. Certainly, there was a gulf between the emotional comfort he expected and that which he received:

> I cannot tell, whether from my own unhappy temper or that of my friends and relations, but in this day of trouble, they seem to stand aloof and as it were staring at me like a stranger. Not one, no! not one that attempts to pour that healing balm of compassion into a heart wounded and torn to pieces with trouble. Whenever it shall please the almighty to take from me the wife of my bosom, then shall I be like a beacon upon a rock, or an ensign on a hill, destitute of every sincere friends, and not a friendly companion left to comfort my afflicted mind and yield that pleasing comfort of consolation to a mind quite worn to the grave with trouble.[33]

There was a recognition in Turner's words of the hazards of too solitary an existence, a theme that is discussed in Chapter 1 of this book. And yet God was present in Turner's everyday world, and the potential (and actual) loss of Peggy would be His decision alone; in which case Turner depicted himself in religious terms, like a 'beacon on a rock' or an 'ensign on a hill', wanting earthly company in ways that echoed not modern-day loneliness but a religious state of 'desolation', akin to that of Jesus in the wilderness. Turner's loneliness, then, was comparable to the earlier sense of 'oneliness', rather than its modern equivalent.

The Oneliness of Thomas Turner

As a widower, Turner experienced the practical and emotional loss of his wife, both in 'the disburthening my mind...when it was almost even overloaded with trouble'[34] and in running his household. He also had to contend with the accusation that he had been responsible for her demise by encouraging her doctor to undertake an unnecessary and violent operation:

> That Mr Snelling at my request (and by force) castrated my wife, whose operation was the immediate cause of her death. And with such amazing swiftness is the report spread that there is hardly a child of four years old or a woman of four score within ten miles of the place but has it at their tongue's end.[35]

Castration referred to an ovariectomy, in which a woman's ovaries were removed, or a more total hysterectomy, in which the uterus was excised. While the first such procedure was recorded in the sixteenth century, there are very few authenticated instances of it taking place before the nineteenth century. In the time of Peggy Turner, it was not a procedure that she would have been expected to survive.[36] There is no doubt that Turner felt himself isolated and slighted by this lack of community regard, which was crucial for social standing and financial credit as well as emotional well-being in eighteenth-century England.[37] Turner girded his loins against such accusations with reference to his own conscience, 'which I am sure sings peace in that affair', as well as the 'over-ruling providence' of God that 'orders everything according to infinite wisdom'.[38]

Marriage, for Turner, when he was at his most optimistic after the death of Peggy, had offered a 'secret pleasure' that could not be found outside of it, 'whatever the libertines may say or think'; a secret pleasure made up of the 'solid foundation of friendship and domestic happiness', a certainty that could not be found elsewhere in life.[39] Perhaps Turner was already preparing himself to marry again, as would have been expected for a man of his station and lifestyle in the eighteenth century. He enjoyed some forays into the dating world—such as tea with his 'old acquaintance, Mr Coates's servant' a few months later, on 16 October 1762, but 'not one word of courting, no, not even a kiss as a preparative thereto. Of sad disappointment this must be', he adds, 'to the busy censorious world to find their conjectures are never like to prove true'.[40] Turner was responding to the gossip that accompanied the previous visit of Mr Coates's unnamed servant to the Turner household just a few weeks earlier.[41] By the time Turner's diaries end, however, in June 1765, he had remarried. On 19 June Turner wed Mary Hicks, servant to Luke Spence. And he was characteristically pragmatic about the union:

> [T]hank God I begin once more to be a little settled and am happy in my choice. I have, it's true, not married a learned lady, nor is she a gay one, but I trust she is goodnatured, and one that will use her utmost endeavour to make me happy, which perhaps is as much as it is in the power of a wife to do. As to her fortune, I shall one day have something considerable, and there seems to be rather a flowing stream.[42]

The marriage lasted until Turner died in 1793, and the couple had seven children, only two of whom outlived their father. We can learn much about eighteenth-century emotional expectations in marriage and society from Turner's diary. The polite sociability expected of marriage, as well as the complex rights and responsibilities that went into being a husband and wife, were well rehearsed in eighteenth-century manuals and guidebooks. We can make certain presumptions about the frustration experienced by Turner when his wife did not act according to expectation, as well as his sadness when he felt disrespected at home and unvalued by society at large;[43] particularly when, in Turner's own view, he consistently acted in accordance with social expectations as a responsible figure in the local community, as a husband, and as a true Christian.

For all his difficulties, I do not believe that Turner's experiences as an often-solitary man, or as a widower, can be equated to a modern definition of 'loneliness'. He pursued holistic medical treatments designed to care for the whole person, he believed in God, he sought out civil companionship, and he lived according to the desires and expectations of a middle-class eighteenth-century shopkeeper. He did not receive as much companionship from others as he had hoped, and he frequently felt a gap between what he gave to others and what they gave to him, in terms of time and attention. And he mourned his son and mother and wife, all of which made him aware of his temporal isolation, his 'oneliness', and the guiding hand of God. But he was not lonely in any modern sense.

In Turner's time 'loneliness' had not yet emerged as a linguistic or emotional state; although David Vaisey, the *Diary*'s modern editor, writes that 'Thomas was a lonely man', Turner never used the term 'loneliness'.[44] He was solitary, but he was also of the belief that his sufferings were for a purpose. His experiences were framed and described in reference to a higher power which never deserted him, through difficulties, illness, and even death. He did, however, expect kinder treatment from others, in accordance with the expectations of eighteenth-century sociability.

It is impossible to know the extent to which Turner's emotional state parallels modern discussions of loneliness, because the nature of language is that it shifts and transforms over time. There is also always a gulf between what is expressed and what is felt. But I am suggesting that the qualitative experience of being alone described by Turner, even though it was associated with feelings of resentment that he wasn't receiving the friendship and companionship he felt he deserved (including from his family), was framed within discourses of civic identity, politeness, and the certainty of God's presence. And even allowing for the conventions of eighteenth-century diarizing, this is markedly different from the bleakness of alienation described as characteristic of the modern self.[45]

I want to turn now to another instance of widow(er)hood, from the following century, in which the loneliness of loss is figured differently. While widow(er)hood was, and is, a great leveller, the ways that it was conceived and talked about differed according to class, gender, economic and social status, and time. One of the most famous examples of widow(er)hood was that of Queen Victoria, whose life was defined by the death of her husband Prince Albert. The monarch's grief was described in far more detail. And for Queen Victoria, widowhood became a defined social and emotional identity. Her mourning was constructed through the world of goods—which was not absent in Turner's writing (in the food that was served, for instance, and the architectural structure of the household), but which had become far more expansive and theatrical than it had been in the eighteenth century. This reflects the fact that Victoria was a monarch, and as such had a wider variety of consumer goods at her disposal, but by the nineteenth century, more material objects were available than they ever had been before, thanks to mass production and consumerism. Thus, even the middling levels of society would be able to commemorate Albert's passing with a factory-worked cup or figurine.[46] Even by the mourning practices of Victorian culture, Queen Victoria's mourning was seen as excessive, suggesting cultural differences in defining widow(er)hood that are not only individual and gendered, but also collective and nationalistic. Yet it is possible to discern a core of loneliness in Victoria's writings that is not expressed in the writings of Thomas Turner.

Of course, it is not possible to be certain that the emotional sentiment described by Queen Victoria defines any 'authentic' experience. Besides conventions of the text, there are differences in diaries written by unknown individuals and monarchs who might expect them to be read by others (indeed, this motivated the rigorous censorial work that was undertaken after Queen Victoria's death by her daughter, Princess Beatrice).[47] Nevertheless, even allowing for such variation there are significant differences of style and content in the diaries of Thomas Turner and those of Queen Victoria. Unlike Turner's, Queen Victoria's writing is filled with references to the specific loneliness of a widow, and the creation of a space that nothing and nobody (not even a sense of God) could fill.

The conventions and expectations of Victorian marriage were more expansive, and more emotionally constructed, than those of the eighteenth century; marriage was widely understood to include material comforts, romantic love, and friendship, just as it had in the seventeenth and eighteenth centuries. But the domestic sphere was pictured, even within the royal household, as a buffer between the individual and the outside world. Victorian culture identified gender differences, moreover, that focused on women's emotionality and need for companionship and protection, and men's superiority in areas of governance and finance. This seems to have been a running theme of tension in Queen Victoria's journals as she felt Albert's irritation at being regarded as second best to his wife and not even receiving what he regarded as a proper title, being known only as Prince Consort. In looking at the widowhood of Queen Victoria, we can also trace a broader context in which widow(er)hood might be depicted not only as an event (the death of a spouse), but also as the development of a particular social role characterized by individual loss and loneliness.

The Widow of Windsor

Queen Victoria was monarch of the United Kingdom of Great Britain and Ireland from 20 June 1837 until her death on 22 January 1901. In May 1876 she also adopted the title of Empress of India, reflecting the United Kingdom's colonial influence. The daughter of Prince Edward, Duke of Kent and Strathearn, Victoria became queen at the young age of eighteen, after a reputedly unhappy childhood that was dominated by an overbearing mother.[48] Amid much concern about securing the future heir, Victoria married her first cousin, Prince Albert of Saxe-Coburg and Gotha, in 1840.

The love story between Victoria and Albert has received significant attention, as befitting a post-Romantic society, in books and television dramas as well as films. She reportedly was attracted to him from their first meeting, recording in her diary that he was 'extremely handsome; his hair is about the same colour as mine; his eyes are large and blue, and he has a beautiful nose and a very sweet mouth with fine teeth; but the charm of his countenance is his expression, which is most delightful'.[49] After their wedding night in 1840, Queen Victoria wrote in her diary:

> I have NEVER NEVER spent such an evening!!! My DEAREST DEAREST DEAR Albert...his excessive love & affection gave me feelings of heavenly love & happiness I never could have *hoped* to have felt before! He clasped me in his arms, & we kissed each other again & again! His beauty, his sweetness & gentleness—really how can I ever be thankful enough to have such a *Husband!*...to be called by names of tenderness, I have never yet heard used to me before—was bliss beyond belief! Oh! This was the happiest day of my life![50]

The sexual as well as emotional contentment experienced by Queen Victoria is apparent, and throughout her journals she describes the fondest of feelings for her husband, to a point that was quite exclusive; more than once Prince Albert admonished her for not getting enough satisfaction from their children, or for not being quite so affectionate to them as he was.[51] The couple had nine children and were by all accounts devoted to one another during a period marked by political and economic upheavals, assassination attempts, and periods of ill health.[52] Albert became unwell with stomach problems in 1861, exacerbated, it was believed, by family problems, after a public scandal involving their eldest son's affair with an actress. Albert was subsequently diagnosed with typhoid fever and died on 14 December 1861. Queen Victoria was devastated. Commentators have noted that she blamed Albert's death on the worry that the Prince of Wales had caused. He had been 'killed by that dreadful business', she said, a view that made her relationship with her son understandably fraught for some time.[53]

When Albert died, Queen Victoria entered a state of mourning, in which she would remain for the next forty years.

Figure 4. Royal portrait of Queen Victoria, 1871.

She lived a largely secluded existence and undertook fewer public duties. Historians have observed that Queen Victoria continued to act, in many ways, as if Albert were with her until her own death on 22 January 1901; she required that his clothes were laid out each morning, and she slept with one of his night shirts.

She was buried with one of Albert's dressing gowns at her side, and with a plaster cast of his hand. Queen Victoria was interred beside Prince Albert in Frogmore Mausoleum at Windsor Great Park.

The characterization of Queen Victoria as a sombre woman is well rehearsed, though that is not what comes across in her journals. Aside from the film *Mrs Brown*, which explored the monarch's relationship with her servant and friend John Brown (who was rumoured but never proven to be Queen Victoria's lover, though a lock of his hair was buried with her), most discussions focus on her relationship with Albert.[54] Queen Victoria wrote extensively in journals during her life—according to one biographer, she wrote an average of 2,500 words a day. She kept a journal from 1832 until the end of her life, and though these extensive journals were destroyed by her youngest daughter, Princess Beatrice, Beatrice did publish edited versions of the diaries, which had been previously transcribed by the historian and Liberal politician Reginald Baliol Brett, or Lord Esher.[55]

There is extensive evidence in Queen Victoria's journals of the painful loneliness she experienced after Albert's death. From her marriage, the monarch became dependent on Albert for his companionship and friendship as well as his political advice, and during his short illness she often reported feeling alone and anxious. In December 1861, Queen Victoria's journal agonizingly traces his declining condition. Irritated by having to attend to state business while her husband's health worsened, and isolated by the prospect of losing her confidant in life as well as business, on Wednesday 4 December, Queen Victoria reported that her 'anxiety is great & I feel utterly lost, when he to whom I am want to confide all, is in such a listless state & hardly can smile!'

'Dr Jenner' (Sir William Jenner, 1st Baronet) was constantly on hand. Jenner specialized in cases of typhus and typhoid, and he had been appointed Physician Extraordinary to Queen Victoria in 1861; Physician in Ordinary to the Queen in 1862. She consulted him hourly in the hopes of some improvement. Prince Albert was also attended by Sir James Clark, 1st Baronet, who had been Physician in Ordinary to the Queen from 1837 to 1860. Clark 'was grieved to see no change for the better' when he attended, Queen Victoria lamented, though he managed to eat a 'little orange jelly' and rested in his room, sometimes read to by his wife and sometimes by one of their daughters. After a walk in the grounds of Windsor Castle, Queen Victoria returned to see Albert's 'looks & manner were very disheartening & sad. He can take no nourishment only sip a little raspberry vinegar in Seltzer water'.[56]

There can be few things in life more difficult than witnessing the pain of a loved one. The next day, Albert looked 'dreadfully wretched & woebegone', and the monarch found herself 'quite overcome & alarmed by his appearance'. Queen Victoria surrounded herself with attendants. In addition to her children and her own ladies in waiting, Sir Charles Beaumont Phipps, Private Secretary to Prince Albert (and later Private Secretary to the Sovereign), was also present. Albert was given ether for pain relief, and he managed to sleep a little overnight but, Queen Victoria reported, remained 'very restless, haggard & suffering'. Seeing her husband alternately 'suffering' and 'better' put the Queen under dreadful emotional stress: 'It is terrible these ups & downs of hope & fear!'[57]

Like Turner a hundred years earlier, though from a very different socio-economic perspective, Queen Victoria referenced her belief in God as a crutch through the sickness of a spouse. Unlike Turner, whose diaries could juxtapose intense outbursts of anxiety about his wife with a meal that included some good ham, the monarch figuratively or physically stayed at Prince Albert's bedside. She walked or rode or drove a little with family and friends occasionally, but spoke and thought of nothing else, monitoring Albert's condition closely with apprehension and fear and occasional relief. Dr Watson slept at Windsor Castle on 10 December to keep an eye on his patient. He was 'much struck with his improvement', as was Dr Jenner. The following day, the Queen sat with Albert while he ate his breakfast, supporting him with her shoulder. 'He said "it is very comfortable like that, dear Child", which made me so happy, though it almost moved me to tears!' Albert was checked on by Dr Clark and Dr Watson (1st Baronet, a cardiac specialist), who both appeared 'quite satisfied with the progress', though Queen Victoria admitted 'distress' that bulletins would need to be issued to keep the public up to date with Albert's condition.

On 12 and 13 December, the monarch began to be concerned about Albert's breathing. The doctors reassured her that it was at first merely a little 'sneezing', and that his shortness of breath was 'nothing of consequence'. Dr Jenner said the breathlessness and confusion was simply the fever, and that in another week Albert would be convalescing. On the evening of 13 December, Queen Victoria went to bed hoping for a 'quiet night'. There was no journal entry for the following day, 14 December. The Queen had gone in to see Albert at 7 a.m. 'It was a bright morning, the sun just rising and shining brightly', she later recalled. The room was sad and expectant, however, the candles being burned down, the doctors looking anxious. By 4.30 p.m., after a difficult day of waiting and watching for signs, a bulletin was announced, letting the public know that the Prince Consort was critical.[58]

Queen Victoria sat by his bedside most of the time, a lonely and anxious figure, worrying and listening to his breathing. Finally, the death rattle could be heard, and the monarch 'started like a Lioness…bounded on the bed imploring [Albert] to speak and give one kiss to his little wife'.[59] Queen Victoria later recorded the moment of Albert passing: 'Two or three long but perfectly gentle breaths were drawn, the hand clasping mine, and…*all, all* was over—the heavenly Spirit fled to the world it was fit for, and free from the sorrows and trials of this World!'[60] Gone, too, was Queen Victoria's social and emotional buffer against the world, and the most significant person to her, bar none.

The monarch did not begin her journals again until 1 January 1862, when she began to record the depth of her mourning:

> Have been unable to write my Journal since the day my beloved one left us, & with what a heavy broken heart I enter on a new year without him. My dreadful & overwhelming calamity gives me so much to do, that I must henceforth merely keep notes of my sad and solitary life. This day last year found us so perfectly happy now!! Last year music woke us! Little gifts, new year's wishes, brought in by maid, & then given to dearest Albert. The children waiting with their gifts in the next room, all these recollections were pouring in on my mind in an overpowering manner.—Alice slept in my room! & dear Baby came down early. Felt as if living in a dreadful dream…[Later on]…saw the Duke of Newcastle in dear Albert's room, where all remains the same. Talking for long of him, of his great goodness, & purity…Alice gave me my beloved Albert's Xmas present—so precious & so sad.[61]

Queen Victoria's children tried to comfort her during a period that must also have been difficult for them, having lost a father.

In her biography, Julia Baird recounts through an exploration of private correspondence the peculiarly attentive and emotionally close relationship Albert had with his children, especially given the traditional conventions of domestic relations within the Victorian upper-class family. 'He is so kind to them and romps with them so delightfully, and manages them so beautifully and firmly', reported the Queen.[62] 'Sweet Baby [Princess Beatrice, the youngest child] came down whilst I was dressing and remained with me whilst I had my breakfast. The other children came to wish me good morning'. Queen Victoria occupied her mind with plans for a mausoleum to remember her late husband, though even then she missed her 'beloved one's assistance terribly'.[63] Since their marriage, Albert had advised the Queen on all aspects of her life, and she bitterly missed his involvement. Occupying herself with conversations about her 'beloved one, of the terrible fatal illness,—of the Memorials, which will be numberless' ensured his presence was a constant one.[64]

The memorials were important for a number of reasons. In addition to engaging in conversations about Albert, which helped to keep him present, Queen Victoria structured her memories of Albert around the world of goods. Material culture is crucial not only in understanding the ways in which emotional experiences can be structured through physical interaction with the world around us, but also in forming an individual and shared sense of belonging. The importance of ensuring that Albert's bust was perfect (however many times it needed to be worked on), and spending time with belongings that reminded the monarch of her husband, helped her to engage with her emotional loss. 'Went to look at my precious Albert's Xmas gifts', she wrote on 7 January; 'a beautiful statue of Psyche by Müller ordered same [*sic*] years ago, which is really lovely & a lovely water colour picture of a girl in an antique dress, holding a small bird'.[65] Rearranging photographs and looking at images of her husband was comforting—especially a 'beautiful photograph of my precious Albert, coloured by Harrach, the eyes of which quite look at me, as if to tell me what to do!'[66] The bust of Albert she found particularly engaging; as it was 'a perfection, really a "chef d'oeuvre". The expression is admirable'.[67]

There was something nostalgic about Queen Victoria's grief that became more apparent as the months and years passed. Each anniversary of sorts was a reminder of all she had lost, and she indulged in them with a morose satisfaction. The sensory experience of Albert's lack, amid the sights and sounds and smells of family celebrations, was particularly difficult to bear. Consider, for example, the monarch's journal entry for 10 February 1862:

> This blessed anniversary, what a strange unusual one! Woke from hearing people walking about & the rustling of silver paper. When the maid came in, it reminded me so much of my little gifts & surprises brought in, for me to give to my beloved Albert, as I always did on this dearest of days. I asked for the girls to come, Alice first & the dear Child came in with the usual nosegay, the bridal one... Alice gave me such a pretty allegorical drawing she has done for me & Feodora a pretty bracelet with the hair of all my children & of beloved Albert. I also gave them all souvenirs & wept oh! So bitterly... Dreadful as all was still the day was to [*sic*] blessed & precious, having brought me 22 years of such happiness & I felt a sort of reflection of the past, which nothing can rob me of![68]

The Loneliness of Loss

Immediately after Albert's death, the painful monotony of the grief-filled mornings had been too much for the Queen to bear:

'such miserable waking, but I feel it must get better'.[69] Certain times of the day were worse than others, as common in the state of bereavement; these included not only the mornings, when one might relive the loss again and again, but also in the evenings, the time that Queen Victoria would ordinarily spend with Albert. But the evenings alone had become 'so long & dreary'.[70]

Some six weeks after Albert's death, the monarch first began to refer to herself in her journals as lonely and 'forlorn', being 'all alone & in misery'.[71] It has been suggested that the first wave of grief Queen Victoria felt for Albert was tempered by shock, which is not uncommon for those who have been bereaved. Only when the shock had passed could loneliness and depression set in. When she was at home in the royal residence of Osborne House, she lamented, 'I feel my loneliness & desolation more & more'. She was not short of dining companions or people to take a walk or a drive with, but she was lonely for Albert, and nobody else. Being lonely for just one person, rather than being generally lonely, is an important reminder of the particular significance of a marriage, or a partnership, in which all aspects of life, practical, physical, sexual, and emotional, are singularly shared.

Very few people understood Queen Victoria's loneliness, other than her half-sister, Princess Feodora of Leiningen. It was she who sat with and 'cheered' the Queen, and who the monarch believed 'quite understands my awful misery & loneliness'. The refrain that 'nobody really understands me' has been analysed through attempts to measure loneliness since at least the 1940s, and it appears in discussions of social isolation through a wide range of studies, and from childhood, through adolescence to old age.[72] Queen Victoria's fourth daughter, Princess Louise, Duchess of

Argyll, also became someone who helped keep the memory of Albert alive; together the mourning women sat and 'arranged photographs of my beloved Albert'.[73] Yet on 12 May 1862, Queen Victoria wrote that the 'the feeling of loneliness [was] ever increasing'. She spent her time walking, with friends, with her daughters, and with the baby that brought joy, but there was a gulf left by the death of Albert that nothing seemed to fill.

'Everything [was] the same every day', she lamented, with constant reminders of Albert's absence, whether that meant looking through political papers concerning Albert's position and title ('heartrending, as all is ended now'), or finding his room empty. It comforted her, however, to feel that other people shared her grief and mourned with her. A community of grief, in other words, shielded her from the isolated loneliness of her own sadness—at least in the early days: 'The expressions of universal admiration & appreciation of beloved Albert are most striking & show how he was beloved & how his worth was recognized. Even the poor people in small villages, who don't know me, are shedding tears for me, as if it were their own private sorrow'.[74] The 'sympathy' of others gratified the Queen and made her feel comforted; a theme that would recur again and again in the years after Albert's death, particularly in relation to her subsequent caricature as a lonely and isolated figurehead.[75]

While the monarch's advisors believed that Queen Victoria should move on from her loss, and should show herself more at events, in reality she was suffering from depression and intractable grief. Her journals record how 'absolutely wretched' she felt; 'the evenings so long & dreary'.[76] The sights and sounds that surrounded her had taken on a new meaning, since Albert was not there to share them. Indeed, their existence reminded her of what she had lost. Even walking with her daughter Alice, the monarch found that 'All the trees & shrubs make me so sad to look at now. Dear Albert loved them so'.[77] Visits to the church became visits to '*his* church, which he had been so keenly interested in! [emphasis added]'. And yet Queen Victoria was unable to restrain herself from focusing on memories of her husband, on spending time in his room and with his belongings, though that brought pain rather than comfort: 'Looked at all my dear Albert's things, which upset me dreadfully'.[78]

Most of the time the comfort and companionship of her children helped the Queen in her grief, but sometimes 'Dear little Baby [Beatrice]...quite upsets me by her tender affection'.[79] Besides, there was something rather different about the companionship of a child or friend to that of a husband and lover, a theme that would become all the more pronounced when Queen Victoria's children married and went on to have children of their own.

For more than three years after Albert died, the monarch chronicled her 'awful loneliness' that she somehow 'managed to live through'.[80] Gradually, loneliness became something that Queen Victoria wrote less about in her journals, but whether that reflects a lessened sense of its existence, the speculative importance of her servant Mr Brown in providing a meaningful other, or simply that the Queen chose not to record it is uncertain. There were moments, however, when the loneliness returned, usually when she was reminded of the loss of Albert, as when Charles Phipps, Albert's Treasurer, died:

> Alas, another heavy blow has fallen on me & my valued, faithful, devoted friend, Sir Charles Phipps is no more! It seems like an awful dream, which I cannot realise, for I had seen him only 10 days ago, apparently quite well, & had received a letter from him on the 20th!

> How devoted he was to beloved Albert & me... A crushing sense of increased loneliness came over me, & I felt miserable.

Again, Queen Victoria was supported by her half-sister Feodora, and she found the act of going to visit Phipps' widow both comforting and distressing, for it brought back memories of her loss of Albert, as well as her own confirmed isolation as a widow:

> Went upstairs to see poor lady Phipps, who was terribly overcome & clung to me, but she soon recovered her composure. After talking a little while to her & to the eldest son, Charlie, asked if I might have one last look, on our dear Kind friend & Harriet took me into his room. There he lay, quite unaltered, just like himself, looking so happy & peaceful. I was naturally much affected & it brought back everything before me, which occurred in Dec: 61... he was at rest while the poor sick wife, whom he watched over so tenderly, never being absent from her, even for a night, was left!—We only got back at ½ p.2.—Quite late drove down to the Mausoleum... Sat for some time with dear Feodora & talked much of this sad loss, which reopens all past wounds... Felt very tired & upset.[81]

The loneliness of loss could be reopened at any time, then, for that is the nature of bereavement. A moment's recollection, a familiar scent or sound, an object, an idea of a person could plunge an individual back into an awareness of the solitude of widow(er)hood. Through the emotional displays of others and the objects and environments that were so redolent of Albert's presence, Queen Victoria managed her own sense of loss while being under national and international scrutiny.

Scattered notes of the monarch's loneliness appear during the later years of her journals, especially in relation to those moments when she felt reminded of the absence of Albert. In 1868, when she met with Prince Albert's brother Ernest and his wife, 'both looked extremely well, but he, very stout & aged. To see him, always recalls, so painfully, my loneliness & the blessed past!'[82] Here, the reminder of what would not pass, as well as the impact of nostalgia, must have contributed to Queen Victoria's sense of abandonment. Equally lonely was her sense of distance from other people, as the dual identities as Queen and grieving widow kept her apart from others. 'May God help me, in my ever-increasing loneliness & anxieties', she wrote in her journal of 20 June 1884, which was apparently the last time she wrote on the subject.

It is unsurprising, in this context, that the perpetually mourning monarch—in dress and habit, in behaviour and social perception—has been immortalized as the 'Widow at [or of] Windsor', from the eponymous poem by Rudyard Kipling. Narrated in the tongue of a lowly soldier, the poem critiqued the social impact of the Empire over which Queen Victoria reigned, the monarch's 'mark' being found on everything from 'cavalry "orses"' to 'medical stores' and 'ships on the foam'. The Queen herself is simply 'the Widow at Windsor/With a hairy gold crown on 'er 'ead', reduced among such splendour to a cypher of loss, loneliness and abandonment.[83]

Queen Victoria outlived Prince Albert by forty years. All that time her public grief became central to her self-definition. She continues to be remembered in the twenty-first century by her unsmiling pose, her rounded figure, and her black garb. She cuts a lonely figure in portraits made after Albert's death; not merely in the traditional sense of being alone, but representing a more intense emotional loneliness that is characteristic of a modern sense of self, and more consistent with twenty-first-century descriptions of widow(er)hood as a life stage. Queen Victoria was religious, as was Prince Albert. But she seemed not to find any real comfort in religious expressions, or the belief that Prince Albert's soul was destined for Heaven. Rather, she seemed determined to keep him with her on earth for as long as possible, preserving Prince Albert's rooms at Windsor, Osborne, and Balmoral; creating numerous busts and statues in bronze and marble; sending a lock of Albert's hair to their son Leopold, and a handkerchief, which he was instructed to always keep at hand; sending miniature photographs to friends and family members; and building, of course, a stone mausoleum. It was not just an empty chair that was kept in place for Albert.

There is something reminiscent of Charles Dickens' Miss Havisham in Queen Victoria's response to widowhood, in the latter's desperate attempt to stop time, to preserve Albert's life in the present, just as Miss Havisham captures the moment of her jilting by wearing her wedding dress and presiding over a cobwebbed banquet. Though the circumstances were different (Miss Havisham having been abandoned rather than widowed, and turning insane with grief), there is a shared quality of extreme and solitary sorrow and a dedication to ritualistic clothing (a bridal gown in Miss Havisham's case; widow's weeds in Queen Victoria's). *Great Expectations* was published in book form in 1861, the same year that Albert died, but serialized a year earlier.[84] Miss Havisham certainly captures Victorian attitudes towards death and memorialization, and reveals contemporary concerns that it may have been pathological to cling to the past, despite considerable contemporary investment in the memorialization of death.[85]

Whatever the reasons for Queen Victoria's prolonged mourning of her husband, it is clear that she not only missed him, but felt lonely without him; lonely in a highly specific, modern sense that was based on shared connections, shared experiences, and the unique relationship that they enjoyed as husband and wife. All in all, there are sixty-two entries referring to the state of being 'lonely' in Queen Victoria's journals, and all but eighteen refer to the period after Albert's death. And of the twenty-two recorded instances of 'loneliness', twenty-one took place after widowhood. Loneliness was just as much of a companion to Queen Victoria as widowhood. Linguistically, if nothing else, this marks a dramatic shift from the eighteenth century, when Thomas Turner wrote about loss, but never mentioned loneliness.

Although Thomas Turner and Queen Victoria were both young when widowed, most modern widows and widowers are elderly (and without a monarch's economic and social resources). More research is needed into how widow(er)hood—which is recognized as producing a distinct form of loneliness—can be triangulated with other challenges confronting the elderly, including neglect, physical illness, and social isolation. Studies suggest, too, that the length of widow(er)hood is a key factor in feeling lonely; remarriage can resolve the experience of isolation connected to the loss of a significant other.[86] Here, as elsewhere, there is a temporal aspect to loneliness—as in Queen Victoria's marking of the passage of years by the trees at Windsor, or the arrival of an anniversary. All emotions are impacted by time—sadness can feel unending if one is lonely; joy can be fleeting—and loneliness is no exception. Chronic and persistent loneliness, of the kind recorded by Queen Victoria, as opposed to transient or situational loneliness that is temporary and more easily remedied, requires particular attention in the twenty-first century, associated as it is with far more negative health and social consequences.[87]

Along with other experiences of loneliness, the effects of widow(er)hood depended on a range of variables, including wealth, family, and friend networks, and whether a person actually liked their spouse. Bereavement could, and can, bring ambivalence, as well as relief, anger, guilt, excitement, and sadness as well as loneliness, however loved a spouse might have been. What of widows who are lonely after the death of a spouse even though their spouse was unkind and abusive? Thomas Turner was far more flattering about his wife's characteristics once she had died. Was this nostalgia? Guilt? Or something else?

Loneliness in widow(er)hood, as any other pinch-point of experience, will be felt differently according to circumstance, and according to the survivor's ability to forge new relationships. Sometimes this means experimenting with new ways of interrelating, such as elderly people engaging with Internet dating.[88] The convenience and accessibility of dating online has advantages and disadvantages for elderly people as well as younger people; it provides a means to form and maintain romantic and friendship relationships, while overcoming a variety of physical and psychological limitations, from immobility to shyness. There is growing evidence, however, that use of the Internet prevents or encourages loneliness according to how it is used. And most research into the impact of social media on loneliness has been carried out not on the aged or the widowed, but on the millennial generation, to whom I will now turn.

CHAPTER 5

INSTAGLUM?

Social media and the making of online community

> *FOMO n. colloq.* fear of missing out, anxiety that an exciting or interesting event may be happening elsewhere, often aroused by posts seen on a social media website.
>
> 2004. *North Coast Jrnl. Weekly* (Humboldt County, Calif.) (Electronic ed.) 12 Aug. It's a great event; I feel like I have to go, since it's free for me. The real reason is this thing called FOMO; it's a disease, the Fear of Missing Out syndrome.
>
> *Oxford English Dictionary Online* (2018)

In 2014, a thirty-two-year-old woman from North Carolina died when her car hit a recycling truck. It was 8.33 a.m. and Courtney Sanford had been driving to work. As she drove, Sanford took selfies with her phone and posted a Facebook update about how happy she felt while listening to a Pharrell song: 'The happy song makes me HAPPY'. The authorities received the 911 call one minute later. 'In a matter of seconds, a life was over just so she could notify some friends that she was happy', a police spokesman reported.[1] We can only speculate about why Sanford was taking selfies and updating her Facebook page while driving, but it was clearly important to her to share her emotional 'status' at that moment in time. Without inferring any psychological intent in this case, and despite legislation against using mobiles while driving, many people text or take selfies on the road. 'Distracted driving' linked to mobile phone use killed 385 people on US roads in 2011 alone. Mobile phones were involved in 21 per cent of fatal crashes in which drivers aged fifteen to nineteen were involved.[2]

There are many different aspects of this story that are relevant to the study of loneliness, and by contrast a sense of connectedness or belonging. What is it about mobile phone use that makes younger people in particular feel connected, and what is the FOMO that allows careless or dangerous decisions to be made? It is important to understand the complex emotional relationships individuals might have with their mobile phones and social media; for some, the inability to connect for whatever reason causes intense anxiety, depression, and obsessive thoughts.[3] FOMO has been linked specifically to loneliness, and to a spectrum of emotional states that are associated with a lack of belonging, social identity, and approval.[4] Defined as 'a pervasive apprehension that others might be having rewarding experiences from which one is absent, FOMO is characterized by the desire to stay continually connected with what others are doing'.[5]

One of the difficulties of being constantly connected on social media, given the conventions normally depend on giving the best possible appearance of self, is that other people's lives can look better than one's own. This comparative dimension is one of the main reasons why Facebook users report dissatisfaction and loneliness, when other people's lives seem more successful or loving.[6] This chapter considers the rise of social media in order to address an entangled twenty-first-century dilemma: is excessive social media use a cause, or a consequence, of millennial loneliness?[7]

The Rise and Emotional Impact of Social Media

Social media have been widely adopted comparatively recently, since 2003.[8] They include social networking sites like Facebook, online discussion and review sites, video-sharing and user-generated sites (like blogs and vlogs), and virtual gaming. Most users are consumers rather than producers. Some 60 per cent of Internet users were thought to use social media in 2009, with the highest proportion of users being aged between eighteen and thirty-four.[9] Research suggests a number of different reasons for investment in social media use and the perceived outcomes (emotional, social, practical). While use of social media is influenced by differentials that include cultural, socio-economic, and technological factors—including access to services—the perceived individual outcomes include social capital (the ability to fit in and stand out), identity formation (as both a personal and a social goal), psychological and emotional wellbeing, physical wellbeing, and behavioural change.[10]

The emotional search for social networks online is arguably most profound at the early and mid-adolescence stage, as it is associated with 'imaginative audience behaviour', meaning an intense focus on the self and concern for how the self is being perceived by others, especially peer groups.[11] So-called 'digital natives' who use the Internet to develop and secure a sense of community and identity online can be particularly vulnerable to negatively perceived judgements and exclusions, especially if those individuals are otherwise socially isolated.[12] There are many reasons why this might be emotionally and socially problematic, including the existence of the 'dark web' and the negative self-esteem impacts on girls of images of the body that are disseminated online, both problems that connect with the broader challenge of living in a patriarchal society.[13]

It is therefore unsurprising that where loneliness and mental ill health have been considered among young adults, it is often social media that is held to account. Millennial loneliness has galvanized political concern—second only to loneliness among the aged. A 2018 study from the Office for National Statistics found that young adults were more likely to feel lonely than any other age group.[14] Loneliness among the young was also shown to be significant in the 'world's largest loneliness survey', undertaken by the BBC in 2018.[15] In fact, the study concluded that the young were lonelier than the old, despite the stereotype of the lonely aged. Yet youth loneliness has fewer visible social care and health implications, which is one of the reasons it has received less public health concern. Where loneliness in the young has been addressed, it is routinely (and perhaps automatically) linked to social media use, and to changing offline relationships. A 2015 study funded by health insurers found that loneliness was being exacerbated by the breakdown in face-to-face social relationships associated with social media.[16]

The long-term impact of social media use on psychological, emotional, and physical wellbeing, as well as the ability to network and form relationships in real life, has been the subject of intense debate. It has been argued that social media reduces real-life relationship skills, creates violent behaviours, and encourages obesity, making it difficult for younger people to conform to socially approved behaviours.[17] In a 2012 article, the marketing specialists Marcel Corstjens and Andris Umblijs referred to social media as 'the power of evil', arguing that the 'damage of negative social media strongly outweigh positive contributions'.[18] Excessive social media use is often associated with poor self-esteem and loneliness among the young. In 2017 *Forbes* magazine ran an article on the loneliness of millennials.[19] It concluded that the number of Americans with no close friends has tripled since 1985 and that this is particularly prevalent among the young.

Loneliness has been widely associated with excessive online use, along with other emotional states like anger, jealousy, and resentment, which are often connected to the tendency of some social media sites to promote 'bragging' behaviour that leads to a lack of self-esteem and self-worth.[20] There is a cyclical relationship between negative feeling states and social media engagement: loneliness and boredom, and life dissatisfaction, encourage yet more engagement with Facebook—especially when users are isolated from others—which produces a self-fulfilling, negative thought spiral. Nearly three-quarters of young adults reported FOMO in a 2012 survey.[21]

Loneliness is more prevalent in societies where social media use is at its highest, including the US and the UK;[22] this is unsurprising, since loneliness as a whole is most prevalent in the post-industrial West. Related health and safety concerns around social media include the cultural anxieties of intimacy on the Internet: there is a false sense of security that comes from 'knowing' a person online, or feeling part of an online community.[23] Loneliness is just one manifestation of a pathologizing effect of social media that can include poor self-esteem, an inability to socialize, and a detachment from social networks in real life.[24]

One of the lesser explored aspects of social media is its influence on solitude, with physical and social effects.[25] Solitude, the act and capacity of being alone, which is linked to creative and mental health benefits, is less of an option when screen culture has become so profound and an individual is connected to many different people at the same time. For many teenagers, there is the ever-constant blue light of a screen and a psychological, social, or physical impulse to connect virtually with others. Lack of rest, persistent anxiety, and poor sleep hygiene can characterize adolescents' engagement with social media, which impacts negatively on wellbeing.[26] Allied to this is the prevalence of 'Internet addiction', which has implications for the 'self-soothing' ability of adolescents to exist without the constant background noise of other people.[27] The term 'Internet addiction', like the allied term 'Facebook depression', demonstrates a widespread conviction that social media is detrimental to the individual and social fabric, and a prime cause of millennial loneliness.[28]

Social Media as Minefield or a Mirror?

While it is true that the communication of emotions and the construction and maintenance of relationships have undergone wholesale changes as a result of social media, including the birth of new emotional 'pathologies', such as FOMO, it is important to look at social media in context. Individual needs and affiliations searched for online are not separate from the needs sought offline; at the heart of the promise of social media are the combined desires of connectedness and belonging. The shape of those needs and the ways in which desires are met are not separable from, but related to, the ways individuals communicate in offline, social relationships. Though the speed and number of attachments made is faster online than in the offline realm,[29] social media behaviours reflect behaviours that take place in real life. What is different is the nature and expectations of belonging and 'community', a complex but important concept that is not easily translatable between the online and offline realms. Before considering this in more detail, however, I want to explore the ways in which concerns about social media connect to the 'moral panic' around twenty-first-century loneliness.

Social media is characterized by its speed and diffusion; a transitory emotional state can be expressed and shared widely within a matter of seconds. These communications can appear secretive, taking place on individual screens and according to distinct languages and logic. Emotional responses can themselves be affected and intensified by the speed of communication through digital networks, which destabilizes the idea of an individual feeling. A 2014 study of Facebook, comparing the data collected in negative and primary posts, concluded that emotions expressed on Facebook could influence respondents' emotions non-verbally, creating ripples through large groups of people who may never have met.[30] At its most extreme, this behaviour has been linked to suicidal depression and copycat suicides.[31] From a historical perspective, this research is reminiscent of 'moral contagion' as a psycho-social category in the eighteenth century, and the idea that an emotional experience or belief could contaminate a large group of people; in the 1960s, historians described the European witch-hunts as an example of moral or emotional contagion, and there are modern examples that explore how emotions can 'infect' individuals and crowds.[32]

This view of social media is consistent with social neuroscience research that argues loneliness is contagious; that the risks of being lonely are increased for people who know others who are lonely.[33] John Cacioppo and others used data from the population-based

Framingham Heart Study to explore the topography of loneliness in social networks, and the ways that loneliness occurred in particular clusters extended up to three degrees of separation and spread through emotional or moral contagion. The diffusion of loneliness was stronger than the spread of friendship (supporting Cacioppo's argument that loneliness is a biological signal that one's survival is threatened), and stronger in friends and in women than in men and family relationships. The answer for Cacioppo was clear: strengthen the networks for the individuals that are most likely to experience loneliness, and the social framework would also be strengthened.

The framing of loneliness as contagion is problematic. While on the one hand, it posits loneliness as a social emotion, linked to the individual's need for a collective sense of belonging, it also presumes that loneliness is always negative, which it is not. Attitudes to social media, with its parallel implications of contagion, nevertheless form part of the moral panic around loneliness in twenty-first-century Britain. New technologies of communication have always generated cultural anxieties. In the 1880s, when the telephone was an innovative and alarming form of technology, it was regarded with some suspicion as well as excitement. Contemporaries believed that it might 'save the sanity of remote farm wives', as the American Professor of Communication Lana F. Frakow identifies, 'lessening their sense of isolation' (Figure 5).[34]

This statement tapped into gendered ideas about women as 'talkers' as well as the potential for loneliness created by the urban/rural divide. Use of the mobile phone has similarly played into existing gender roles and ideology, with implications for the ways that mobiles are desired, acquired, and used.[35]

EVERY FARMER NEEDS A GOOD TELEPHONE

A telephone on the farm is a "saver" in a great many ways. It increases the working force by decreasing the necessity for so many trips to town and to the neighbors. It adds security by providing means for quick communication in time of misfortune and distress. There is no question as to the telephone being a paying investment for the farmer. The only question is, which telephone is the best for the farmer to buy?

IT'S CHEAPER TO TALK THAN WALK

Stromberg-Carlson Telephones

are built better than the ordinary telephone, so that they are especially adapted to the farmer's use. Every piece and part that goes to make up a complete telephone are made by skilled specialists in our own plant—the largest independent telephone factory in the world—made with minute care and thoroughly tested before leaving our hands; that's why they give the best service; that's why there are more of them in use than of all others combined; that's why it is the telephone to buy. Many other good reasons are contained in our new book, "How the Telephone Helps the Farmer," which will interest you if you are going to buy one or a hundred telephones. Write today—ask for book No. 123—we send it free.

Stromberg-Carlson Telephone Manufacturing Company

Rochester, N. Y. **70-86 W. Jackson Blvd., Chicago, Ill.**

Figure 5. A 1905 advert for telephones aimed at socially isolated farmers.

In addition to being seen as a positive technology, however, the telephone gave rise to fears of ill health, addiction, and a withdrawal from everyday social activities, as well as the blurring of gendered boundaries between work and home. In the 1920s, the American-based Knights of Columbus Adult Education Committee (the Knights of Columbus being the world's largest Catholic fraternity) asked whether the telephone made men 'more active or more lazy', whether it broke up 'home life and the old practice of visiting friends'.[36] The American sociologist Claude S. Fischer has analysed the findings of a rare systematic survey on telephone, letter, and telegram use from the 1930s. Of the 200 women and men consulted (the gender balance is not broken down), sixty-six felt discomfort about the telephone. Social perception of the telephone's effects was ultimately ambivalence, with the study's authors concluding that though this new technology may 'reduce loneliness and uneasiness', its 'likely contribution to the malaise of urban depersonalization should not be underestimated'. No evidence from the survey actually demonstrated 'the malaise of urban depersonalization', indicating that the telephone as an invention tapped into broader existing anxieties around modern rural and urban lifestyles.[37]

Concerns about social media should be viewed in the context of such broader historical arguments. Moreover, there are many studies in favour of social media that suggest its benefits, rather than its disadvantages.

Those who experience social anxiety, for instance, are less inhibited about connecting with others online. Networking sites like Facebook can help those with mental health problems navigate complex social and family relationships, and facilitate emotional sharing which might lead to greater social support. Social media also has a significant health and social role in conveying information and providing spaces for both the dissemination of data and communication between people who might be incapacitated or infirm.[38] And they enable distance-relationships, such as those between families living far apart, to be continued in a convenient, online space.

It is unhelpful, then, to lament the rise of social media as an inevitable cause or repository of social ills.[39] And it is crucial to keep fears of technology and emotional change in historical context; each new form of communication from the telegraph to the Internet has brought uncertainty and panic about its uses and abuses, as well as a presumption that 'old ways' of sociability would be threatened.[40] As with many forms of technological innovation, then, it's not what social media is, but how it is used that creates impact, for good or ill. Users who experience positive connections as a result of using Facebook, including social support, social influencing, and feelings of being cared for and being connected—all of which are regarded as opposite states to being lonely—also experienced those connections in real life. Facebook as a platform for maintaining existing relationships is therefore more helpful than when it is used as a retreat from face-to-face social interaction (for instance, college students who feel shy about meeting new people and rely on social media as an alternative report decreasing levels of satisfaction with online community).[41] Where emotional difficulties like unwanted loneliness arise in relation to social media, it is when the online world overrides and replaces offline connections, rather than being supplementary or linked to those physical, embodied connections.

The most significant questions to ask, therefore, in relation to loneliness and social media are not how often it is used and when, but whether it replaces or supplements offline relationships. Does the construction of online community, however defined, substitute for a lack of connection in other areas, and does that lead to reduced sleep and social functioning? And to what extent is the 'digital divide' between people on the basis of health, economics, and other variables contributing to the problem? After all, many of the general pitfalls associated with social media, including 'social snacking', a term used to describe reading other people's posts rather than actively participating in online communities, are also found in real-life situations, as shy and socially anxious people will 'hang back' from contributing to personal conversations.[42] Social media therefore benefits and disadvantages lonely people in precisely the same ways as other forms of social interaction.

Social Media and the Meanings of Community

The term 'online community' is used everywhere, as though its meaning is inevitable and common sense and—crucially—the same thing as offline community. But it is not. Virtual communities are social networks that involve individuals—regardless of geographical and political boundaries in many cases—in a shared idea or belief, or interest. As such, they are reminiscent of what the political scientist and historian Benedict Anderson referred to in his 1983 analysis of modern nationalism as an 'imagined community'—an emotional and creative process by which a sense of shared values are created across wide geographical and social differences.[43] For Anderson, the nation is a constructed community that inspires people to feel as though they belong sufficiently to die on a battlefield in pursuit of a shared goal, or to follow a football team around the world.

Social media also creates imagined communities by promoting a shared sense of values and beliefs, by speaking a common 'language' of images, rhetoric, and beliefs and the sense of an online world to which certain people can belong. An online community seldom generates the strength of feeling identified by Anderson, for which one would lay down one's life for a cause, as is the case with modern nationalism (though extremist groups do use social media to the same end).[44] But it is nevertheless a sense of identity and shared meaning that outwardly identifies mutual interests and goals.

In 1993 the American critic Howard Rheingold defined virtual communities as 'social aggregations that emerge from the Net when enough people carry on these public discussions enough, with sufficient human feeling, to form webs of personal relationships in cyberspace'.[45] While traditional definitions of community were boundaried (normally by geographical or familial limits), virtual communities exist in cyberspace. They can be exclusive and define themselves by what they are not—such as the 'Reddit' comment board 'The Donald', which describes itself as 'a never-ending rally dedicated to the 45th President of the United States, Donald J. Trump'.[46] This 380,000-strong group refers to Donald Trump as 'daddy' and 'the God Emperor', and gains its identity by standing *against* liberalism, feminism, intellectualism, and much more besides. Belonging to 'The Donald' is cultivated by symbols, from red 'Make America Great Again' baseball hats to the recurring motif of a wall between the USA and Mexico, and the coiffured, cartoonish figure of a portly white man, unhampered by intellect or nuance.

Such virtual communities resemble real-life communities in that they offer a shared view of the world and one's place in it; they reflect back and echo the feelings and opinions one might have about the world. And often, they provide a reassuring sense that one is right. And they can spill over into the offline world, through rallies and public gatherings in which symbols and chants—'Make America Great Again'; 'Build the Wall'—create an emotional sense of belonging and safety, at least for Trump supporters. Not for the many millions—women, black, and immigrant populations—who are endangered by Trump's policies and the cultural stirrings of hatred and violence generated by his right-wing, white supremacist, and misogynist support base.

Just as print media and national newspapers brought people together in Anderson's 'imagined communities', social media sites can create a sense of shared values, ethics, and support; what is different is the sheer proliferation of social media reports and the multiple, competing interests they support. Virtual communities need not be defined by conventions of geography, gender, ethnicity, or economic status, though there remain barriers in terms of affordability, Internet access, and language skills. Virtual communities build on the traditional idea of a group of people that are defined through a common goal and defined against others by the sharing of that goal. Virtual communities also resemble real-life communities by providing support, information, acceptance, and friendship between people who may not have met in person (and conversely, of expressing disdain and condemnation of views they do not regard as central to that community's values).[47] Social ostracization or online 'shaming' can cause as much loneliness and isolation in the virtual world as online, as the writer and journalist Jon Ronson has shown.[48]

Myths of Intimacy

Online community, between people who have usually never met and share only select aspects of their lives, presumes inclusion and belonging through communicational modes that borrow from successful real-life intimacy. It prioritizes openness and transparency, encourages emotional response (albeit in a limited way through, for example, Facebook's ever-powerful 'like' button), and claims to promote consensus.[49] This rhetoric of openness and sharing—a presumption of egalitarian transparency—is inherent in the corporate mantra of Google ('Do no evil'), Facebook ('making the Web more social'), and Flickr-Yahoo ('Share your pictures, watch the world').[50]

Yet just as inner-city windows might present an illusion of togetherness in which isolation is actually the norm,[51] this presumed openness of virtual communities hides the fact that inclusion in social media can be fickle and conditional; digital citizenship hides multiple power dynamics and relations, not all of which are explicitly stated.[52] Whereas there has been some discussion of the meanings of digital citizenship (to mean the accepted norms of appropriate, responsible technology use), online 'community' is invoked as a given. The Professor of Media Studies at Utrecht University, José van Dijck, refers in her discussion of social media's history to 'community function' and 'community character'; 'community collectivism' and 'community utilization'; and to 'community' itself as being innovative, organizational, self-selecting, and open. But community, like citizenship, carries an enormous functional, symbolic, and practical weight.[53]

What kinds of 'community' are being forged online, and how do they impact on self-esteem, a sense of belonging, and self-identity?

How does online community differ from offline community, and how and why does loneliness result? In the case of 'The Donald', connections are formed through a sense of purpose or character, which is consistent with sociological accounts of group identity.[54] These kinds of groups do not usually involve interpersonal ties beyond the group's purpose. Sociological discussions of attachment in online communities distinguish between 'identity bonds' (e.g. to Trump or Starbucks) and bond-based attachment, such as meet-up and support groups that might connect via Facebook but are based on interest in the individual lives of their members.[55]

A related difference between online and offline communities is accountability. A defining characteristic of community has historically been not only shared characteristics, which is the modern usage (and which is entirely compatible with a shared interest in Kim Kardashian's pregnancy or what colours are in fashion for autumn), but also a sense of responsibility for others. The *Oxford English Dictionary* gives a variety of definitions of community that include 'a group of people living in the same place' and 'a body of nations or states unified by common interests', as well as a 'particular area of place considered together with its inhabitants', such as a rural community or local community. There is a more nuanced usage, however, which derives from an historical sense of a 'community of interest' that means connectedness of people with place, values, and responsibilities. The origin of the term 'community' is late Middle English, from the Old French *comunete,* reinforced by its Latin source: *communitas* and *communis,* terms which are suggestive of people being in some sense equal and acting together.[56] In this sense it seems more compatible with such terms as 'commonweal' or commonwealth, which has at its base the idea of a general good.

Social media does not ordinarily conform to a conventional idea of a community of interest, especially where it is identity- rather than bond-based. I am not suggesting that 'communities' in the past were all about collective compassion, or that there is an artificially rigid line between online and offline community. Rather, I am suggesting a general watering down of the essence of accountability as a precondition of belonging to communities online. There are important instances where this is not the case; crowdsourcing for a charitable cause, for instance, in which personal identification with a cause can run parallel with concern for a named individual or nation.

Emotional engagement with online communities is, moreover, impacting all areas of offline life, including the social contract between government and citizens. One example is the way social media, especially Facebook, was instrumental in the outcome of the 2016 US Presidential election.[57] Digital citizenship takes places alongside other forms of citizenship. This has implications that are not merely passive, but also politically active and capable of mobilizing real-world change. Consider, for instance, the ways social media can stimulate and engage users in political action, such as the street demonstrations during the Arab Spring that were followed by the ousting of leaders in Tunisia, Libya, and Egypt.[58] What are the implications of these developments for the shaping of community in the twenty-first century? Can social media be used to support and shape identity formation, to complement and develop responses to loneliness?

The digital revolution is changing other aspects of life too, including the ways people interrelate emotionally; at its most extreme we find computerized alternatives for physical contact that include android dogs and sex robots.[59] But again, online connectedness seems to heighten rather than diminish loneliness when there is no corresponding or simultaneous offline attachment. In other words, where social media is an individual's sole or exclusive way of engaging with the world, loneliness is more common.[60]

One of the most important claims in this book is that the commercialization of the individual, at the expense of the social, was dominant from the late eighteenth century in Britain, and that loneliness developed as a result. Some forms of social media in the early twenty-first century can be seen as evidence of modern isolated individualism: the articulation and consumption of the self, the production of multiple identities, and the focus on individual wealth as a manifestation of networking success.[61] By arguing that loneliness and social media are linked, I am not claiming that social media itself is negative. On the contrary, I believe that the digital world has the potential to transform individual and social lives for the good. The pressing consideration in loneliness interventions then becomes how to utilize social media in successful and collaborative ways.

Online communities that are bond- rather than identity-based might offer solutions for people who are physically isolated from others, sick, or infirm. By bond-based, I mean communities that share an interest in the wellbeing of the members of a group as individuals, rather than merely a shared interest in norms, goals, activities, and beliefs.[62] Bond-based community groups might also offer a lifeline to rural inhabitants who are unable to access crucial, tailored information about health and wellbeing.

The value of social media needs to be considered in relation to existing and changing social relations, then, and the kinds of emotional experience that are presumed and conveyed through online communication. What intimacy at a distance lacks, however, is a consideration of the physical, lived experience of loneliness, and the importance of touch. It is different to see a beloved grandchild through a Skype call than to hold that child, smell its forehead, and feel the small, curled weight of another body against your own. Virtual reality technologies, which are already used successfully to mediate health information and support for elderly people, might hold the clues to the future of digital engagement as a haptic, full-body experience.[63]

Rather than worrying about whether social media is good or bad for young people, it would be more productive to consider how it might bridge the relationship between the mental and physical worlds, to nurture relationships between the individual and society, and to forge new meanings of community that bring together the virtual and the real world. This would be of benefit not only to the millennial generation, but also the whole spectrum of society, including the oldest old.

CHAPTER 6

A 'TICKING TIMEBOMB'?

Rethinking loneliness in old age

I remember the moment when my Grandma Rose went into a care home. She had been increasingly demented after my Grandad died, and she needed full-time care. When I had visited her in hospital, before she was admitted into a private home (no NHS places being available), she had been wild-eyed and confused. 'What is it?' she said again and again, looking at my toddler in his pushchair. His head had toppled forward so that his shock of blonde hair was visible, and my Grandma could not make sense of the collection of limbs and hair in the pushchair. As is common with people living with dementia, she also asked about people long dead and confused the people around her with deceased relatives. I was my mother; my mother was her aunt; Grandma Rose's dead husband Sidney was late for dinner.

I thought at the time what a particular kind of loneliness was linked to dementia; it wasn't just the fact that Grandma Rose was locked into an entirely different world to those around her; that nobody understood anything she said. It was also that the moments of lucidity would drop without warning, bringing a horrified realization to my grandmother, and to those around her, of a palpable and unbridgeable isolation from others. When

I subsequently visited my grandmother in a care home, she was thin and quiet, and kept to her room. My glamorous grandmother, who had won multiple beauty contests in the 1980s and swore by a beauty regime of Oil of Ulay, peroxide bleach, and Superkings, was wispy-haired in hand-me-down sweatpants and socks of different colours. 'People keep stealing things', she complained, pointing at a woman wearing a skirt with a familiar tear at the hem, the empty biscuit tin sitting on her dresser. That tall, powder-blue biscuit tin, which sat on a cheap chipboard dressing table, was the only object I recognized from her home. Aside from the biscuit tin, it was the bed that caught my eye. A thin, grey camp-bed that was easy to move and to get in and out of. And so cheap and plain, compared to the aesthetic of the grandmother that I knew, with her powdered cheeks and her love of canary yellow.

Grandma Rose didn't live much longer. Each time I saw her, she was thinner, frailer, more disconnected from those around her. Sitting around a Formica kitchen table, surrounded by other old people in different degrees of disconnect, was traumatizing for my children, so they didn't go again. It wasn't just my grandmother's mouth stretched open like that of a baby bird, guzzling down whatever slop she was being fed, or the tiny, beady-eyed woman who sat opposite, staring earnestly into my eyes and pleading, again and again: 'will you take me home? Please take me home'. (Nobody paid her any heed, and to my shame I looked away. I didn't know what to say.) It was the recognition of the degrees of separation between the care home residents; the neat, tidy newcomers, who looked around as though they couldn't believe decent people could let themselves go so comprehensively, the confused middle-grounders, who knew who they were one minute but not the next, and the ones who were completely lost, like Grandma Rose, existing only to be shuffled from one room to another, to be prized in and out of flimsy cardigans and plonked in a corner of the room while the clock ticked on.

I was conscious then of the discrete and erratic unravelling of identity for old people with dementia. That a person could pass from one stage to another, and—less often—back again, with little warning or fanfare. That each of these elderly people, with their locked-up lives and stories, was isolated from the others around them with a decreasing recognition of that isolation. Flashes of intense loneliness aside, they merged into a single organ; a living, breathing amorphous huddle of bodies to be kept clean, fed, and watered. A large part of my response resulted from the way that they were cared for. Uniformed women who moved around these elderly men and women, not seeing difference, not remembering preferences for flavour, seating, companion. They acted—as they laughed and chatted to each other about nights out—as though Grandma Rose was interchangeable with another old lady, whose kids didn't visit that day. The care was not cruel, but indifferent. Nothing marked those old people out as individuals as they were gathered together like cattle at feeding time.

Not all elderly people develop dementia, though like Alzheimer's, dementia has been recently linked to loneliness. Feelings of loneliness even in a crowd, rather than simply the state of being socially isolated, are seen as a predictor of dementia.[1] This is related to the distinction between 'oneliness' and 'loneliness' that I made earlier; loneliness is an entirely subjective emotional state, which is why we can be lonely in a crowd. Loneliness is also a relatively high predictor of neurological problems in later life, so tending to loneliness throughout the life stage may be important to preventing loneliness in old age.[2]

It is as though the breakdown in social relationships in people with dementia is mirrored by a breakdown in neural connections: metaphor made flesh. Elderly people have many other ailments, physical and mental, that can result in a disconnect between what is needed—companionship, practical support, emotional and sexual fulfilment—and what is received. This disconnect can represent undesirable feelings of solitude for isolated elderly people that are linked to everyday social tasks—nobody to help you get dressed in the morning, to help with shopping or putting the bins out—as well as loneliness that exists in care homes as well as hamlets: a deep, emotional need for an empathetic, engaged human connection.

There is much research needed into loneliness among the aged and infirm, who are lonely as a result of their lack of face-to-face social interaction, as well as those who live in remote rural communities, whose families have moved away in search of work, and who may have also been widowed. And while most research focuses on urban communities and their differences from rural ones, there are vast swathes of the population living in retirement in poor coastal villages and caravan parks who are not merely socially isolated and alone, but also experiencing economic deprivation, physical limitations, and mental ill health.[3]

As with other social groups discussed in this book, it is not being alone that is in itself the core of loneliness among the aged, but rather an emotional alienation from other people. There is considerable uncertainty about the numbers of elderly people who are lonely, largely because approaches to loneliness have been under-theorized. Stereotypes of the aged and lonely predominate; the spectre of an ageing population, unable to be cared for by an increasingly disparate community, and by an overburdened NHS, have helped fuel the narrative of an epidemic of loneliness that accompanies an ageing demographic. Attributing old age with a presumption of loneliness is also problematic because it becomes a self-fulfilling prophecy. Fear of loneliness taps into and perpetuates the moral panic around loneliness as an inevitable and negative human condition. A Swedish study (2009), which examined elderly people's perceptions of ageing and care, found that a pervading fear of the healthy elderly was that they would lose their sense of identity and become 'a nobody with no meaningful relations'. Recognizing and affirming that individuality, researchers found, as well as providing 'care with dignity to the end', was necessary to assuage such fears.[4]

Fear of a social death, of ceasing to exist in a meaningful way with other people, lies at the heart of the panic around loneliness and old age. The implication is that staying relevant, connected, and at the centre of social and familial networks, is the key to avoiding elderly loneliness. Yet that is harder than it sounds. And the incidence of loneliness and old age tends not to be considered through the lens of the individual searching for meaning, but rather as a social problem linked to the inevitable hazards of ageing. The 'lonely old' are an economic burden, infantilized, or homogenized as a socio-economic category in search of a cure.

Despite the moral panic of the headlines, there is no inevitability that old people will be lonely, and much depends on individual circumstance, as with each of the life experiences or pinch-points considered in this book. This chapter uses a starting age of around sixty-five as the beginning of old age, since this relates to government policy around pensions. I will consider first the nature of the UK's ageing population, and then the specific ways elderly people can be lonely, before considering the political and social systems that perpetuate loneliness, and their underpinning beliefs about ageing. Finally, I will consider the ways in which we might tend to elderly loneliness in more embodied, culturally specific ways that target an evident current need.

The UK's 'Ticking Timebomb'

Firstly, let's look a little closer at health and social policy discussions of elderly loneliness, currently framed as an economic 'timebomb' as the UK's population—and that of the Western world more generally—is becoming older. With an ageing demographic comes the associated practicalities, cost, and need for a more joined-up philosophy of health and social care, though that need not lead to social and political panic.[5] The practical challenge is not simply that people are living longer, to an average of eighty-two for women and seventy-eight for men. The proportion of older people in the country has also increased. In 1901, people over sixty-five years old formed 4.7 per cent of the population of Britain; by 1961 it was 11.7 per cent. That figure continues to rise.[6]

From a narrowly economic perspective (that, in my view, should never be applied to health, social care, or education), the challenge of an ageing population is that a high proportion will live for years with life-limiting illnesses and disabilities, from high blood pressure and heart problems to diabetes and cancer. In the last few decades, loneliness has been linked to these conditions and to physical and mental illnesses, even death for aged people. Not only the aged and ill, but also their families and carers, can experience intense loneliness.[7] In the case of life-threatening or chronic illness and loneliness (among the old and young alike), it is the existential questions raised by the condition that can make people lonely, from 'will I die?' to 'will I lose my hair?' and 'who will look after me?', as well as the disconnect experienced by other people's discomfort with that illness, the distancing language of the medical profession, and the unexpected loneliness, too, of being a survivor.[8]

Isolation through illness produces a sense of emotional loneliness, especially if comfort is not forthcoming. Moreover, all forms of social isolation can provoke loneliness, particularly if not chosen. This is often the case among the vulnerable old due to limited mobility, and the death of friends and loved ones, especially in the case of the 'oldest old' (the term used to describe people aged over eighty). The NHS Choices website warns that older people are 'especially vulnerable to loneliness and social isolation'.[9] According to Age UK, which has a concerted campaign against elderly loneliness, more than 2 million people over the age of seventy-five live alone in Britain, and more than a million older people can go without speaking to another living person for over a month (Figure 6).[10]

Current estimates suggest anywhere between 10 and 43 per cent of older people living in the community experience social isolation, while between 5 and 16 per cent report loneliness.[11] After the age of eighty years, however, 50 per cent of all people define themselves as lonely; a situation that is likely to worsen over the next few decades as established patterns of family dispersal continue, but life expectancy increases.[12]

This isolation—which is different from the self-selected solitude discussed in earlier chapters—will inevitably be worse for people

Figure 6. Age UK advert for loneliness, 2018.

who live in remote areas with a lack of friends and neighbours, with grown-up children who have moved away, and in rural areas where a person is living in poverty or infirm. It is not liberating or refreshing to be alone when all efforts to find companionship have failed. Dealing with bereavement and mental illnesses, such as depression and anxiety, as well as loneliness and ill health is also a reality of life for many elderly people. And yet, despite this backdrop of intense difficulties, mental health problems, physical health problems, loneliness, and isolation for vast numbers of elderly people in the UK—and the government's recognition of those problems—there is the ever-present problem of unmet need.

The Vulnerable Old and the Problem of 'Unmet Need'

Physical, mental, and social vulnerability of ageing populations might be an undeniable reality in the early twenty-first century. Yet there has been a systematic lack of care for many older adults who need it. Sometimes the care needed is physical, and sometimes emotional; often, as in the case of my Grandma Rose, it is both. Older people who live with chronic conditions, like Alzheimer's, diabetes, or arthritis, whose everyday health is negatively impacted in multiple ways because of that condition, and/or those who need help dressing, bathing, eating, shopping for groceries, cleaning, and getting to medical appointments, are all too often bereft of care. Some receive social care assistance; others get help from family and friends, neighbours, or privately paid healthcare workers. In one recent study, a woman called Monica described the hopelessness of living alone and suffering from limited mobility, painful arthritis, and fatigue:

> Because of my breathlessness, I can't walk any great distances. I'm slower these days. I've got a walking stick now but it's hard to manage a walking stick sometimes. It's difficult getting groceries into my house, carrying the groceries up the stairs—I have to make several trips. I can't carry too many at a time now. But I haven't really got anybody that I could ring up and ask them to come. That's where perhaps I feel isolated.[13]

It is unsurprising in such circumstances that isolation can become loneliness; what more certain way of feeling a disconnect between oneself and the rest of the world than having nobody to help at times of need? For decades in the UK there has been awareness of an unmet need among older members of the country, but no sustained approach to understand why and how this unmet need is so prevalent.[14] Partly, it reflects a lack of confidence and low expectations on the part of those needing care. In a study of older people in inner-city and suburban London, researchers sampled the experiences of one in twenty people aged seventy-five years and older. Help had been sought in 24 per cent of cases and offered in 18 per cent of cases. When asked why they did not press for help, people cited withdrawal, resignation, and low expectations. Experience of failure in service delivery was another deciding factor.[15] In other words, many older people felt that there was no point expressing a need for help. When it was answered, what was given was inadequate. And it takes a particular quality of will to keep asking for support when that is not forthcoming.

The problem of unmet need is far more widespread than this quoted study might suggest. In 2008 the Commission for Social Care Inspection found that this lack of vital care and support was a key policy challenge for social care, and that an accurate measurement of the shortfall was crucial for fair provision.[16] The problem of unmet need sits at the heart of the policy agenda, but the problem continues. And that is unlikely to change if the struggle for older people in getting support is long-winded and often unsuccessful.

Unsurprisingly, it is governmental changes in social care provision that have been linked to this unmet need. Changes in the composition of the population since the 1970s (including people travelling further away from their homes for work, divorce, working single-parenthood leaving traditional carers overstretched, and the anonymity of urban living), combined with changes in social care provision, mean there is less support to go around. Between 2003–4 and 2008–9 the gross expenditure of Councils with Adult Social Services Responsibilities in England for people aged over sixty-five years increased by over 8 per cent to approximately £9 billion, according to one recent study, but the cost of providing services has increased by 15–26 per cent.[17] Some services have been dropped by councils, and contact hours in home care have also decreased from 200 hours in 2007–8 to 183 hours in 2008–9.[18] A rise in private social care has replaced, in many cases, what councils used to provide. Since the mid-1980s, local authority care home spaces have declined, while private sector provision has increased. At-home social care has also increased, though the threshold for support has in general been raised to 'critical need' which more than 25 per cent of people may not meet.

Clearly there is a significant problem with the fulfilment of need in British health and social care, which has direct links to the number of vulnerable elderly people experiencing unacceptable levels of chronic and intermittent loneliness. There are individual and social differences between elderly, lonely people and that is important. Inevitably it is those who cannot afford to supplement social services who will be most hit. So, too, will those who for whatever reason—lack of language or confidence, Alzheimer's—cannot articulate need or follow up repeated requests for assistance.

Ageing and Neoliberalism; or When Did Old Age Become a Liability?

There is a remarkable discrepancy between this recognized deficit in social care in ways that perpetuate isolation and loneliness and the government's insistence that it wants to combat loneliness. I believe the reasons for this disconnect lie in a complex blend of political ideology about health and social care as well as ageing, and how those beliefs relate to the complex, historically situated nature of loneliness. Firstly, governmental responses to ageing in the modern age presuppose familial and social rather than state responsibility. In accordance with a range of neoliberal approaches to the concept of wellbeing, families are supposed to step in to provide what older people need. The welfare principles of government are different than they were when the welfare state was formed, with individualistic policies replacing social planning, and extending to health and wellbeing as well as ageing, as seen in the extension of the pension age and the emphasis on private and employer pensions.

This shift from the collective to the individual has not been restricted to the UK. The trend towards neoliberalism and globalization throughout the world, which has focused on consumer 'choice' and privatization (and the encouragement of competition in the pursuit of care contracts), is characteristic of political developments across the Western world.[19] Fragmentation of care, the lack of a joined-up approach to ageing policy, and the creation of unmet need is the inevitable result. Moreover, this approach, which regards ageing as a liability rather than an asset, does not tend to the subjective experience of ageing, or the complexities around loneliness as an individual and social phenomenon that can also be historically situated. The experience of loneliness, like the experience of ageing more generally, needs to be considered in relation to the overall value system of society. Differences in value systems and the integration of aged people into all aspects of cultural life might provide a way ahead. Can the history of ageing in the UK provide any insights into the emergence of ageing as an economic liability and the social contexts in which isolation and loneliness have become normalized?

Ageing in History

Age is just a number. A range of perceptions and expectations attach to that number, depending on individual perspective as well as what any given society expects of that age. Studies of subjective age, which assess how people suppose they feel, look, act, and would prefer to be, have found a wide range of judgements that have little to do with any objective number. In one such account, younger people had older subjective identities, older people reported younger age identities, and there was a discrepancy between subjective experience and actual age that was associated with a fear of growing old, with all that involves.[20] Fear of growing old and lonely are prevailing cultural stereotypes that are part of the moral panic associated with loneliness in the early twenty-first century. This sense of foreboding about ageing is not transhistorical. And neither is the experience of loneliness among ageing populations.

Unlike other disciplines, including sociology, history does not have a strong track record of tending to the bodies, identities, sexualities, and experiences of elderly people. The question of ageing in history has only recently attracted historical interest.[21] It is not surprising, given its general neglect, that there has been even less about the history of loneliness among aged populations.[22] Historian Pat Thane's *Old Age in English History: Past Experiences, Present Issues* (2000) explores changing medical and philosophical perspectives on ageing. Ancient Greek writers, for instance, worried about old age not in terms of its emotional burden or isolation, but as a cautionary tale about physical health; the importance of looking after oneself when young and tempering extremes of passion, helping the journey towards old age, and eventual death. This sense of *preparing* for old age is missing in the postmodern, youth-obsessed West, with its cultural narratives of the need to stay young for as long as humanly possible.[23] Yet viewing old age as something to be accepted and incorporated into one's sense of self from youth might enable loneliness to be addressed and prevented before it occurs.

Throughout the medieval and early modern periods, elderly people lived and worked alongside younger people, and were not necessarily stigmatized for being old or cast aside as a result of infirmity. There is more evidence about the living habits of elderly people and their families from the nineteenth century, with the collection of census data. There is also evidence of the gendered impact of caring practices, either by older women of the poorer sectors of society providing childcare (much as happens today via an invisible economy of workers), or by educated women acting as companions to older, wealthier women. The economist and writer Harriet Martineau, for instance, was called on to act as a companion to her mother in Norwich in the 1830s, while the writer Charlotte Brontë resented becoming a carer for her cantankerous father in the 1840s.[24] According to the Irish writer and anti-vivisection advocate, Frances Power Cobbe, caring for one's parents was an obligation to be borne by daughters.[25]

Ageing and dependency might have created gendered notions around 'care', which remain with us, but there was nothing intrinsically negative about ageing as an experience. Though there was a lonely 'old crone' foreshadowing of folklore and fairy-tale, in which an old woman might possess evil or sinister qualities marking her out as different from others. The term 'crone' comes from the fourteenth-century Anglo-French word *carogne*, which was itself an insult, meaning literally 'carrion'.

The stereotype of the crone, who often possessed a 'wise-woman' knowledge that the village might need, through herbal medicine, for instance, could be vilified and resented. This trope taps into a Western tradition of patriarchal fears of older, sexually undesirable, but powerful and independent women, and has been associated with moments of historical victimization of elderly women, as in the European and North American witch trials.[26] But it also corresponds with the historical tendency for vulnerable members of society to take the fall for negative socio-economic conditions. It is important to note, too, that older male bodies have similarly been ridiculed, either because of their declining muscle strength and presumed feminization as a result, their diminishing potency, or their loss of patriarchal power and descent into madness, as in the 'poor, weak, infirm and despis'd old man' motif of Shakespeare's *King Lear* (1606: Act 3, Scene 2, line 23).

Perceptions of the older body that sags and grows weak are clearly central to the objective perception of ageing in the West. But aesthetic cultural concern about *looking* elderly—experiencing grey hair and wrinkles, drooping breasts and erectile dysfunction, and all the rest of it—didn't become mainstream until the 1950s, when more emphasis was placed in British and North American culture on looking youthful. The veneration and monetization of youth and the creation of the 'teenager' have certainly been linked to the post-war period. A cultural shift towards perfecting physical standards of attractiveness was boosted by the intersection of surgical skills with an advertising industry that tapped into ideological ideas around self-improvement.[27] There is surely something emotionally alienating about looking old in a culture that values youth above experience. Or worse, trying to 'fit in' with youth culture, even though one doesn't quite pull it off. The 'mutton dressed as lamb' attack on women who are seen to dress younger than their years is not, however, a new phenomenon, but one which was prevalent in eighteenth-century culture.[28]

For all of the mockery and contempt displayed towards ageing bodies before the nineteenth century, there was not such a strong trend of economic threat as there is for the government in the twenty-first century. And let's be clear: it is only old people without financial independence who are of concern to the government; ageing when one has wealth means that the practicalities of ageing, including increased domestic help and private healthcare, are experienced differently. Among working populations, ageing did not become a liability until individual bodies were judged by their ability to be productive in a global, comparative, and competitive sense. There is an extensive biography on the transition from a domestic economy in the UK, in which poorer people had more flexibility, where multiple household members from old people to children would pull together in the pursuit of a family income, towards the industrialization of production and the gradual erosion of traditional working practices towards a male breadwinner wage norm.[29] Historian Pamela Sharpe has shown how women were marginalized by or adapted to this new economy, which also had implications for the economic participation of elderly people as a whole.[30]

In many ways, then, we can identify a notably modern sense of being elderly as a life stage in relation to the Industrial Revolution in Britain, when patterns of work moved out of individual homes, where there had been flexibility around employment, into factories, where there was anything but. I am not glorifying a halcyon age of pre-industrialization. There was poverty and social inequality in the domestic economy, just as in industrialization. Most evidence of working life from the seventeenth century, moreover, suggests older people who were incapable of being productive were regarded as 'infirm' (as in the 'Poor Law'), or neglected and even resented within family groups. Through the early modern period, care of the elderly and 'deserving' poor was administered at a local level by churchwardens, overseers of the poor, family, and the aged themselves.[31] In 1834 the new 'Poor Law' offered a more condemnatory approach to those who were dependent, redefining those eligible for aid, grouping parishes into unions managed by elected officials, building workhouses, and forbidding 'outdoor relief' to the able-bodied poor. Through such mechanisms the traditional Christian ideal of charity and support based on natural rights was transformed into a welfare system based on self-help, economic individualism, and (crucially for the development of mass industrialization) a 'free labour market'.[32]

With industrialization, the social and economic function of older people shifted. Older people who had served key roles in domestic manufacture might still help with smaller children who were not employed in factories, but once those children were brought into the factory system, they fulfilled less important economic functions and could be viewed as a burden. Wealthier people, on the other hand, could invest in something like a modern 'retirement' plan, based on moving from a productive cycle of life to another, less productive stage.[33] In keeping with the rise and influence of economic individualism addressed by this book, then, with its corresponding impact on social and emotional experience, we can trace the classification and even the pathologization of old age to the time when it became economically unviable; those who were too slow or too infirm had no place in modern industrialized industries. The subsequent emergence of a definitive objective marking of old age (by the state pension) can be associated with this marketization of employment. Ironically, the 'cradle-to-grave' ideology that marked old age out as a distinct period where society should take care of the less able precipitated its definition as economically unviable.[34] The emergence of old age as a definitive state is therefore wrapped up in ideological questions about obligation, financial responsibility, and duty of care.

The physical identification of old people as a specific social group, regardless of individual difference, has also been established through the design and implementation of architecture. Quite literally, cultural attitudes to the aged are built into the environment. The geographer Glenda Laws has shown how the segregation of the elderly into purpose-built blocks and age-defined housing developments, as well as, we could argue, nursing homes and geriatric hospital wards, has created a division between old people and the rest of society that is economically viable but not necessarily emotionally positive. State policies are wittingly or otherwise complicit in the creation of what Laws calls 'ageist' built environments. This is important because gathering old people together (which may offer less isolation than in individual homes, but not necessarily less loneliness) both pathologizes the status of being old and presupposes homogeneity between people on the basis of age. Care in the community is no alternative if old people are living with unmet need, and otherwise isolated from family and social networks, but there must be a middle ground in which elderly people with their varied experiences, which may or may not involve loneliness, are considered as valid and significant members of the social fabric.

The Complexities of Loneliness Among the Elderly

The experience of loneliness in old age is not universal, or inevitable. It is dependent on the dominant ideologies of ageing and social care, as well as individual, familial, and societal qualities of experience. There can be no standardization of approach because the elderly and the lonely are not a homogenous mass—though they might share the psycho-social traits of the so-called Silent Generation (those born between 1925 and 1945, who were brought up to work hard and keep quiet). Elderly people are every bit as complex as other generational groups who experience loneliness differently according to their wealth, psychological experience, health, gender, ethnicity, mobility, family and friend networks, and much more besides. Some elderly people are Internet-savvy.[35] Others have limited digital capacity through factors that include infirmity, economic access, and social capital, or knowing how to engage with online communities. These differences are overlooked if we focus on the elderly and lonely purely through an economic lens, or as part of a crisis in health and social care.

As with loneliness at any pinch-point, then, elderly loneliness intersects with a number of other variables. And it changes over the course of a person's life, and old age. The fleeting moments of intense and terrifying loneliness experienced by my Grandma Rose in which she was aware of an unbridgeable gulf between herself and others would not have been the same as the chronic loneliness experienced by a person who is disabled, compos mentis, living in an isolated farmhouse and fearful of intruders.[36] Loneliness among the aged depends, like loneliness in younger groups, on the relationships and health of the individuals concerned; on their quality of life and resilience. There is a significant body of work to be done on understanding loneliness as a life stage, which means that interventions will need to start earlier, if loneliness in adolescence and youth can be, as some studies suggest, a predictor or indicator of loneliness in old age.[37]

There have been few systematic, evidence-based attempts to find out what loneliness means for individual elderly people. Researchers have consistently shown that the presumption is that older people in industrialized societies are overwhelmingly in poor health, physically isolated, unable to work, and living in poverty. Yes, many people need support, and old age can be a period of intense isolation and loneliness. But we need to look at who is *not lonely* rather than who is, in order to prepare for old age as the ancient Greeks advised. Paying attention to the absence of loneliness in old age would enable us to develop appropriate health and social care interventions while taking account of individual difference. And global comparisons show that it is the context in which ageing occurs, the closing down of options available to the individual, that causes loneliness, even for the elderly infirm. It is not ageing itself, which can be an opportunity for reflection and growth.[38]

Clearly there are socio-economic factors at play, as well as environmental ones. The basics of wellbeing must include support for everyday activities and a safe and comfortable home. Moving outwards, however, a defining principle is whether a society is integrative or segregated; whether it provides opportunities for support and social integration by older and less mobile members of society *with others in society*. Gathering old people together in a care home or at a tea dance might make economic sense but it will not necessarily ease the feeling of loneliness; shared experiences and meaningful connections are not made entirely on the basis of age. One of the most important steps in developing individualized approaches towards loneliness in old age must be a better awareness of its variability.

Gender, for instance, remains a significant variable in the identification of loneliness, just as it is with every life stage. Traditionally, and for older generations in which men were the sole provider in individual working-class households, their homosocial or same-sex networks revolved around work. Work brought companionship as well as status and income; one of the challenges levelled against mass industrialization, of course, is that it created a piecework mentality that reduced an individual's ability to feel pride in the 'end product' of a task. Could retirement similarly provoke feelings of loss and loneliness, through a withdrawal of these social networks and the means by which gendered identity is reinforced? Loss of work and retirement is similarly difficult for older women. For some married women, gendered identities tend to be clustered around family and social networks rather than exclusively paid employment. Yet widowed and single old women are among the poorest members of society, and unlikely to be part of extended, familial networks. They are also more likely to be physically isolated.

Geography matters, as well as a sense of place. Loneliness is higher in deprived inner-city as well as remote rural areas, though the intersection of these environmental issues with age, gender, and ethnicity needs more attention.[39] Ethnic differences can play out across space and place and are critical to the creation of a sense of lack. Sociological studies into the use of playgrounds and community spaces, for instance, suggest that some ethnic groups find it easier to engage with and explore shared social spaces than others. One primary site of investigation among elderly people might be public libraries. Although increasingly shut down by local authorities under social cuts in the 2000s, libraries have long played a civic role in bringing people together across a wide social demographic, and in providing a shared social space in which community can be enacted. There are very few physical spaces where people can meet in the twenty-first century without paying for the privilege of being there. It's not just books, in other words, that libraries provide, however critical books are to the social fabric, and to the ability of individual people to find companionship through reading. So, there are medical and health reasons to protect libraries, as well as moral and educational ones.[40]

The 2014 CentreForum report on 'Ageing Alone' recommended a number of social interventions to prevent older people becoming a burden on the NHS and social care through being admitted and readmitted to hospital, and since 'supporting additional services will not be easy in the current financial climate'. The emphasis must be on the 'willingness of individuals of all ages to get involved in their local community', the report affirmed. Formalized and structured opportunities for togetherness were suggested, so that 'modern society can organise itself to help address loneliness'.[41]

This is an interesting historical moment, then, when individualism is prioritized by governments on the one hand, yet a revised notion of community thinking is encouraged on the other. The ideal of community prioritized by an individualist government is one that acknowledges the need for accountability (which exists in traditional notions of *communitas*), but the government does not play a role in that; it is a mere observer and facilitator to community as enacted by others.

Elderly Futures

I have focused, in this chapter, on philosophical and economic approaches to the lonely elderly, and I remain convinced that a historically situated, joined-up approach to loneliness among the aged, as with other social groups, is the only way beyond the 'loneliness as epidemic' narrative. I want to conclude with a consideration of elderly futures in the digital age, and what role social media might play in the meaning of community. Loneliness at all levels can be impacted by technological innovation, and it is not inevitable that 'intimacy at a distance' (a term used to describe the circumstance of many millions of elderly people who live at some remove from family but communicate via video calling or messaging) is necessarily worse than close-living, with all the irritations that can result. But there is a problem in how elderly attitudes towards social media have been framed.

In an article entitled 'The Rise of the Silver Surfer: How Technology Is Enriching the Lives of the Ageing Population', Fran Whittaker-Wood wrote in the *Huffington Post* that it was patronizing for people to presume elderly individuals cannot benefit from digital technologies, especially those linked to the creation of new social networks to replace those that are dying. Rejecting the notion of a 'digital divide', Whittaker-Wood argued that seniors were getting online at a faster pace than ever before. Citing research by the Office for National Statistics, she observed that 75 per cent of adults aged over sixty-five years use the Internet, with women over seventy-five reflecting the greatest increase in any demographic group. This reflects the fact that 'technology can significantly improve the quality of later life and seniors are finally beginning to wake up to how it is changing the face of ageing'.[42]

The simplistic terms of this article are instructive in considering how elderly loneliness has been framed as a disease in search of a cure. Yes, digital technologies can provide a wide range of solutions for elderly lifestyles, including connections with family and friends, social groups, and accessibility to a range of goods and services, including medical healthcare and technologies. But there is no simple correlation between loneliness and digital technologies among the elderly. Digital technologies do not provide a quick-fix solution for loneliness among the aged any more than they do among the young, nor are they a resolution for a lack of physical connectedness 'in real life'. They do not solve the embodied loneliness or the craving for physical touch that, say, a pet might. Nor do they necessarily assuage the feelings of disconnectedness that accompany grief and widow(er)hood, or a sense of isolation from one's peers. Some of the conventions of social media use, in which particular versions of the self are presented to others—usually 'happy', airbrushed selves with close family connections, economic safety, friends, and a harmonious home—might even increase feelings of isolation and loneliness by resulting in negative comparisons and low self-esteem.[43] Social media and digital technologies do not transform social relations but reproduce them; how people engage on social media tends to sit alongside existing forms of connection, reproducing the patterns and habits of interacting that already exist. Lonely old people who feel socially disconnected are not going to feel more embedded in real life by using Facebook.

To positively influence health and social interventions, to support the government's targets for reducing loneliness at all levels of society, and to ensure the elderly are not left behind, we need to develop evidence-based, historically informed understandings of what loneliness means for different social groups, according to their specific contexts, experiences, and expectations. This is a more complex matter than comparative assessment between the UK and other nations, although that would be helpful in understanding the impact of national and cultural influences. What is needed is a clearer understanding of the architecture of loneliness for the aged, as for adolescents, single parents, the poor, and the homeless, and any other identified vulnerable group. As part of this closer attention to detail, we need to consider, as a society, the ways words take on different meanings in different times and places; words like 'elderly' and 'community' as well as words like 'loneliness', 'belonging', and 'home'.

CHAPTER 7

ROOFLESS AND ROOTLESS

No place to call 'home'

Home, *noun.*

- Te where a person or animal dwells.
- A dwelling place; a person's house or abode; the fixed residence of a family or household; the seat of domestic life and interests.
- A refuge, a sanctuary; a place or region to which one naturally belongs or where one feels at ease.
- A person's own country or native land.

Oxford English Dictionary

What does 'home' mean for you? Maybe it's marshmallow-soft images of smiling family, tables laden with food, snuggles on the couch, or playful squabbles over the remote control. Parents coming around for a roast; hanging out in cafés with loved ones on a Sunday. Arriving at Heathrow and getting collected by a friend. Perhaps it means something different. 'Home' can suggest a physical structure, a house, a flat, a room; or something bigger: a county, a country, a continent. But home can also be a battleground; a place of fights and hate. Or an elusive ideal, connected to a sense of safety, of belonging, that one has lost, or never experienced. In Brian Bilston's 2017 poem 'Refugees', home is something that can be shared or not shared, depending, quite literally, on the way that the story is read.[1]

In earlier chapters I have talked about lonely childhoods and lonely marriages, lonely widow(er)hood and lonely old age, all of which takes place within and through the spatial arrangements of domestic space—be it the palatial environment of Windsor Castle or a single room in a Lancaster care home. And much of the material culture of our worlds, the things we surround ourselves with, gives shape and meaning to our lives, and provides us with a sense of individual and collective identity. I will continue these themes in relation to consumer culture, the language of the body, and loneliness in Chapter 8.

I am going to explore, here, the meanings of loneliness for people who do not have a home, who are defined as homeless, and refugees, displaced from one home in search of another. Common to both groups is a vulnerability, and an exclusion from conventional social groups and support networks (Figure 7).

Figure 7. Homeless man seeking emotional engagement as well as relief.

Homelessness is a growing problem in twenty-first-century Britain, as it is in other industrialized countries. So, too, is rootlessness, as a result of a European refugee crisis.[2] In the case of both homelessness and refugee isolation, however, loneliness is one of the neglected areas of health and social policy. Partly this is because loneliness is understudied. But it also reflects a wider lack of concern for the complex psychological needs of the displaced, despite the fact that emotional and physical trauma can make everyday life and cultural integration impossible.[3] And without a clear sense of how loneliness is constructed and experienced among the rootless and the roofless, there can be no joined-up, multiagency response to negative experiences for refugees and the homeless.

There is something fundamental about the interconnecting themes of national identity, home, and belonging that draws together rooflessness and rootlessness as distinct problems in the history and culture of loneliness. This chapter asks what a cultural understanding of loneliness can bring to health and policy interventions, and conversely what the experience of loneliness for homeless people and refugees might bring to our understanding of loneliness as a twenty-first-century emotion cluster.

Rooflessness: Homelessness as a Recent Historical Problem

Homelessness is a new phenomenon—at least insofar as the term denotes the lack of a stable home, accompanied by psychological, physical, and social problems. 'Homelessness' only began to be discussed in printed works from the 1850s, under the influence of industrialization, urbanization, and slum clearance. Before the seventeenth century, homelessness was rare, largely because of the hierarchically ordered nature of society, and the paternalistic ordering of extended family structures ('family' meaning not only birth and intermarital relations, but also servants) that made one person accountable for another.

The *Oxford English Dictionary* defines the state of being 'homeless' (before the noun 'homelessness' was created) as 'having no home or permanent abode', though the term was seldom used before the seventeenth century.[4] In 1613 the self-styled 'water poet' John Taylor in *The eighth wonder of the world* made the first reference to homelessness: ''Twere best he iog'd from his commanding Mayne: And with his troupes of homelesse, rouing slaues'.[5] Fear of homeless troops and 'masterless men' was also prominent in seventeenth-century discussions of soldiers coming home from battle.[6] In 1729, the Irish author Samuel Madden in *Themistocles: The lover of his country, a tragedy* referred to 'an homeless, hopeless, friendless Foe'.[7] But it was not until the nineteenth century that homelessness was regarded as an urban problem: in the first volume of the *Monthly Repository* (1831) Francis Wiggins invited readers to '[i]magine yourselves the rudely dressed and ungainly boy wending his way, homeless, and penniless, through the streets of Philadelphia'.[8] And in *The brain and the nerves: their ailments and their exhaustion,* the physician Thomas Stretch Dowse (who wrote extensively on the ubiquitous nineteenth-century nervous condition 'neurasthenia') remarked that '[i]f the thousands of people who waste their money in galvanic appliances were to spend it upon the destitute and homeless poor of London, it would be far better for their nerves and their consciences'.[9] The reference to the 'conscience' is important, for here we have evidence of a shift in attitudes towards homelessness as constituting a blot on the moral landscape of society. Although the distinction between the deserving and undeserving poor had long been the concern of philanthropists, homelessness was culturally complex, and that there was a charitable compunction on the part of the more fortunate tapped into a much longer Christian charitable tradition.[10] Not until the twentieth century, however, was there a shift towards representing homelessness as a social and political 'problem'.

On 16 November 1966, the play *Cathy Come Home* (written by Jeremy Sandford and directed by Ken Loach) was shown on BBC1.[11] Its main theme was homelessness, a subject that had seldom been explored in the mainstream media. The play was greeted with public shock and critical acclaim, due to the provocative subject matter: the descent into poverty and homelessness by the eponymous Cathy and her husband Reg. It gave rise to a number of charities aimed at supporting the homeless, as well as political campaigns to demand governmental action. The homeless charity Shelter was coincidentally established a few days after the film was broadcast, and Crisis the following year. Housing policy was gradually reformed over the next decade, with the passing of the Housing (Homeless Persons) Act in 1977.[12] The Act gave councils the legal duty to house those considered 'priority' and provide advice and assistance to all others.[13]

Despite the social reforming nature of *Cathy Come Home*, and an expansion in both housing and welfare reforms to prevent homelessness and to support homeless people, there was a sharp increase in homelessness in the UK during the 1980s. House price inflation, the selling of council accommodation, rising unemployment, increased mental health and drug-related problems, and a ban on sixteen- and seventeen-year-olds claiming housing benefits saw the numbers of people on the streets increase. By the 1980s homelessness as a social problem linked to rapid urbanization was politically entrenched. J. David Hulchanski, Professor of Housing at the University of Toronto, studied the *New York Times* historical database from 1851 to 2005. He found that the term 'homelessness' was used in 4,755 articles—but nearly 90 per cent were published in the twenty years between 1985 and 2005. Before 1980 it was rare to find the term used.[14]

There has been a further rise in homelessness in the twenty-first century. Since 2010, with sweeping benefit reforms, the problem has become worse. In 2013, more than 112,000 people were declared homeless in England alone, a 26 per cent increase over the previous four years. The number of people living rough in London also grew over the same period, but by 76 per cent to over 6,000 individual bodies. Critics have blamed this rise on a £7 billion cut in housing benefit, welfare reforms, and a lack of affordable housing.[15] And rough sleepers represent a fraction of the total homelessness population; pregnant women, parents with dependent children, and people categorized as 'vulnerable' by local councils are housed, however temporarily. These 'hidden homeless' are not visible on the streets but inhabit bed and breakfasts and the spare rooms and couches of friends and family members. They are overwhelmingly trapped in a cycle of poverty, abuse, misfortune, or dependency.

In 1981, the United Nations announced that 1987 would be the 'International Year of Shelter for the Homeless', in recognition that homelessness had become a serious international problem. At that time, the term 'homelessness' was not used, largely because it was insufficiently well known. The condition of being homeless was linked to a lack of social and familial support and connectedness, which is a critical component of what is being argued here: homelessness, with its accompanying links to depression and anxiety, loneliness, deprivation, poverty, and abuse cycles, means more than simply being unhoused. Although this is commonly the implicit suggestion in debates about housing—that homelessness is merely the state of not having a house—it means much more besides, including a far higher incidence of addiction, mental health problems, and loneliness.

Who Are the Homeless?

Homelessness is gendered and class-based. It is also skewed by age and vulnerability. Men are more likely to be homeless as a result of unemployment or addiction; women as a result of physical or mental illness, or abuse. Migrants and those without support networks are also more likely to succumb to homelessness; Eastern European migrants made up 30 per cent of London's rough sleepers in 2013.[16] Young people, especially those aged between sixteen and twenty-four, make up 8 per cent of homeless people. Many homeless people have no formal education or qualifications and have been in local authority care or prison. In the main, then, homelessness afflicts people who have the least, and are correspondingly regarded as less productive to a consumer-orientated, individualistic society. Against a backdrop of self-promotion and self-resilience, homeless people are not regarded as efficient contributors to society. They are also, overwhelmingly, denied the social networks that provide a sense of community and identity (other than that forged through deprivation), or safety.

The widely recognized fragmenting of community through individual pursuit of wealth in the 1980s, reinforced by a series of legislation in the twenty-first century, including the 2011 Localism Act, which allowed less secure tenancies and market-rate rents (benefits for which are capped by the government), and the Welfare Reform Act, has exacerbated the homeless problem in the UK. It has also created greater divisions between the 'haves' and the 'have nots'. What this means in practice is that it is not only the physical safety of a home that is disappearing as a reality for many people, but also a range of associated services, including health and social support. Up to 70 per cent of homeless people have a mental health problem, for instance (either contributing to the homelessness or directly resulting from the homelessness), and are caught in a cycle of deprivation and dependency.[17]

Given the sheer scale of the problem, it is understandable that loneliness is one of the least studied aspects of homelessness. With a reduction in funding, fire-fighting immediate crises necessarily takes precedence. But the reality is that homeless people, like other marginalized social groups, experience loneliness as a disconnectedness from physical, emotional, and social forms of contact and wellbeing. And loneliness might also be significant in the creation of homelessness, as the latter is often linked to familial and social isolation. Homeless people are among the most marginalized members of society, and widely understood to feel 'disconnection, disassociation from society at large, and a sense of aloneness and loneliness'.[18] The intersection of loneliness and homelessness is especially problematic given the stigmatization of the homeless and negative stereotypes that have been linked to feelings of 'worthlessness, loneliness and social alienation, and even suicidality'.[19]

Perhaps unsurprisingly, research into the homeless and the lonely suggests a higher incidence of loneliness among homeless people than within the general population as a whole.[20] There were five factors assessed by researchers in one study into loneliness among the homeless, which included: 1. emotional distress (including 'pain, inner turmoil, hopelessness, and feelings of emptiness associated with loneliness'); 2. social inadequacy and alienation; 3. 'growth and discovery'—meaning the potential for inner strength and self-reliance that might emerge through the experience of loneliness; 4. interpersonal isolation (which included the absence of close relationships or a primary romantic relationship); and 5. self-alienation—a degree of 'detachment from one's self that is characterized by numbness, immobilization and denial'.[21] Homeless people reporting loneliness described higher levels of interpersonal isolation, and lower levels of 'growth and discovery'. Homeless people are not always acknowledged or interacted with by the general population, meaning that the capacity for isolation is higher among those living on the street.

The Significance of 'Home' and Its Lack

We might expect, given modernity's emphasis on the home and domestic interiors, and the separation of work from home since the nineteenth century, as well as the complex dynamics of shame and responsibility that are associated with homelessness, that the homeless experience a distinct kind of loneliness. We might also expect that experience to differ by such circumstances as age, gender, ethnicity, disability, mental health, and length of time on the streets. For instance, women who are homeless more commonly report histories of sexual or physical abuse, higher rates of mental illness, more frequent suicide attempts, and major health problems.[22]

So homelessness is part of a much broader emotional problem in which loneliness plays a role. Finding a lack of research into homeless women in the UK in their own right, and equally importantly, a paucity of studies examining homelessness from the perspective of women, a sociological analysis by Annabel Tomas and Helga Dittmar of the University of Sussex (2007) showed how 'influential the concept of "home" as a place of security and safety (as opposed to the less emotional concept "house") is among those who are safely housed, but not those who were homeless'. Similarly, the themes of safety and security, associated with the term 'home' among women who were securely housed, were missing among those who lacked homes and who also had experienced abuse in childhood, adolescence, and adulthood.

The point to bear in mind is that homelessness is not only a structural condition denoting the lack of a roof—though this is how homelessness tends to be framed. More profoundly, it is a social and emotional experience, characterized by a lack of physical safety and social belonging. In order to understand the psychological impact of homelessness, we need to examine the emotional context in which it occurs, in relation to the individual and social meanings of home, and related concepts like 'family' and 'belonging'.

Refugees and Loneliness

I want to turn now to the particular status of refugees and asylum seekers, who are subject to a distinct set of political, social, economic, and social pressures as well as stereotypes, and are—like the homeless—an increasingly prevalent group, thanks to global conflicts and climate change.[23] Adult and child refugees have often experienced multiple traumatic situations, which are revealed through a range of psychiatric and physical complaints, as well as a chronic sense of loneliness. This perilous emotional state is linked to precarious, unknown, and frequently hostile environments, including in the UK and especially after the Brexit referendum in 2016.[24] In a 2011 study into the psychiatric needs of refugees, almost 90 per cent of respondents experienced 'psychological distress', including grief and sadness when thinking about their homes of origin, and loneliness about their isolation in a new environment.[25] The challenges of a new, refugee identity were associated with comparisons made between the self and others, from whom one was isolated: 'When I look around me, I see so many people who feel happy and safe, and I think "Why not me? Why can't I be that person, why can't I have what they have?" It makes me want to cry all the time'.[26]

This subjective, negative comparison is common to all manifestations of loneliness; the recognition of a lack is based on a sense of what one wants, as well as what others may have. Refugees are also torn apart from their homes and families, the familiar environments and sensory experiences—sights, sounds, smells—associated with home. Material culture is crucial in structuring individual emotional lives (and loneliness), and a loss of these objects of identity, combined with a lack of community recognition—and even, in many cases, social ostracization—can be devastating to those unable to belong. Being lonely because of feeling 'left out' has been specifically linked to younger refugees and asylum seekers in particular, who might be alienated from others and unable to form new relationships. Loneliness among refugees and asylum seekers can be overlooked by health and social services that focus on trauma and practical considerations rather than wellbeing, social connectedness, and loneliness.[27]

In a recent article on the health status and health needs of older refugees from Syria in Lebanon, researchers explored the mental and physical wellbeing of those over sixty years old receiving charitable assistance.[28] In ways that correspond to the types of social change traced in this book, Jonathan Strong and colleagues at the Center for Refugee and Disaster Response at Johns Hopkins Bloomberg School of Public Health found that older refugees faced a variety of age-specific disadvantages. These disadvantages remained constant despite the specificities of conflict and displacement. Impairments in mobility and health can lead to dependence on others, but social networks can diminish over time, and self-esteem, connected to jobs and relationships earlier in life, can decline. There is the added disadvantage, too, of an economically precarious existence compared to younger generations. In common with a global growth in older populations, due to better health and fertility and increased longevity, people might expect to live longer. So, the same kind of health and wellbeing issues that affect the elderly, including loneliness, affect refugees. Nevertheless, there are some specific characteristics of loneliness among refugee populations that need to be considered.

Firstly, in a crisis situation, medical services, such as hearing aids for age-associated conditions, are not necessarily viewed as socially urgent. Older people can, therefore, become even more sensorially detached from their surrounding environment and communities. Older people are seldom included in the 'vulnerable' services offered for women and children, and mental health services tend to fall behind other kinds of interventions. In crisis situations there are also negative impacts on the availability and consumption of food, in which older people tend to lose out to younger people, and the related impacts on cultural practices around food that tend to promote sociability and inclusion. Given how important food and practices around eating are to maintaining social cohesion and a sense of wellbeing, it is easy to imagine how marginalization around mealtimes is damaging to a sense of wellbeing and how it might promote loneliness.

The report by Strong and his colleagues also focused on domestic environments and the material culture of everyday life. In addition to fragmented and fractured habits around food and consumption, physical accommodation for refugees can be crude and unfurnished. Around 26 per cent of older Syrian refugees lived in tents, and 11 per cent in public buildings, unfinished structures, or other dwelling sites. Around 40 per cent were also carers, either for spouses or grandchildren. And one of the most underexplored aspects of health and loneliness in the UK is the emotional isolation of carers, especially if there is insufficient social support,[29] since elderly people are often carers for their spouses and struggling with the vulnerabilities linked to ageing as well as the additional responsibility of looking after others.[30]

In addition to the vulnerability experienced by elderly refugees around health, financial stability, and the precarity of domestic situations, further strains were produced by the circumstances of being a refugee: these included missing and worrying about relatives left behind in war zones, the grief associated with the death of loved ones, and the trauma of living through and fleeing from danger. Routinized existence of the kind that might bring stability and comfort, including familiar food, smells, and sounds, was also largely absent. Negative feeling states were reported that included anxiety (especially when there was no friend or family member to support individuals in an emergency, which is also a theme for elderly loneliness), depression, especially among older, educated refugees, and feelings of loneliness. Those feelings of loneliness were associated by Strong and his collaborators with 'poor financial status', living in poor conditions, and 'lacking a friend who could provide care if the older refugee became sick'.[31]

Significantly, loneliness comprised a range of different emotional states, in keeping with this book's description of loneliness as an emotion cluster. These feelings included sadness, insomnia, and powerlessness, which are characteristic of depression, with anxiety about the future, as well as grief for family members who might be missing or dead. What this important study of Syrian refugees has identified, in relation to loneliness, is how persistent and ongoing loneliness might be among refugee populations. In addition to a variety of health and social difficulties, including being accepted among new and often culturally diverse communities, and continuing traditions and practices that keep refugees connected to the idea of 'home' (and often in difficult financial, medical, and social contexts), the impact of loneliness can be as emotionally debilitating as grief and trauma.

These insights into the meanings and experiences of loneliness from homeless and refugee populations, characterized here as roofless and rootless, have relevance to the study of loneliness as a matter for health and social policy. In each case, it is the lack of safety associated with an insufficient home that brings additional feelings of loneliness, along with the difficulties of integrating into community, being accepted, and often experiencing mental and physical disabilities as well as economic precarity. And the experience of loneliness is linked to an embodied existence, related to an emotional sense of wellbeing (and its lack) through the physical and built environment.

As these examples suggest, loneliness as a subjective experience is not merely a mental, but also a physical state. It produces a series of visceral and embodied reactions that might range from fear and resentment to anger and sadness. The body languages of loneliness are complex, but there is no reason why we might not attend to reading the body in understanding where loneliness occurs, and for whom. Embodiment is not only about the body, of course, but also the material world in which we belong; our experiences and engagement in the world are always mediated through our bodies as well as the things that define us: from clothes and crockery to cars and carpets, objects give rise to individual and social meanings. This embodied sense of loneliness is a subject that has been neglected in the study of loneliness, which is why it is time to address materiality and the body.

CHAPTER 8

FEEDING THE HUNGER

Materiality and the lonely body

> It sort of feels like shallow, and often you find yourself lulling into a false sense of 'I don't care, it doesn't matter', just pushing all the feelings down so that you don't have to face the cold. The isolation too. It just feels heavy and it makes you feel small, like you're in the middle of a giant swarm of orange dots and you're the one blue.
>
> Anon., twelve years old

Loneliness can be difficult to define. It has no opposite; it is entirely subjective, being perceived differently across times and places, between people, and even according to one's own life stage. The loneliness of children will be different to that of adults and each of the individuals and social groups covered in this book. In uncovering loneliness, moreover, we are engaging as researchers and as human beings with psychological experience, representations of language, and embodied experience. While the psychology of loneliness is well explored, reinforcing the idea that loneliness is a mental and individual rather than a social and physical experience, the embodied experience of loneliness has been neglected. So, too, have the ways in which the lonely body engages with the world around it. Part of the reason for this is the difficulty in defining, accessing, and describing loneliness as a physical, lived experience, a difficulty that is exacerbated for the historian.

The material culture of *solitude*, on the other hand, is easy to uncover; a single toothbrush in a bathroom; a single fork in a kitchen; a single pair of shoes placed neatly in the hall—the objects of singledom are not the same as objects of loneliness, bringing us back to the difference between being alone and *feeling* alone. There have been exhibitions on the material culture of solitude, such as the online exhibition by the Romanian-born researcher and artist Jean-Lorin Sterian.[1] The material culture of loneliness is more neglected. And yet it is central to the experience and communication of loneliness. New materialist approaches to health, for instance, use the concept of 'assemblage' to describe the siting of the body within a network of physical and interpersonal 'relationships and affects'.[2] Loneliness, like any other emotional state, is defined in and through the principle of embodiment: individual experience is material and physical as well as symbolic and linguistic.

Bodily and material practices provide fundamental means by which belonging (one of the limited, unsatisfactory terms that has been considered throughout this book to explain the problematic absence in language of a loneliness 'opposite'). The objects and gestures of everyday life, of inheritance, of cultural, religious, and ethnic identity, are key sources in the construction of individual and social identity.[3] The stories that we tell ourselves about our own identity and history, our place in the world, and our relationships with others—past, present, and future—are structured through material goods: food, books, movement, clothes, photographs, furniture, buildings, soft furnishings, and everyday ephemera. Along with verbal narratives and gestures, to which I will return, material objects are the means through which we structure our physical and mental worlds and communicate our emotional experiences to ourselves and others.

Because material objects tell stories about who we are, and where we are in the world, they become especially important in signifying meaning when other aspects of ourselves and our identities are cut off and adrift—among refugees and migrants, for instance. Being displaced 'by definition changes one's relationships with the material world to which we belong', as one scholar has put it: 'the world of places, things and other people'.[4] Studies of food memories among Mennonite women refugees in the 1920s and 1940s, for instance, identify narratives of selfhood and identity around food and cooking that are formed in relation to the bigger, inherited themes of hunger and deprivation.[5] It is particularly interesting, then, that the neuroscientists John Cacioppo and Patrick William have compared loneliness to a kind of bodily hunger, a signal that something is needed for the survival of the individual or tribe.[6] The imagery of a bodily hunger is consistent not only with the physicality of the lived experience, but also with the material culture of food and the practices of living that surround the individual body and help us to make meaning out of social experience. We can see this at work in the artist Daria Martin's film *A Hunger Artist*, which is based on the Franz Kafka short story of the same name (1922).

Kafka's book explored the author's familiar themes of death, art, suffering, and isolation. The eponymous artist starves himself for forty days—on multiple occasions—against a backdrop of waning public interest. The final of those cycles is represented in Martin's film, with an empathetic response from the viewer curated through careful choice of music, lighting, and angles that allude to the sensory body: the hollowed-out cheeks of the artist, the sad pools of his eyes, the ringing in his ears, the heartbeat that becomes a clock marking time.

Most accounts of *A Hunger Artist* focus on what it tells us about the real-life spectacle of hunger artists in nineteenth-century Europe and America (the subsequent inspiration for the American illusionist David Blaine), or about the role of the artist, swallowed up by society.[7] I am interested, rather, in what it tells us about embodied loneliness, and the lonely body in the material world. Viewers eat and drink and make merry, performing togetherness while the artist is alone. By contrast to the dowdy colours of the artist, the audience is suffused with colour, their mouths lascivious, their eyes glazed. In Martin's film we are reminded of the sensory nature of embodied belonging as well as, by extension, the absence of that feeling in the case of loneliness. The hunger artist cannot speak or hear properly by the end; he cannot participate through the senses; his body is withdrawn, isolated, making contact only with rough fabrics and dry straw.

The hunger artist is denied the humanity of belonging. He is starving not only for food, but also for human contact, eating with others being just one of the rituals of togetherness that allow us to feel part of society. It is not just the bars of the cage that keep the hunger artist from the realm of the other, but also his internalized sense of disconnect. The single, saving moment of humanity is when a young girl approaches the cage and reaches out her hand to touch the artist. Touch, the most neglected of the senses when it comes to emotion, provides a moment of hope and connection, literal and symbolic, that is all too fleeting. Finally, the skeletal figure, increasingly separated from the realm of the human, slips beneath a bed of straw, before transforming into a sleek black panther.

The hunger artist is not solitary, but he is lonely; his psychological imprisonment as manifest as his physical separateness. Looked at but never *seen*, the artist's loneliness is conveyed by shapeless clothing, downcast gestures, a physical and emotional retreat from the world of the human. People look at the artist, but do not see 'him'; they see the body as object, as spectacle. The empathic gaze needed for social belonging is absent. Loneliness can be a prison, when it is unwanted. It can occur in social isolation as well as in a crowd. Martin's film makes us think about the placing of the individual, lived body in relation to others, and of the different gazes in which the lonely body can be positioned. 'I always wanted you to admire my fasting', the artist says to the impresario at the end. He has not been admired; he has been the subject of scorn, derision, pity, and most withering of all: indifference.

Yet the individual's engagement with the social and material world necessarily leaves traces. This chapter considers how we might understand the physical impact and experience of loneliness—firstly, as it produces distinct emotional feelings, and as those feelings are communicated to others through the language of the body. And secondly through the ways in which embodied experience takes place within the realm of material culture. The objects that we surround ourselves with, as well as the bodies we inhabit, are fundamental to any understanding of loneliness as a kind of hunger. And it is particularly important to put the body back into discussions of loneliness in the neurocentric West.

Modern medicine and health interventions view loneliness as a mental affliction; in part this is because pathologized loneliness tends to be linked to depression, anxiety, and low self-esteem. The separation of emotion from the realm of the mental is a product of nineteenth-century scientific classifications.[8] But loneliness causes illnesses of the body as well as the mind. And loneliness is a physical, lived experience that connects us to the material world and to the world of other people. Our connections to that material world are always emotional; they need not be linked to consumerism and excess, though they frequently are in the commodified West, which has in turn been associated with the rise of loneliness. Before we turn to the language of the body, then, I want to explore the relationship between loneliness and material culture.

Loneliness and the Material World

In the twenty-first century, rampant consumerism and materialism have been cited as symptoms of excessive individualism and blamed for a variety of social ills. Psychologists and neuroscientists, like Duke University's Monika Bauer, have concluded that 'materialistic people' (though the definition is surely problematic) are unhappier than their less materialistic counterparts.[9] Materialistic values are believed to damage social connectedness, and decrease an individual's ability to satisfy the need for intimacy and closeness. The insatiable process of acquisitive demand and consumption of goods, and the subsequent need for more or different goods—without the need being satisfied—has been identified as a 'vicious cycle' of consumerism that affects many levels of society, including teenagers in search of peer approval and the economically deprived.[10] Materialistic people are, as a result, likely to be viewed as self-centred, selfish, and less socially adapted.[11] The links between materialist consumption and individualism are clear, and indicative of a tendency to define oneself in relation to one's possessions, and usually in competition rather than collaboration with others.

In this context, there is a growing body of literature on the links between material culture and wellbeing. There is rather less, however, on the specific relationship between loneliness and material culture.[12] Loneliness might actually increase materialism, rather than being seen solely as its product; a critical link has been made between loneliness and materialism that works in a cyclical fashion. This means that the more consumer goods people crave and acquire, the less their apparent need for social connectedness, and yet the less connectedness they experience, the more they desire consumer goods. This model presumes a basic need for 'relatedness' and connection between people; a need that can result in material goods being substituted for human relationships.[13]

As I have argued elsewhere in this book, we do not need to adopt a reductionist biological approach to the human psyche in order to appreciate the historically important basis of social connectedness, or the 'individual in society'. Remember, for instance, the poet Alexander Pope's *Essay on Man* (1734), which explored the foundations of the individual and society in relation to God, and along with many writers in an age of politeness and civility, viewed that: 'Self-love and Social be the same'.[14] The mutual cooperation of the individual in society is one of the many aspects of the eighteenth century that faded from view with the rise of individualism.

What sociological studies of loneliness in the twenty-first century suggest is that material comforts and compensations—so much more numerous and widely available today than in Pope's time—might substitute for fulfilling human relationships, if only on a temporary basis. Moreover, it is more common for lonely people to anthropomorphize objects (and non-human companions) and to see faces and emotional expressions in material objects.[15] This is reminiscent of the behaviour of Chuck Noland (played by Tom Hanks) in *Castaway*, who was stranded on a desert island. An injured Noland makes a bloody handprint on a basketball that he tosses aside. Later, in a moment of reflection and—it is implied—loneliness, he uses a tongue-dampened finger to draw an eyes, nose, and mouth on the ball, and gives it a trunk by placing it on a rock. 'Wilson' becomes his main companion.

Since material comforts and compensations are often more readily available than fulfilling human relationships, they can also substitute for their lack. In psychology this approach is consistent with attachment theory, in which early childhood experiences (including the inability to connect to a human caregiver) can lead to later dependencies on material objects.[16] Yet material objects tend to provide only short-term satisfaction, reinforcing the acquisitiveness that led to consumerism in the first place.

At the beginning of this book I suggested that loneliness is best understood as an emotion cluster, rather than a single state, and one which brings together a range of disparate, often conflicting emotional states, into a coherent whole. In the realm of material culture, we can see the emotional states attached to loneliness, including desire, jealousy, resentment, and disappointment, being played out through the cycle of acquisitive materialism. There is an extensive sociological and psychological literature on consumer emotions, and I don't intend to reproduce those here. What is relevant for the purposes of this discussion is that emotions like anxiety, jealousy, and desire are targeted by the advertising industry, and that the cycle of consumer emotions can turn rapidly from acquisitive desire to disappointment once a material object has been obtained.[17] The 'fire of desire' of consumerism, like the passion of coveted love, is depicted as hard to quench.[18]

I recognize that the term consumerism can be overused, and it is difficult to define any notion of 'excessive' consumerism (especially when material culture as a whole is integral to defining the self and the social group). There is evidence that spending money on objects might increase when loneliness is perceived, and that loneliness is not satisfied by, but increased by, a person's purchasing habits. Retail therapy, for this reason, has been identified as a pattern and behaviour associated with loneliness in the twenty-first century (Figure 8).[19]

Yet consumption can also take place in the pursuit of social cohesion rather than individual self-representation. While the quest for material objects to support social identity tends to be

Figure 8. Consuming passions: does materialism make us lonely?

equated with youth culture, it is also apparent in immigrant groups, who might turn to material possessions in order to cement or celebrate shared roots and inheritance. And it is notable among elderly people, for whom the concomitant slackening of the skin and social ties provokes a yearning to belong, to have meaningful connections, that might attach to specific material objects. In a paper published in the *Journal of Ageing Studies*, the Professor of Anthropology Robert Rubinstein explored the significance of personal objects to older people, reinforcing a view that 'object relations' theory is not merely connected to an individual's psycho-social development as a child, but rather that it shapes and enfolds an individual's entire life, since 'valued material possessions…act as signs of the self that are essential in their own right for its continued cultivation'.[20] The making of the self is an ongoing process, after all—why shouldn't it continue well into old age?

As elderly people in the West are typically characterized by declining social ties (as a result of the death of friends and family, geographical separation from loved ones, or mental and physical infirmity), the material objects through which their selves are preserved and perpetuated tend to be linked to other people; to 'family' and inheritance, themes that continue to give meaning to an individual's life beyond the here and now. Material objects serve to preserve and convey community; not just one's individual relationship to others, through gifts, for example, but also through transgenerational objects such as antiques and heirlooms.[21] The acquisition, care, and passing on of these objects, moreover, conveys a special role and responsibility on the possessor, putting them into a broader social and historical context, and perhaps also providing an extra source of meaning and connectedness.

Material culture therefore provides a shared 'sociocultural code' of belonging for individuals, as well as internal and individualistic meanings that can prevent, or conversely structure, feelings of loneliness.[22]

Loneliness and the Body

Objects do not exist in a vacuum, then; they are linked to the individual and the community through emotions, as well as the physical bodies of users. What is interesting, to me, about the engagement between objects, emotions, and physical selves is the way in which behaviours around objects provide clues to emotional states, including loneliness. One instance of this, especially relevant to elderly people, is found in the American writer Julius Fast's book, *Body Language*. Fast explores the case of an elderly woman who is contemplating being put into a care home.[23] In a section called 'The Body Is the Message', Fast describes how the subject in question, 'Aunt Grace', kept quiet in family discussions, not wanting a say in whether she should be put into a home because she didn't want to be a burden to anyone. Instead she 'sat in the middle of the family group, fondling her necklace and nodding, picking up a small alabaster paperweight and caressing it, running one hand along the velvet of the couch, then feeling the wooden carving'. When the family couldn't decide what to do, they eventually took note of what Aunt Grace was doing: 'Aunt Grace had been a fondler ever since she had begun living alone. She touched and caressed everything within reach. All the family knew it, but it wasn't until that moment that one by one, they all became aware of what her fondling was saying. She was telling them in body language, "I am lonely. I am starved for companionship. Help me!" '[24]

This story about Aunt Grace reminded me of my Grandma Rose. Though she did not seem conscious of her physical appearance when experiencing an intense episode of dementia, it became very important to her, in moments of lucidity, that her hair was properly groomed. Her hairbrush sat proudly on her bedside table, however infrequently it was used (and on the occasions when a hairdresser visited, of course she would use her own equipment). But that didn't matter; the hairbrush, along with a biscuit tin, were the material links to my grandmother's lifelong social and psychological identity. Physical grooming reminds us of one's emotional engagement with the world, the social self presented and confirmed through daily interaction. My Grandma Rose won beauty pageants all her life; looking groomed was central to her sense of self as well as her connections with others. This was apparent in the way she moved, the way she made herself up—including, to widespread mortification, the yellow sundress and matching hat she donned in order to sit on a muddy bank to watch my brother fish. (My urban grandmother, on a rare visit to Wales, had envisaged, I am sure, an environment closer to Henley's Regatta.) I wonder about that hairbrush now, in relation to Grandma Rose's loneliness in those moments of lucidity; whether it connected her to times when she was more embedded in social and familial networks, and whether those memories made her more or less lonely.

There are numerous historical and contemporary examples of loneliness being enacted in and through the body in relation to material objects, as well as landscape and the built environment. Loneliness as an emotional state is triggered by sensory experiences, as well as by memories and a sense of loss, in many cases, for what one no longer possesses. Loneliness can provide a bridge between one world and another, shifting from companion to tormentor, from shadow to ache. When Queen Victoria felt lonely for her husband Albert, for instance, loneliness was both a constant presence and an occasional visitor, triggered by moments of sadness and nostalgia. On 3 June 1862, some six months after she was widowed, Victoria described in her journals how she felt upon returning to Windsor, the principal royal residence where Albert had died:

> Poor sad Windsor, which was in its summer verdure, & all just like at Ascot time in former years. What a contrast!...drove down to Frogmore with Alice [Queen Victoria's second daughter], which is in such beauty, quite full of blossoms & flowers, azaleas, rhododendrons, seringa, &c, & the air quite perfumed. Oh! how it brought back the memory of former happy happy days & made my heart sick within me...The sense of my loneliness & desolation overwhelms me.[25]

Victoria's sensory engagement with the physical world through which she remembered Albert was perhaps second to none; the monarch was surrounded by busts, casts of his hand, photographs, and 'numberless' monuments and mementoes.[26] Echoing the mass production of commemorative items at a national level (plaques and busts, plates and handkerchiefs, and every imaginable token for the masses), Victoria preserved Albert's rooms at the royal residences at Windsor (where Albert had died) as well as Osborne and Balmoral, and gifts Albert and Victoria had exchanged, from the first bouquet Albert had ever presented her, to her bridal wreath. She commissioned busts and statues, sent parcels of Albert's hair and handkerchiefs to her children, and began the habit of dressing in black that she would continue for the rest of her life.[27] Victoria furnished her home and environment with a complex architecture of loneliness in the wake of Albert's death, and spoke to material objects as though they housed his spirit. This included the ivory miniature she would keep in her pocket and a locket that she would open to reveal his image whenever she wanted to share with him some aspect of her experience, such as a particularly beautiful view.[28] She also commissioned a royal mausoleum at Frogmore, to which she returned again and again in mourning:

> In the afternoon drove with Louise down to the beloved Mausoleum, where I felt peaceful and calm! There was such blessed repose there & I can always realize the blessed regions in which my Darling dwells now, & where I too yearn to be, far away from the strife, anger, abuse & evil passions of this world.[29]

'Thank God', she later recorded in her journal; 'I feel more and more that my beloved one is *everywhere*, not only there'.[30] And when she was surrounded by so many mementoes to Albert, how could he not be present?

Victorian grieving practices are different to those that exist in twenty-first-century Britain. Yet within marriage as well as in widow(er)hood, material objects could narrate loneliness and unhappiness, just as they could signify love and companionship through gifting and memorializing. In the 1990s I worked extensively on matrimonial disputes from the seventeenth and eighteenth centuries, when the church courts were responsible for oversight of marriage laws. At the time I was researching, most historians were focused on emotional life as becoming more sophisticated and nuanced from the eighteenth century, in respect to marriage, as to other areas of civilized culture (a decline in blood sports and theatrical displays of punishment, for instance). My work, which brought together sociological and anthropological perspectives on marriage, focused on how love and anger were played out through the domestic spaces of the home, meaning that material culture, from cutlery to beds, from custard to fireplaces, became symbols of love or hate within the domestic context.[31] For women who were refused access to material goods, this was a rejection of the community of marriage, and the expected behaviour of husbands, reflecting a domestic intimacy between husband and wife that stretched far beyond the marriage bed. That work is being rediscovered, as the relationships between emotions and material culture are receiving more historical attention.[32]

Princess or pauper, in the twenty-first century as in the seventeenth, individual engagement with material objects and the physical environment illuminates much of the emotional world of that individual, their social relationships, and the balance of power that exists between the same. It is harder to trace loneliness through material cultures of the past, especially since loneliness only becomes a linguistic entity in the late eighteenth century. Prior to that time, 'oneliness' denoted the state of being alone, rather than corresponding to any emotional lack. In *A Sociology of Religious Emotion* (2010), Ole Riis and Linda Woodhead show how far body modifications (such as fasting or posturing, or dancing), in addition to sensory stimulation (through, for instance, drumming or strong tastes and smells), have long been common in social performances of religion, but not necessarily in private, solitary communion with God.[33] Religious solitude was 'a private relation' between an individual and God rather than an integral part of a complex relationship between the individual, material objects and symbols, and social groups.[34]

It is not only in religious contexts where emotional engagement with objects would reveal much about the intersections of loneliness and solitude. It would be interesting to compare embodied loneliness over time, or between different cultures, to see whether changes in an individual's relationship to material goods in relation to loneliness can be detected. Related themes are the anthropomorphizing of material goods and the use of animal therapy in substituting for human companionship. Many studies show that animal-centred therapies are important not only in providing an emotional connection to elderly people, but also for encouraging human–human relationships; pets provide something to talk about as well as an excuse and opportunity to get out into the world. In one investigation into experiences of care home residents, a single interaction with a domestic animal once a week was enough to significantly reduce loneliness.[35] Where pets are not possible, robotic dogs have been introduced, with positive benefits.[36] Introducing companion animals into care home situations may help alleviate loneliness among aged populations.[37]

Lonely Bodies

It is impossible to perceive or experience the self without a body that thinks, feels, and believes. However our bodies might be viewed, and not simply in our own minds, but according to science, medicine, and theology, they are the meeting point between self and world.[38] Emotions are also a mediating point between mental and physical experiences, organized in narratives and memories that are passed down through the generations, and embedded in physical structures and the world of things. The language of the body, in representing emotions, in communicating ethnicity, genetic inheritance, habits, and behaviours, is therefore central to the understanding of loneliness.

I have explored in other chapters the ways in which loneliness has been figured as a physical and emotional affliction, as well as an emotional state. Accounts of loneliness tend to focus on the mind—whether in terms of mental health conservation and promotion, or through the presumption that 'mind' must be prioritized over 'matter' to force oneself to undertake exercise, sociability, and the like (sportswear company Nike's 1988 slogan, 'Just do it', being a case in point).[39] Given the twenty-first-century emphasis on emotions as psychological states, that is perhaps an understandable position in modern medicine. And yet, loneliness *is* physical as well as mental. It is not only that it has negative physical effects, including a higher incidence of strokes and heart disease, that creates such economic concern among an ageing population.[40] Loneliness is also a felt experience with links to other embodied and intensely visceral emotional states, including but not limited to sadness, jealousy, anger, and resentment.

By tending to loneliness principally as a mental condition, linked to depression and anxiety and other pathologized states, modern Western medicine tends to the mind (or the brain, in a narrow biomedical sense), rather than the body. The reasons why allopathic medicine separates mind and body in this way are rooted in the philosophical and practical development of scientific medicine as a field since the nineteenth century.[41] Today there is little emphasis on the medical prevention of loneliness, though there is an extensive pre-modern history of medical attempts to view the excesses of solitude as a whole-body rather than a psychological affliction. Since loneliness can be associated with depression, moreover, it is today treated obliquely through antidepressants, either as a stand-alone treatment or in conjunction with therapy. Some doctors do suggest other forms of treatment, including exercise, diets, acupuncture, and so on, but these bodily targeted activities are a second resort, intended to reintegrate the individual into healthy socialized habits. This is different to developing a meaningful holistic approach—or even a necessarily relevant social network—since enforced social connections (as in the injunction to get out there and see more people) tend not to be sustainable.[42] It is meaningful connections based on a shared understanding that are needed to prevent loneliness, even if that connection is made with a cat or dog, rather than another human.[43] Spending time with people one is emotionally alienated from can be even more lonely than being alone. By contrast, petting animals is now said to increase pleasurable hormones, including oxytocin, and to reduce stress, in much the same manner as a companionate touch from a friend or loved one.[44]

Feeding the 'Hunger'

The terminology of being lonely around other people, or 'lonely in a crowd', is remarkably similar to the language used in substance abuse and recovery programmes when social alienation is common. The physical symptoms described by the Professor of Preventative Medicine Steve Sussman in relation to dependency, withdrawal, and recovery include a sense of 'discomfort in [one's] own skin' and a desire for food or drink to alleviate that unpleasant sensation.[45] Intriguingly, in relation to the cluster of emotions that are linked to the state of loneliness, food or drink are often used as metaphors, symbols, and practical tokens to ease and comfort the individual and the collective body. The neuroscientist John Cacioppo, who compared loneliness to a psychological 'contagion' that could spread between individuals, also referred to loneliness as an internal 'hunger'. This is because, in Cacioppo's social-neurological approach, 'disconnection from others' is viewed as 'a life-threatening circumstance [in which] loneliness evolved as a signal to change behaviour—very much like hunger, thirst, or physical pain'.[46] The mental health charity Mind uses the same metaphor when advising people how to overcome loneliness: 'It can be helpful to think of feeling lonely like feeling hungry. Just as your body uses hunger to tell your body you need food, loneliness is a way of your body telling you that you need more social contact'. The implicit suggestion is that in the same way we might feed a deprived body with food, meeting 'more, or different people' satisfies the hunger of loneliness.[47]

In addition to food, another prevalent metaphor for talking about loneliness (and assuaging it) is temperature: literal and figurative cold and heat. And loneliness is cold. As a German psychiatrist, and contemporary of Sigmund Freud, Frieda Fromm-Reichmann was one of the first to identify loneliness as a pathological mental condition. She recounted in a 1959 essay how a woman suffering from schizophrenic depression had exclaimed: 'I don't know why people think of hell as a place where there is heat and fires are burning. That is not hell. Hell is if you are frozen into a block of ice. That is where I have been'.[48]

By contrast, physical warmth has a physical and symbolic compensatory effect when a person is feeling disconnected from others, and lonely. While hot baths might not effect the sense of inner warmth a person feels when she or he is already connected to family and friends, they do make a physical and psychological difference to isolated individuals.[49] As if mirroring a lack of social warmth, lonely people have been found to demonstrate a greater desire for warm food and drink, as well as baths and showers. These links to food are important; eating disorders, including binge-eating, have been similarly associated with feelings of isolation and loneliness.[50]

Women who are obese report far higher levels of loneliness than non-obese women; a characteristic that is understandable given the high degree of social stigma around obesity in the Western world. Yet obese men did not report higher levels of loneliness than non-obese men in the same study, reflecting the probability of gender-skewed appearance expectations.[51] It remains to be seen what difference class and ethnicity make to these experiences. Numerous psychological and sociological articles, for instance, suggest that black women are 'more satisfied with their bodies than White women', and that black women therefore experience fewer insecurities linked to body mass index and body image than their white counterparts.[52]

Links have also been identified between sleeplessness, loneliness, and obesity; given increased awareness of a link between lack of sleep and weight gain as well as the role of anxiety in preventing sleep, it is understandable that loneliness has an impact on such basic functions as eating and sleeping. Yet psychiatrists argue that there is a material change in the body as a result of loneliness and sleep deprivation, as changes in cortisol (the 'stress hormone') production impacts on both sleeplessness and weight gain. This is a particular problem for young adults.[53]

Taking care of diet and sleep were among the 'habits of the body' that ancient and pre-modern physicians linked to self-care. The so-called non-naturals (circumstances external to the body that acted upon it) included not only sleep and nutrition, but also exercise, the condition of the air, and emotional regulation. Before the nineteenth century, the body and its habits were central to discussions of all emotional states. Physicians bled patients to get rid of 'bad blood' or offered vomits and purges to remove negative and stagnant humours; though the humoral context had all but disappeared by the nineteenth century, the practice of bleeding has continued in various guises.[54] Eighteenth-century excesses of solitude were addressed through therapeutics that included exercise and the physical proximity of one body to that of another.

This physical perspective on loneliness has been apparent in the history of therapeutics: non-pharmacological interventions prior to the twentieth century were in line with, and incorporated, traditional ideas about the non-naturals: fresh air and exercise (eventually for the good of hormones rather than humours[55]), nutritious food and drink, sufficient sleep, staying connected to people, and developing a balanced way of being in the world rather than withdrawing from it. The possibility of twenty-first century therapeutics that are stimulating for the body, rather than the mind, in oneliness is intriguing. Instead of enforced forms of sociability that rely on talking and thinking (including cognitive behavioural therapy or CBT), that might mean dancing, petting animals, cooking and eating in groups, and a wide range of activities that bring the mind together with the sensorial body and the social body. Charitable activities in the UK that promote sociability and independence—from the 'men in sheds' movement to Age UK Doncaster's 'circles for independence'—recognize at a practical level the importance of physical activities and skills to prevent loneliness.[56]

Few health and social care recommendations for overcoming loneliness deal with embodied experience or preventative strategies. There has been a move towards 'social prescribing' in the UK, which means that doctors can prescribe not only medication, but also opportunities to engage with local volunteer groups. Critics have argued that social prescribing is being rolled out across the UK with insufficient rigour or evidence of success; at its worst, social prescribing takes financial pressure off NHS budgets and leaves individuals without sufficient support.[57]

Moreover, social prescribing does not reframe the mind/body division of modern medicine or put the physicality of loneliness centre stage. It does not address the sensorial aspects of loneliness, or the ways that sounds, smells, sights, and touch impact on lived experience: from the rattle of railway carriages to the scent of apple blossom, the material environments of our lives and memories reflect physical, lived experiences. And these are not generally considered in relation to the loneliness 'epidemic'. Aside from pets, for instance, the desire for physical contact, especially among elderly populations, is not tended to. In elderly populations this reflects not only the division between mind and body that we take for granted in Western medicine, but also a more general neglect of elderly sensory experience. As a society and in medicine, we tend to imagine elderly bodies as sexless and breaking down, rather than the continued vehicle of the self with the same desires and needs as younger people; certainly, the lack of sexual intimacy is not tended to in discussions of elderly people.[58]

Speaking With and Through the Body

Part of the reason that loneliness is so hard to see in others is that it is not a single emotional state, but a cluster.[59] Arguably, this could be said of all emotions, partly as a result of their transitory nature and also because emotions are connected to both triggering event and cognitive context. Thus, anger at a romantic slight might be tinged with humiliation or sadness; jealousy of a sporting rival might be connected to disappointment and anger. There is no single emotional state that remains static and unchanging and unconnected to both perception and environment. Unlike most other emotional states, however, loneliness is not signified by a distinct set of socially understood gestures. Consider anger, which has been associated in Western culture with flashing eyes, clenched fists, and a reddened complexion, or love, which might reveal itself in a rapid heartbeat or facial blush, or even shame (bent head and slumped shoulders). By contrast to these distinct and recognizable experiences, there is no history of conventional gestures or display codes that communicate loneliness.[60] Even sadness, characterized by downcast eyes and slumped shoulders, is not consistent in representing loneliness. For lonely people are not always sad; sometimes they are angry, resentful, ashamed, resigned, or even at peace.

There are therefore a variety of postures and behaviours linked to the body that might suggest loneliness. One of these behaviours is, ironically, an inability on the part of lonely people to interpret and understand the emotions of others; this has been characterized as an 'impaired' coding system.[61] Learning to read and interpret body language is, after all, a social skill; lack of practice and engagement in this area by enforced solitude, and/or an overwhelming concern that one might not be performing sociability *correctly* (and might be rejected), could make emotional communication difficult.

The languages of the body can be intentional or unintentional, intended to convey social meaning (tears are a case in point, whether 'crocodile' or authentic). *Withholding* emotional body language, for instance repressing angry gestures, is also a form of embodied language. Reading the emotional body requires attention to posture, demeanour, tone, and movement, as well as grooming rituals and the external layering of the body through clothes and modifications. 'There is no attribute of the human body, whether size, shape, height or colour, which does not convey some social meaning to the observer', the historian Keith Thomas argued in the 1990s. Differences of health, occupation, education, environment, gender, class, and ethnicity leave their marks, while the perceptions and prejudices of the beholder add to the meanings created by the body's physical stance and gestures.[62]

In the example given above of an elderly woman whose relatives debated her living in a care home, Aunt Grace's behaviours around a physical object provided clues to how she was feeling that were otherwise inaccessible. Such feelings may well also have been inaccessible to Grace, herself; it is unclear how many of her behaviours were conscious or deliberate. Lonely people are not always conscious of themselves as such. And there is no single pattern of behaviour that might have followed: Aunt Grace became overly attached to an object; another person might have smashed it. In tending to the presence of loneliness in aged people in 1998, Anne Forbes from the Catholic Agency for Social Concern in London wrote for the *British Medical Journal* of the need for general practitioners (GPs) to be more attuned to the manifestations of loneliness in their patients, especially those who might be aged and vulnerable. Forbes identified a number of bodily characteristics of lonely people that included: verbal outpouring; prolonged holding of one's hand or arm; a defeated demeanour; tightly crossed arms and legs; and drab clothing.[63] It is a shame that Forbes' ideas seem not to have been developed further in the medical context. As they stand, each of these physical signifiers is insufficiently specific to help identify loneliness, for they are associated with depressive disorders, and with the emotions of fear (verbal outpouring), anxiety (prolonged holding of one's hand), shyness (tightly crossed arms and legs), and a lack of financial resources (drab clothing).

Yet there are some interesting parallels between Forbes' comments and the work of medical sociologists who have explored 'materialities of care' in health and social care contexts,[64] as well as the work of cultural and emotional geographers, who have long been attentive to the emotionality of space, place, and material culture.[65] Social historians have also been attuned to the relationship between physical appearance and mental state. Consider Michael McDonald's still significant *Mystical Bedlam* (1981), which explored ragged clothing and appearance as linked to depression in the seventeenth century.[66] Similar claims can be made about women's appearance within early modern marriage, which was linked to social respectability and status as well as mental health. Women who were denied clothes by their husbands were therefore similarly denied social acceptability and standing.[67] On the other hand, the presumption that clean and tidy clothes and outward forms of agreeableness (including open-armed and expansive gestures) are linked to an absence of loneliness, rather than to internalized, 'civilized' behavioural codes, seems problematic and blind to communicational differences according to gender, ethnicity, and nationality. Deliberately covering up feelings by smiling when one is sad can also be part of 'putting on a brave face' to avoid the shame of loneliness.

One of the most neglected aspects of embodied loneliness is how loneliness might, along with ageing and bereavement, limit the desire and capacity of people to seek out companionship, however meaningful that might be. This withdrawal from social life can be characteristic not only among lonely people, but also their carers—one of the most understudied but lonely sectors of (paid and unpaid) employment.[68] Understanding the language of the body and of material culture in which loneliness is articulated is therefore crucial to a more nuanced understanding of loneliness in the twenty-first century. It can offer insights into how loneliness might be experienced, communicated, and prevented, as well as how to 'read' loneliness on the bodies of others. It might also allow for an understanding of the absence of loneliness in defining the gestures, rituals, and habits that indicate wellbeing; this is critical to discerning the difference between solitude as a choice and undesirable loneliness, and when people might welcome intervention.

The kinds of intervention that might be helpful when loneliness is viewed as a physical condition are, unsurprisingly, physical. Movement, like touch, offers a sensory way to commune with others, whether that takes the form of swimming, dancing—which has the added emotional dimension of music—walking, or sculpture.[69] If loneliness is a whole-body experience then its sensory engagement—and by extension the individual's sensory participation in the world—is important to address. The sounds we hear, the smells we experience, the touch of another (loving, nurturing, sexual) all play a role in our experience of ourselves as embodied individuals that are also connected to others. When I lived in East Finchley in London, the sound of the Northern line tube at the end of my friend's garden was an irritant to her, but comforting to me: it reminded me that I was never alone but part of a much wider network of existence which I could engage in, or remove myself from, whenever I wished.

The element of choice was important. Solitude (and even loneliness in the right context) can be both empowering and emotionally restorative, especially when it is chosen. We tend to have an entirely negative association of loneliness in the West, but loneliness, as well as solitude, can be healing and even creative. Much depends on whether it is enforced, prolonged, yearned for, or interpreted as a sign of social and emotional deficit. One of the challenges for the study of loneliness, then, in addition to recognizing its differences between people, times, and cultures, is knowing when it enriches rather than impoverishes human existence.

CHAPTER 9

LONELY CLOUDS AND EMPTY VESSELS

When loneliness is a gift

> I have entered into a sanctuary; a nunnery; had a religious retreat; of great agony once; and always some terror; so afraid one is of loneliness; of seeing to the bottom of the vessel. That is one of the experiences I have had here in some Augusts; and got then to a consciousness of what I call 'reality': a thing I see before me: something abstract; but residing in the downs or sky; beside which nothing matters; in which I shall rest and continue to exist.[1]
>
> Virginia Woolf, *A Writer's Diary* (1928)

Loneliness can be terrifying, both existentially and on an everyday basis. Loneliness, especially when connected to disability, infirmity, mental health problems, and vulnerability, can be a terrible bind. But loneliness can also be, as the influential English modernist writer (and pioneer of the stream-of-consciousness writing style) Virginia Woolf put it, necessary even when painful—at least for the creative process (Figure 9). 'Seeing to the bottom of the vessel', experiencing a different reality to the busyness of everyday life, allows a new understanding of the self and the world to emerge.

Figure 9. Virginia Woolf, 1927, Harvard Theatre Collection.

I am not talking, moreover, simply about solitude, though certainly that has also been linked to creativity and the time and place to write, or paint, or just to think. I am talking about loneliness as a conscious sense of a lack between what one has and what one needs, in terms of meaningful connections and sociability, that can nevertheless become an asset rather than a liability—particularly when it is chosen, handled carefully, and taken in small doses.

In this chapter I will explore the relationship of artistic creativity to loneliness, and the ways in which the pursuit and tolerance (and reframing) of loneliness can be conceived as a positive as well as a negative experience. I will chart some of the ways in which writers and artists have engaged with the desire for loneliness in their work, and the literature around loneliness as an active pursuit that carries on a much earlier, spiritual form of retreat associated with monasticism and closeness to God. This is manifest in 'Daffodils' by William Wordsworth, which is one of the best-known articulations of the particular communion with the natural and the spiritual world that can be reached through contemplation in solitude:

> I wandered lonely as a cloud
> That floats on high o'er vales and hills,
> When all at once I saw a crowd,
> A host, of golden daffodils…
> For oft, when on my couch I lie
> In vacant or in pensive mood,
> They flash upon that inward eye
> Which is the bliss of solitude…
>
> William Wordsworth, 'Daffodils' (1804)

Loneliness could provide, via solitude and a conscious recognition of one's social isolation, a divine communion with nature. The ambivalence of loneliness as a positive as well as a negative experience took on new meanings in the context of romantic individualism. The theme of necessary isolation in pursuit of creativity has since become part of the cultural iconography of the artist: lonely and starving in a garret, suffering for the purposes of the creative project.

But can we learn anything from the pursuit of loneliness as an active rather than a passive state? Is it possible to reframe loneliness in ways that will be of benefit to twenty-first-century classifications, when loneliness tends to be regarded as overwhelmingly negative? To begin to answer that question, we need to turn to the Romantics, for whom humanistic ideas of selfhood had begun to replace the need for the orthodox divine.

The Lonely Romantics

In the critically acclaimed *The Lonely City* (2017), the writer Olivia Laing extolled the pleasures as well as the pains of loneliness, identifying loneliness as a creative enterprise as well as a manifestation of a particular urban identity.[2] Laing illustrates beautifully the paradoxical situation of loneliness in the modern urban landscape, where one is theoretically closer to others, yet also anonymized and placeless. She links her personal story of loneliness in a vast city to works of modern art, including the anonymity of the self in the work of the American realist painter and printmaker Edward Hopper (1882–1967). Hopper's representations of modern American life, of solitary figures in a hotel lobby or a diner, for instance, surrounded by the possibility of companionship yet somehow removed from others, have become synonymous with the alienation of the urban environment.[3]

For the Romantic poets, loneliness intersected with the creation of a particular kind of secular, creative identity—one which was gendered and combined ideas about civilization versus nature with the pursuit of beauty, love, and the soul. The vision of loneliness as a Romantic ideal in the broadest sense, linked to the poetry and writings of the Romantic poets in late eighteenth- and nineteenth-century Britain, drew together earlier ideas about the divine and the spiritual, and reworked these for a humanistic and sometimes deistic mood.

The American literary critic and essayist William Deresiewicz has summarized the emergence of Romantic ideals about solitude in ways that acknowledge their eighteenth-century origins and religious roots:

> The self was now encountered not in God but in Nature, and to encounter Nature one had to go to it. And go to it with a special sensibility: The poet displaced the saint as social seer and cultural model. But because Romanticism also inherited the 18th-century idea of social sympathy, Romantic solitude existed in a dialectical relationship with sociability.[4]

The Romantics were not inherently antisocial or in constant need of solitude, then, though that was once a widely held belief.[5] They took moments of solitude, as Wordsworth had, in order to commune with nature, and valued time to reflect on what they had seen, but they were also intensely social when it came to spending time with other poets and writers, to enjoying the conviviality of urbane society.[6] Indeed, the point of writing for the Romantics was to perform a social service as well as a personal and spiritual good; it was searching for answers that might help the individual to negotiate his or her way through an increasingly mechanized, urbanized, and (for some) brutish environment of the Industrial Revolution, and the 'dark, satanic mills' of William Blake.[7]

Like Blake, Wordsworth (and Samuel Taylor Coleridge, who jointly published *Lyrical Ballads* with Wordsworth in 1798, though the second edition of 1800 had only the latter as the author) was part of the first generation of British Romantics. In the 1802 edition of *Lyrical Ballads*, Wordsworth set out the elements for a new type of poetic verse that moved away from the rigid diction of eighteenth-century poetry towards a spontaneous writing style said to be earned through tranquillity in nature and proximity to the soil.[8] The construction of a particular middle-class Romantic sentiment marked by excessive emotionalism and sensitivity to the natural world allowed the self-reflection and introspection needed to commune with God in nature.

Wordsworth remained religious throughout his life, though the same was not true of all Romantic poets. And his 'Daffodils' emphasizes the significance of solitude and quiet reflection for this creative process which paralleled the imagination (the inward eye) and the existence of the divine: 'for oft, when on my couch I lie/In vacant or in pensive mood/They flash upon that inward eye/Which is the bliss of solitude'. There are no negative associations here attached to the state of being alone. Loneliness is less apparent in Wordsworth's writings than solitude, which reflects the eighteenth-century absence of loneliness as a pathologized emotional state.

As an aside on the centrality of the natural world to the early Romantics, particular forms of environment are known to mediate and promote a sense of loneliness. Geographers, particularly cultural geographers, are sophisticated in narrating the emotional impact of the physical world.[9] One of the striking aspects of twenty-first-century loneliness, especially in urban, impoverished settings, is the lack of 'nature' of any kind; people who do not see greenery from one day to the next are prone, in some studies, to mental health problems, including loneliness, and there is increasing evidence of the restorative function of green spaces.[10] The medicalization of the environment as a source of wellbeing is reminiscent of eighteenth-century discussions of climate and 'taking the air' by engaging with nature in relation to health, as well as the concept of holistic health and the habits of the body.[11] It is important to note both the links between urban impoverishment and a lack of green spaces in twenty-first-century life, and the class-based interpretation of nature as a source of solace during the Romantic era. For Wordsworth's 'peasants', the natural world was much in evidence in the pre-industrial landscape, but it was overwhelmingly the context of hard, manual labour rather than quiet contemplation.[12]

By 1818, when Mary Wollstonecraft Shelley, daughter of the writer, philosopher, and women's rights advocate Mary Wollstonecraft, wrote *Frankenstein, or the Modern Prometheus*, solitude and social isolation were widely discussed. Shelley's novel was influenced by the Gothic elements of earlier writers, including Horace Walpole's novel *The Castle of Otranto: A Gothic Story* (1764), but it also explored contemporary social and political concerns that included the fear of mob rule, the bleakness of rural landscapes—including the mountains of Switzerland and the barren hillsides of Scotland—by contrast with the idyllic pastorals found in Wordsworth's writing, and the role of medicine and science in defining humanity (or its lack). There was a deliberate retelling, too, of the myth of Genesis, and of *Paradise Lost* in which an omnipotent creator abandons his creations to isolation, despair, and sin. John Bunyan's words provide an epigraph to Shelley's work: 'Did I request thee, Maker, from my clay To mould me man? Did I solicit thee From darkness to promote me?'[13]

In Shelley's *Frankenstein*, the eponymous doctor seeks solitude as a respite from guilt and regret: 'I shunned the face of man; all sound of joy or complacency was torture to me; solitude was my only consolation—deep, dark, death-like solitude'.[14] There is a hint here of the modern alienation that would become so central to the writers of the early twentieth century, in which solitude was equally respite and torment. Importantly, there is not a single reference to 'loneliness' in *Frankenstein*, and only one reference to 'lonely', which meant little more than the state of being alone. The desolation of solitude could be associated with the abandonment by the creator; this seems compatible with my suggestion that the increasing secularization of society in outward forms from the late eighteenth century contributed to the creation of loneliness as an emotional state: loneliness as related not only to the state of being alone, but to a related sense of abandonment. At the time Mary Shelley was writing, and despite the political and social radicalism of many of the Romantic poets, women's creativity was still marginalized; some recent scholars have argued that women within the Romantic circle nevertheless experienced distinct forms of alienation and loneliness as artists. Certainly, they might not have wandered as freely in search of daffodils as their male counterparts.[15] And women's writing in the Romantic period continues to be downplayed in favour of their male counterparts.[16]

Loneliness and the Modern Project

By the early twentieth century, and the writings of Virginia Woolf, solitude and loneliness were explicitly connected, with loneliness as a distressing emotional state, but also one which was necessary for the creative project. There might be 'great agony...and always some terror' of loneliness, but it was nevertheless necessary for mediating a different 'reality' to that which one experienced when surrounded by the clatter of everyday life, and by friends and acquaintances. Woolf wrote about solitude and loneliness in many of her works, addressing the ongoing challenge of maintaining the 'external' façade of sociability alongside the internal need to be alone to create. It's important to note that by the 1920s, the concept of the external-facing extravert (to use the Swiss psychiatrist Carl Gustav Jung's original spelling) and the potentially neurotic introvert was starting to make headway in discussions of psychiatry and mental health. The writer Sylvia Plath, who was a great admirer of Woolf, was similarly concerned about the relationship between an introverted, lonely personality and neuroticism. So, the association of solitude with mental illness—which was always a potential risk in classical and early modern understandings of the humoral body—became more persistent in the modern age. It continues as a characteristic of the emotionally fragile artist in the twenty-first century, when mental illness and creativity are frequently linked.[17] And though the association of neuroticism and loneliness was not necessarily made by Jung, it is significant that the Western world has, since the early twentieth century, had more regard for extroverted behaviours (gregariousness, social confidence) than their introverted counterparts.[18]

From 1905, a group of writers, artists, and intellectuals had begun meeting at the home of Virginia Woolf, and her sister, artist Vanessa Bell: 46 Gordon Square, London.[19] These members of the self-constructed 'Bloomsbury Group' were liberal, from wealthy, white backgrounds, and their bohemian rejection of conventional attitudes to sex, morality, and marriage was part of their self-definition. Woolf, however, suffered from mental illness all her life, probably exacerbated by the sexual abuse she had experienced as a child.[20] Woolf also recognized that periods of loneliness were central to her ability to write, to imagine, to create new worlds that were removed from the daily routines of everyday life: 'It is going to be a time of adventure and attack', Woolf wrote in her journal on 28 May 1929—'rather lonely and painful I think. But solitude will be good for a new book. Of course, I shall make friends. I shall be external outwardly. I shall buy some good clothes and go out into new houses. All the time I shall attack this angular shape in my mind'.

Sometimes, Woolf wrote explicitly about needing to be alone, not to write necessarily, but to think about writing, especially when a new project was taking shape. There are often tensions, in Woolf's writings, in juggling the expectations of the social and the creative. This is reminiscent of Sylvia Plath's desperate attempts to bridge the cultural expectations of womanhood, as discussed in Chapter 2; her need to be involved in the minutiae of domestic existence, no matter how unconventional the household, and yet retain a foothold on her need to write and be creative. This is a familiar refrain throughout history; women's writing all too often takes second place to the realm of the domestic. 'A room of one's own' may have been Woolf's rallying cry for women writers, but many still write in the gaps.[21]

Woolf recorded that she was '"tired"', in inverted commas, in her diary on 10 September 1929. She was at a picnic at Charleston, the house in Lewes, East Sussex where Vanessa Bell lived. Woolf's husband was away, 'having a picnic'. 'Why am I tired? Well I am never alone. This is the beginning of my complaint. I am not physically tired so much as psychologically'. Part of the problem was the pressure to constantly entertain: 'We have the Keynes; then Vita came; then Angelica and Eve; then we went to Worthing, then my head begins throbbing—so here I am, not writing—that does not matter, but not thinking, feeling everything'.[22] For Woolf, as for many writers, 'incessant company is as bad as solitary confinement'.[23] Similarly, however, too much time alone was problematic: 'I look down and I feel giddy...It's having no children, living away from friends, failing to write well, spending too much on food, growing old. I think too much of whys and wherefores; too much of myself. I don't like time to flap round me'.[24]

Stopping time from 'flap[ping] round' her seems to have been a large part of the purpose of Woolf's diary, in which she set out her anxieties about writing, her achievements, where she stood in relation to other writers, and her fears for the future. Woolf's preoccupation with time passing—seen most clearly in her novel *The Lighthouse*—is also relevant because of the largely unexplored relationship between time and loneliness.[25] Our relationship with time—perception, memory, associations—is central to the subject of emotions and the experience of disconnectedness from others, and ourselves.[26] Time seems to pass more slowly when we are happy than when we are bored, or sad or in pain. And this subjective experience of time connects with the perception of loneliness; when people are lonely as a result of social isolation, the time between seeing people can seem very long, whereas the time spent with a loved one can pass too quickly.[27]

I wonder whether the connectedness of the Bloomsbury Group fulfilled an emotional sense of oneness for Woolf in a way that other relationships did not. For all its difficulties, being in the companionship of others who saw the world the same way—who might not necessarily agree but shared values and belief systems—must have gone some way to reduce the writer's sense of alienation and loneliness. There is, moreover, a community of sorts among those that are lonely. And self-definition as a lonely artist does not mean one is truly separated from the anxieties of the world; rather the reverse. As Woolf put it in a discussion of 'great works of literature': 'masterpieces are not single and solitary births; they are the outcome of many years of thinking in common, of thinking by the body of the people, so that the experience of the mass is behind the single voice'.[28]

At an individual, experiential level, however, some experiences can feel profoundly singular. One example is grief. Woolf's reaction to her brother Julian Thoby's death from typhoid is reminiscent of Queen Victoria's emotional detachment from others during a period that was similarly 'strained and surrounded with silence':

> What I mean by this last word I don't quite know, since I have never stopped 'seeing' people—Nessa and Roger, the Jeffers, Charles Buxton, and should have seen Lord David...and am to see the Eliots—oh and there was Vita too. No, it's not physical silence; it's some inner loneliness—interesting to analyse if one could. To give an example—I was walking up Bedford...and I said to myself spontaneously, something like this. How I suffer. And no one knows how I suffer, walking up this street, engaged with my anguish, as I was after Thoby died—alone; fighting something alone.[29]

The sense of 'fighting something alone' is common in discussions of loneliness, particularly when it is linked to grief and loss. In Woolf's writing, then, we see the multifaceted nature of loneliness as a personal experience: painful if necessary for the production of art but isolating and alienating when it is accompanied by mental illness and prevents one from being in communication with others. This ambivalence around loneliness and the creative project, especially with its links to suffering and sociability, is also seen in the writings of the poet Rainer Maria Rilke.

Rilke was a Bohemian-Austrian poet and novelist, whose writings focused on questions of belief, solitude, and identity. In his existential writings, he tends to be positioned as a transitional figure between the conventions of nineteenth-century writers, like

Charles Dickens, and the challenge to the traditional worldview found in Woolf and the modernists. *The Book of Hours* (1899–1903) is widely understood to be one of the most important of Rilke's works. Dedicated to Lou Andreas-Salomé, a Russian-born psychoanalyst and author with links to Friedrich Nietzsche, Sigmund Freud, and many others, *The Book of Hours* consists of three sections relating to the Christian search for God. These included *The Book of Monastic Life*, *The Book of Pilgrimage*, and *The Book of Poverty and Death*. The title for *The Book of Hours* came from a type of illuminated prayer book that was popular in medieval France.

In the beginning of this book, I described the general influence of existential philosophy and the search for meaning that formed part of the modernist project; in Rilke's work that is apparent by its core influences, including Friedrich Nietzsche, whose oft-cited expression 'God is dead' referred to the killing of the possibility of God by Enlightenment rationalism.[30]

Without God, the human being could be seen as adrift in the world, lacking any paternalistic advisor or companion, of the kind that existed in earlier manifestations of self-in-world. *The Book of Hours* describes a series of attempts to define and identify and communicate with God, while searching for a meaningful basis for life. God becomes a pantheistic 'neighbour' figure, which he sometimes 'in a long night with a loud knock disturbs', since God and human beings are only separated by a 'thin wall'.

Yet it is difficult for the narrator to access God, or indeed his own inner self, partly because of the restrictions of language, and partly because those moments of clarity—summed up by Woolf as 'true reality'—are so fleeting. It is only possibly to grasp that reality when one is alone, isolated from others ('lonely as a cloud', perhaps), when there are fewer distractions. In 1914, Rilke wrote to

Lou Andreas-Salomé, confiding in her his struggles with creative blocks and depression, using these familiar ideas of creativity, solitude, and loneliness, and paralleling them with the vision of the human at the centre of nature, yet cut off from it. He described himself as a 'little anemone', opened wide and so filled with experiences that it was difficult to close at night. His senses were so constantly stimulated by external events and people that he felt depleted: 'empty, abandoned, cleared out'.[31]

The centrality of the natural world, in its imagery, its cyclical nature, and its Zen-like state of being, was frequently invoked by artists and writers seeking to describe the watchful pursuit of loneliness. Bearing in mind that in the twentieth century the natural world, as for the Romantic poets, could be figured both as a retreat from the brutalities of human existence and evidence of the sublime presence of a pantheistic God, getting close to nature could still provide access to a higher power. In a literal sense, the pursuit of a healthy emotional and creative life was embedded in the solidity of the earth, as in the writings of the later twentieth-century poet and essayist Mary Sarton. Sarton recorded her impressions of solitude, loneliness, and depression, and her epiphanies about the nature of existence, while sowing seeds or 'weeding out irises and "dr[inking] in the damp smell of the earth"'. 'Keep busy with survival', Sarton advised; rather than focusing on the minutiae of life, let the natural world be a guide, for 'nothing stays the same for long, not even pain'.[32]

Sarton was born in Belgium, fleeing with her family to Ipswich in England when German troops invaded. They later moved to Boston in the US, where she studied theatre and writing and published her first collection in 1937: *Encounter in April*. At seventy, Sarton wrote about the importance of her closest relationship, with Judith

Matlock, along with her Unitarian Universalist upbringing, to the shaping of her identity.[33] In 1990, while living in Maine, Sarton suffered a stroke, reducing her ability to work, though she dictated her final journals, working up until her death from breast cancer in 1995. In all Sarton's works, she is characterized by warm and honest accounts of her solitary life, her love and relationships, her lesbianism, and her quest for creativity.

Sarton's best-known writing is perhaps *Solitude* (1972–3). Here, Sarton explored the challenges of being an artist and the emotional states she experienced, including depression and loneliness. Like Virginia Woolf, she wrote about the disadvantages as well as the benefits of solitude and loneliness as a means to access a different kind of reality to that encountered in the everyday. The ambivalent value of solitude, for Sarton, was that there was 'nothing to *cushion* against attacks from within, just as there is nothing to help balance at times of particular stress'. The 'inner storm', however painful, sometimes contains 'truth ... So sometimes one has simply to endure a period of depression for what it may hold of illumination if one can live through it'.[34]

The impact of 'minority stress' that has been associated with lesbian and gay people must have historically led to particular experiences of loneliness, depending on individuals' class, status, ethnicity, and gender, and the socio-legal context.[35] Subaltern groups of all kinds in Britain, by which I mean those people that are socially, politically, and economically outside the institutions and ideologies of power, have traditionally been subject to particular forms of alienation and exclusion. Health and social care work in the twenty-first century has explored the particular cultural challenges for 'gay youth' in particular, identifying significant levels of loneliness and 'psychological damage' resulting from alienation.[36] Yet there has been, and is, significant potential for community engagement and social support for subaltern groups *precisely as a result of* their alienation from the status quo. As with other marginalized people who are excluded as a result of ethnicity, race or class, community practices can provide a means for social inclusion.[37] The emergence and development of the LGBT (Lesbian, Gay, Bisexual, and Transgender) initialism since the 1980s to create an alternative and more inclusive definition of 'community' is an important example of this process—as is the subsequent inclusion of Q for Questioning or Queer and I for Intersex, represented by LGBTQI.[38]

The examples given in this chapter of artists and writers pursuing solitude and even loneliness for the purpose of creativity are not unique. For centuries, poets and writers have sought to answer questions about the relationship between individuals and society, and between humans and a higher power, in which they parallel the natural world with the divine and seek to bridge the gap between individual feeling and the social and physical environment. Central to such questions is the relationship between solitude and loneliness, and the point at which time alone became negative rather than positive. In the twentieth century, there was more emphasis than ever before on the essential isolation of the human experience under the influence of existential philosophy. In the words of the French-American artist Louise Bourgeois: 'You are born alone. You die alone. The value of the space in between is trust and love'.[39]

Most twenty-first-century discussions of loneliness focus on its pathologization as an emotional state. In addition to the economic reasons why this might be so—the association of loneliness with a wide range of emotional and physical ailments that incur financial costs and discussions of moral responsibility—there is also an implicit presumption, which has dominated since the emergence of the mind sciences, that solitude and introversion are neurotic, negative states. Yet introversion and solitude are essential for creativity. Can we learn anything, then, from creative discussions of loneliness that might help address loneliness in the twenty-first century?

There is value in quietness, and in solitude. But that value is entirely subjective; loneliness can be restorative as well as destructive, but only when it is a choice. Most of the case studies explored in this book engage with loneliness as a hazard of socio-economic deprivation. The writers and artists discussed here held a privileged status within society. That is not to say that their individual journeys brought no struggles, but rather that, in the main, lonely people are dealing with experiences and life stages that alienate them from others, making it difficult to develop meaningful relationships for reasons that are practical as well as theoretical. It would be unhelpful to tell our socially imagined seventy-five-year-old widow (the face of loneliness for most charity advertisements), who is peering out of the window in search of companionship, to look within; to find self-fulfilment through the creative process, or through weeding. Or to suggest to a homeless mother of three that philosophical introspection is the way out of a socio-economic trap. So class, privilege, and ableism, and the neglect of people who are physically dependent on others, intersect with and challenge the blinkered presumption that loneliness can be intellectually and emotionally rewarding for *anyone*.[40]

One of the most characteristic aspects of the pursuit of solitude and even loneliness as a creative experience, moreover, is that it is temporary. The withdrawal from society for restorative or creative reasons, so necessary for individual focus and the understanding of some psychological or artistic truth, need not be permanent. While there may be a place in everyday life for moments of tranquillity—associated with the twenty-first-century flourishing of 'mindfulness' apps and lunch-hour meditations—the temporal dimension is important.[41] Is short-term, chosen loneliness (or solitude) really the same as day-after-day enforced isolation when all you can hear is a ticking clock? I don't think so.

Loneliness has many forms, then—social and individual as well as creative and destructive. In recognizing those differences, as well as the individual need for different kinds of connection with the external world (and the importance of the body as well as the mind in engaging with and overcoming alienation), we might adopt more imaginative, meaningful, and person-centred approaches to loneliness. We might even find the tools with which to deal with loneliness as a 'modern epidemic' in a neoliberal age.

CONCLUSION

Reframing loneliness in a neoliberal age

Loneliness is not ahistorical or universal. Nor is it a single emotion. It is an individual and social cluster, composed of a wide variety of responses that include fear, anger, resentment, and sorrow. It manifests itself differently according to circumstance: ethnicity, gender, sexuality, age, and socio-economic class, as well as psychological experience, nationality, and religious affiliation. It is physical as well as psychological, and its emergence can be traced back to the end of the eighteenth century, when 'loneliness' emerged as a new way of talking about the negative emotional experiences of being alone. Prior to that time, 'lonely' and 'oneliness' described the absence of another person, without any corresponding emotional lack.

Accounting for broad sweeps of emotional change over time is problematic, but I believe crucial to understanding how loneliness can be prevalent in 2019 but rare two centuries earlier. This linguistic transition from oneliness to loneliness must speak to broader socio-cultural changes. What I have attempted here is consistent with a longue durée or long-term approach to history that focuses on the evolving relationships between people and their environment: cultural, physical, demographic.[1] The use of longue durée history fell out of favour somewhat in the late twentieth century, when social and cultural historians focused on episodic or short-term events to explore the systems of meaning behind them. Influenced by the 'linguistic turn', interdisciplinary analysis of textual meaning recognized the creative rather than reflective power of language and resulted in some extraordinarily creative and pathbreaking works.[2]

In emotion history, however, the longue durée is key to the most influential theoretical approaches.[3] Accounting for emotional change and tracing the nature of that change, and the extent to which 'change' represents conventions in expression or the 'raw feels' of emotion physiology, is central to any understanding of emotions as historical concepts. Key concepts in emotion history include 'emotionology' (to describe the standards of any given society), 'emotives' (to explain the work done by emotion language in creating identities), and 'emotional communities' (to describe the different emotional standards of any behaviours accepted by any particular social group).[4] In some approaches, there is no pre-language of emotion; emotions come into existence by being talked about. The British-Australian writer Sara Ahmed has joined with anthropologists and sociologists to argue for the social construction of emotions as social practices as much as psychological events.[5] Emotions are neither 'out there' nor 'in here', Ahmed argues, but inherent in the individual as social: 'the objects of emotion take shape as effects of circulation'; it is precisely through the engagement of the individual as part of the social world that emotions are brought into being.

How helpful are these approaches in thinking about the history of loneliness? All share an interest in the centrality of language.

And they confirm that the current moral panic around loneliness is unhelpful. It suggests that loneliness is something that is 'out there' in the ether, that happens to us through contagion, rather than through the interaction of subjective experience with social configurations. We carry our individual experiences into the world and they shape us; we are also shaped by our engagements with others, and this bidirectional process is continual and ongoing. This is why we are emotionally embedded in the physical and environmental worlds in which we live throughout our lives and not merely in childhood. Like the million small rituals of our everyday lives, our emotional expectations and beliefs become internalized until they are as natural as breathing.

Is this another reason why chronic loneliness is so hard to change? Embodied habits—from nail biting to overeating—are notoriously difficult to break; so, too, is getting out of negative mind sets. The whole premise of cognitive behavioural therapy (CBT) that is prioritized by the NHS in overcoming anxious or difficult feelings is that we can redefine our thoughts around a subject or situation, and therefore shift our emotional response.[6] CBT is relatively cheap and short-term and so the preferred therapy of choice; it can be successful in specific localized challenges. But it is not helpful in complex cases, or when emotions are deep-seated, bodily, and linked to trauma. And sometimes negative emotions are perversely addictive, even when they are unpleasant.[7] Sometimes unpleasantness has its own sense of comfort. I remember when I was a smoker. That ashy, bitter taste at the back of my tongue after my morning cigarette tasted gross and it made me feel sick. But it was familiar. Without that taste, it didn't feel like morning. Similarly, spending time around people who make you feel lonely and isolated can be unpleasant yet familiar.

Like the bitterness of that first cigarette. If it's part of who you are, it's difficult to change.

Does worrying about loneliness make its experience more likely? Probably. Moral panics presuppose a collective sense of emotions that increase the possibility of contagion. Concern about loneliness can become all-encompassing and, since it connects to multiple themes around identity that include self-esteem, belonging, alienation, and loss, it is a peg on which to hang any number of hats. Which is why the framing of research questions, and a joined-up interdisciplinary approach to loneliness—What does it mean? When and where does it take place? How is it talked about? What does it feel like?—is so important.

In whatever form it manifests, one thing is clear: loneliness is an internalized sense of discomfort defined by lack. I have argued that it emerged around 1800 as a feeling and a way to talk about that feeling because of a distinct set of social, political, medical, philosophical, and economic changes. The ways that these circumstances connect with individual perception are difficult to pinpoint. Unlike Sara Ahmed, I do not believe that the individual and the social realms are the same, though I can appreciate the political power this gives to emotions. I choose to regard self and social as two interacting spheres that shift and develop throughout an individual's life; from birth the self is developed, calibrated, and redefined (literally through neural connections and figuratively through social connections) in relation to the world around us. This two-way process is at the heart of social construction models that, like the French critical theorist Pierre Bourdieu, highlight the importance of *habitus*, or internalized behavioural codes, which make certain ways of being, thinking, and feeling seem natural.[8]

The elements of that internalization have been explored throughout *A Biography of Loneliness*. The shifts in the cultural fabric, including secularization and evolutionary theory, industrialization, competitive individualism, modern psychological and emotional frameworks, and philosophies of existentialism and alienation contributed to a social language of loneliness in which the self was depicted as separate from and different to others. Over time, and through everyday practice—through language and gestures and rituals, as well as via the written and oral word—loneliness emerged as both a linguistic framework and an emotional cluster.

Social structures were also transformed through this dialogical rethinking of self and world. The established system of face-to-face relationships, which had for centuries been based on local networks and extended families, shifted towards relationships that were based on a separation of home and work, and on the economics of paid employment rather than the domestic economy, in which even the poorest members of society could strive towards self-sufficiency. Old people emerged as a distinct category that drained resources. Conditional support for the aged as with other vulnerable social groups formed part of an emergent bureaucracy of power through which the social contract was reconfigured. And the notion of 'community' (however problematic its meanings might be) gave way to a monetized idea of value in which one's place in the world was dependent on one's economic contribution and role.[9]

The proliferation of evolutionary theory ideas and metaphors is one example of a belief system that has shaped both individual expectations and social structures. The term 'survival of the fittest', for instance, has been normalized by becoming part of the logic of social change. As a concept it provides a shorthand for why individualism is important not only for profit, but also survival.[10] Various forms of competitive Social Darwinism have been naturalized into every aspect of human experience, from exams and career ambition to romance and dating, from economic production to neoliberalist *laissez-faire* policies. Evolutionary principles have become an almost invisible, naturalized framework for political, economic, and social decision making, as well as a metaphorical framework through which to order experience. The idea that competition is an evolutionary need has become implicit and internalized in the West through the language of 'drives' and 'instincts' which reinforces the unspoken belief that 'primitive' desires and the pursuit of self-interest are natural and inevitable.[11]

At the most basic level, the presumption that the human 'instinct' is for self-preservation (given a genetic—but not unchallenged—basis via Richard Dawkins' assertion of a 'selfish gene') not only allows but celebrates neoliberalism, a political philosophy invoked from the 1980s in the West around the principles of free-market capitalism and the individual.[12] As its name suggests, neoliberalism invokes the spirit of liberalism, in particular the political theories of the nineteenth century that were associated with *laissez-faire* liberalism: privatization, austerity, free trade, the stimulation of the private economy, and state deregulation.[13]

The pursuit of individualism that emerged in the nineteenth century was framed by both a philosophy of change and an economic ideal. This ideal was gendered and masculinist in its language—of the wild, feminine natural world pillaged by the mechanistic masculine one, a common theme in the imagery of industrialization—and in the ideological frameworks it supported.[14]

In this context, and with the persistent reinforcement of the ideas of individualism, secularism, and competition through science and medicine, philosophy, and economic discourse, it seems perfectly plausible to suggest that 'loneliness' was invented as a term in the 1800s not only to reflect the alienating nature of globalizing change, but also because a new form of emotional experience was born. In the absence of an all-knowing, benevolent Father and the persistent spread of a competitive individualism, a vacuum had emerged in which the self was alone, marooned and dependent on familial and social networks that were, by reason of these global changes, in a state of flux. Religiosity continued to exist and to thrive alongside science, but the outward rituals and performances of society that assured the individual of her or his place in the world had changed. I am not suggesting, of course, that the hierarchical 'Great Chain of Being', in which every single entity from God through angels, kings, and peasants to the soil, was a satisfactory state of affairs.[15] But it prioritized the sense of 'commonweal' in which accountability mattered. And it gave individuals a sense of connectedness to others, to a system, and to a protective higher power.

Throughout this book I have sought to demonstrate the specific ways in which loneliness impacts on individuals and societies, not only in relation to external circumstance, but also according to personal experience. *A Biography of Loneliness* shows how loneliness impacts people's lives differently at different times, and it has a lifespan of its own. All emotions are political: as rhetorical devices, as social entities, and as ways of organizing social and political relationships. But at this historical moment, none is so political as loneliness.

I have argued that we need to historicize loneliness, therefore, not only for its own sake, but also to expose the hierarchies on which its naturalization depends. In political rhetoric in the twenty-first century, the presumption that loneliness is universal and transhistorical means that it is a human condition and not a product of socio-political and economic choices; of decisions made by governments in prioritizing economic freedom over social responsibility.

The writer, journalist, and political activist George Monbiot has suggested that neoliberalism creates loneliness by focusing on consumerism, by suggesting that personal acquisition is the path to happiness.[16] I agree with this interpretation. In keeping with Monbiot's holistic approach to social inequalities and environmental protection, we need to see loneliness as an emotional state created by circumstances. Where I differ from his view is in the historicity and scope of the problem. Yes, neoliberalism is to blame. Neoliberalism encourages privatization, deregulation, and competition, in all areas, including health and care. But neoliberalism as it has emerged in the twentieth century, most often discussed in relation to the free markets of the American president Ronald Reagan and the British prime minister Margaret Thatcher, has a much earlier precedent in the evolution of the 'social contract', which defined the legitimacy of the authority of the state over the individual, and the rights and responsibilities of its citizens.

The antecedents of social contract theory are found in antiquity, and the historian of economic and political thought Dotan Leshem argues that this is where the origins of neoliberalism must be located.[17] The heyday of the social contract was the mid-seventeenth to nineteenth centuries, and included the work of Thomas Hobbes (1651), John Locke (1689), and Jean-Jacques Rousseau (1762).[18] Crudely summarized, Hobbes believed that without law, humans would revert to the natural state in which lives were 'nasty, brutish and short'. Absolute government was the only solution. By contrast, both John Locke and Jean-Jacques Rousseau identified the importance of the individual in society, and the rights and responsibilities that inhered in being governed.

Discussions of the social contract faded in the nineteenth century as discussions of utilitarianism became more pronounced. Classic and economic liberalism, both of which advocated civil liberties under law and prioritized economic freedom, developed in the early nineteenth century and supported the development of industrialization. The core beliefs of economic liberalism moved away from the paternalistic function of government and towards a judgement of individuals as inherently selfish and motivated by profit. Classic liberals (selectively) drew on the work of the Scottish moral philosopher and economist Adam Smith, best known for *An Inquiry into the Nature and Cause of the Wealth of Nations* (1776), to argue that it was in the common interest of society as a whole for people to pursue their own self-interest.

The creation of loneliness as a modern emotional state came about at a time of considerable debate about the rights and obligations of the state, economic independence, personal authority in the absence of a higher power, the jostle for status in the world among the wealthy, and the fight to survive among the poor. In an age where evolutionary ideals were trotted out and used to defend any number of self-aggrandizing policies, neoclassical liberalism, as it emerged in the late nineteenth century, promoted Social Darwinism, which applied the evolutionary concept of natural selection to human society.[19]

The four main tenets behind Social Darwinism included the biological laws governing behaviour, the pressure of population that presumed a constant struggle for existence, physical and sexual advantages that were borne out through competition, and the cumulative effects of this process on future generations.[20] Personal autonomy and individual greed became assets rather than liabilities, as they would have been perceived in the relatively collective world of the eighteenth century, in which, as poets and writers understood, personal and social happiness were always connected.

Health and social care for old people is a case in point. Britain doesn't have a cultural tradition of caring for old people within their homes, as in other European countries, such as Italy. But elderly people had a function in the household of the domestic economy; even the physically infirm could watch over children and participate in home-based work. When that work moved into factories, and old age became associated with economic liability rather than a cultural asset, it became more common to shift elderly people out of households and into workhouses. Poor relief was structured according to externally imposed proto-bureaucracy with the new 'Poor Law' of 1834, rather than involving face-to-face relationships.

Today, old people create government panic. The population of the UK, as in most of the industrialized world, is becoming older and living longer. More and more people are reported to be lonely, with all the accompanying physical, mental, and social debilities that can accompany loneliness in the modern age. Without any systematic research into its diverse and historical meanings, loneliness becomes a catch-all for emotional ills, and an inevitable part of growing old, like grey hair and wrinkles. But old people with poor mobility and poor health who have strong meaningful social and familial connections do not report being lonely. Those who do not have good connections and are impoverished and suffering from 'unmet needs' that are as basic as being washed and dressed or having a meal, do. And these factors are directly within the control of the government's purse.

Yet in 2018, at the same time that the government created a Minister for Loneliness, who proposed to engage communities and understand loneliness as a human experience, it continued to strip the assets and spaces where community was being formed, especially in the poorest sectors of society: libraries, social care, the Independent Living Fund, council housing. It is not only the elderly who are suffering more loneliness as a result of governmental policy: homeless people and refugees also experience considerable loneliness, lacking not only a roof but also the symbolism and safety of a home. Since the 1980s, under neoliberalist policies that have built on the socio-economic, philosophical, and scientific shifts described in Chapter 1, homelessness continues to rise, along with the emotional and social deprivation it entails.

What and where is 'community', then, in the neoliberal age? The term is so overused to have become almost meaningless. The Internet age is, in many ways, the epitome of free-market thinking and the pursuit of individualism—ironically, since it originated as a concept for the common good. This is why the Internet's inventor, the English engineer Tim Berners-Lee, has called for the Internet to have a legal and regulatory framework.[21] The emergence of online communities as forms of social networks has not replaced the essence of a real-life community, founded on mutual accountability as well as shared interests. Social media has been charged with promoting loneliness and preventing people from connecting in real life. But the task for individuals, societies, and governments is to recognize the ways emotional and social patterns of communication online replicate those found in real life

(IRL)—including social anxiety and 'lurking' as well as more unsavoury traits linked to trolling. The Internet might well help to build new forms of community and combat loneliness, but only if it is used in ways that promote self-care and wellbeing in the offline realm.

One of the main uses of the Internet today is the search for love. Or sex. Romantic love fills the void left by God and the search for a significant other. In attachment theory as in the language of romantic films, novels, poems, plays, and songs, love is quite literally all you need. Since the nineteenth century a 'soulmate' has created both an unrealistic vision of love and a sense of lack when that is missing. The implications of the romantic ideal, for girls and women in particular, are self-defeating and problematic, especially when love is figured as controlling and all-encompassing. And when the self is not enough. The historical impact of this ideal on the lives of women who were otherwise accomplished and independent is apparent in the writing of Sylvia Plath, who suffered a lifelong, chronic loneliness and sense of disconnect from the world.

When love is lost, its lack is even more powerful. Divorce can be painful and isolating, but also liberating, especially when being inside a marriage creates loneliness. Widow(er)hood can be desolating, but alternatively freeing, if a marriage is abusive. The grief attached to spousal death has no regard for status. Queen Victoria was levelled by loss, as was the eighteenth-century shopkeeper Thomas Turner. In the eighteenth century, there was no language for loneliness, and Turner was supported in his grief by a conviction that God's will is always right. For Victoria, the death of Prince Albert marked decades of mourning and self-identified loneliness, especially around the objects and landscapes that she associated with her late husband.

Such materiality matters, as does the body. We need to explore new ways of understanding the impact of loneliness across the different pinch-points represented here, the transitions of life where loneliness is known to be likely, in order to prevent it and alleviate it—if action is needed and desired. Embodied loneliness needs to be understood as a physical experience as well as a mental one. Understanding its signs and symptoms, not only through the body but also through material culture and the world of goods, will help to create self- and social-awareness around the occurrence of loneliness as well as helping to shape health and social care interventions that might make a difference. There are steps in this direction—as in the UK government's announcement in late 2018 that it would give permission for GPs in England to prescribe dance classes through the NHS as a way to combat loneliness.[22] But so-called 'social prescribing' will not compensate for a lack of basic social care, or access to the full range of provisions—social, medical, physical, spiritual, intellectual—that are necessary for human flourishing, or that problematic but ubiquitous term: wellbeing.[23]

With some exceptions, the lonely body is neglected in the neurocentric twenty-first century. We don't watch the body language of others to see if we can detect loneliness (which, because it is a 'cluster' of emotions—anger, sadness, grief, fear—has no outwardly conventional expression). Nor are we encouraged to work with and through the body to prevent or alleviate loneliness. Social care has been reduced so far that many old and infirm are denied help with medication, let alone 'body work'. But there is evidence that massage therapies reduce loneliness, especially in those for whom touch is not a part of everyday relationships.[24] Health workers in palliative care found massage produced 'existential respite…by means of warm hands of a human being confirming the dying patient's individual value'.[25] Massage promotes a sense of personal value and self-esteem, and counteracts social disconnect.

Engaging the body and its senses brings people back to social connectedness. The Spitz Charitable Trust has an evolving music programme that reduces elderly loneliness.[26] It is well known that people with dementia can be reinvigorated by hearing the music of their youth; it can also stem loneliness. Music positively affects loneliness in all ages, as seen by the composer Nigel Osborne's use of music and the creative arts to support traumatized children.[27] Dancing brings together movement *and* music, and ballroom dancing has been found to alleviate loneliness among the elderly in Brazil.[28] Dance, researchers found, augments mental, emotional, and physical wellbeing as well as countering social isolation. And what about food? Aside from the rituals of belonging involved in cooking and eating together, comfort food brings a sense of physical belonging: 'chicken soup really is good for the soul'.[29] There is a gendered dimension to loneliness as well as its remedies; the global Men's Sheds Association (which originated in Australia) provides the opportunity for men to work alongside one another, focusing on a shared task—like woodworking—that fosters a sense of wellbeing and connectedness while avoiding explicit emotion talk, which can be off-putting to many people.[30]

Finally, we need to recognize when loneliness is good, as well as bad. Loneliness can support creative thought and activity as well as emotional healing. Since it acts as a buffer between self and world, time alone need not be negative. There are important differences between solitude and loneliness, but even loneliness can be productive. It can provide a space for self-reflection and self-awareness, especially if one is introverted and easily depleted by social contact. There is no doubt that short-term bouts of selective solitude, perhaps even accompanied by meditative contemplation, reading, or relaxing, have a restorative effect on certain people. While the positive benefits of loneliness might be linked to the natural world and to the benefits of artistic creation, these experiences are not available to many socio-economically deprived individuals. Multiple studies have shown how thriving 'against the odds' is the most that many socially disadvantaged youngsters can hope for.[31] And for the exhausted single mother working three jobs, spending quality time alone might well mean folding laundry in front of Netflix rather than reading a novel. Like the concept of slow food, self-care and self-improvement is class-based and dependent on mental and physical capacity as well as time.[32]

I am not suggesting that wealthy people do not experience loneliness, but it is more pronounced among poorer and disadvantaged people for the reasons discussed throughout this book.[33] Without the money to pay for carers, without credit to buy a house, without political influence to get citizenship and the resources to pay for food, clothes, and medicine, socio-economic deprivation produces specific kinds of loneliness that wealth can mitigate. Yet wealth alone does not cushion a person from the existential angst of individualism. The reclusive loneliness of the rich is the subject of multiple cultural images and stories.[34] Wealth is isolating in its own way, since it casts a shadow over the intent of strangers who might otherwise be friends. It encourages a limited approach to socializing in which it is difficult to step outside of one's peers, even though they might not be the most emotionally engaged connections. And the biographical pinch-points discussed in this book, from childhood loneliness to the loss of love, from divorce and widow(er)hood to growing old, pay no heed to income, status, or profession. The cushioning effect of wealth, moreover, becomes less meaningful once one is old. While one might experience more comfort during the declining years, the falling away of friendship and family among the oldest old is the greatest leveller of all.[35]

Reframing Loneliness

How do we reframe loneliness in the neoliberal age? Firstly, we need to recognize the impact of the political and economic structures that have given rise, historically, to its creation. Secondly, we need to situate loneliness within specific individual and social circumstances and acknowledge that loneliness does not mean the same thing to different people; that its links with solitude, moreover, are as significant as its differences. Thirdly, we must stop talking about loneliness as a clearly defined entity; it is fluid and spills over into other areas of health and wellbeing. It mutates even across the biography of a single person. It can be fleeting or chronic. It can be linked to isolation as well as sociability. And despite differences in what is needed or valued, the search for meaningful connection is universal. An enforced lack of such connection, which is often manifested as loneliness, need not be.

Most work on loneliness, including this one, focuses on the Western world. We need more comparative research into the meanings and function of loneliness not only at different biographical stages, but also in different cultures; I have touched on the linguistic differences between 'loneliness' in English and Arabic. It is possible that Middle Eastern countries do not experience loneliness in the same way as in the UK, since there appears to be no common language for loneliness. This is not to suggest that collectivist societies have all the answers, or that the nature of family or community in those societies is all-embracing. Elder abuse, for instance, is a problem outside of the Western context.[36] Rather it is to say that understanding loneliness requires a joined-up approach that considers alternative ways of viewing the individual, the body, society, emotions, and even the self.

One aspect of the 'epidemic of loneliness is clear: we should question such emotive language and the moral panic it invites. Defined as an epidemic, loneliness spreads. Neuroscientists like John Cacioppo, whose work has been invaluable in understanding the social nature of emotional states, reinforce a biological model of loneliness through the language of contagion. And the language of contagion—like that of infection—is culturally seductive (as a powerful and easily applied metaphor) but politically and morally problematic. When associated with negative connotations around 'contamination', the language of contagion is unhelpful.[37] Consider, for instance, the emotive language around the building of a wall in Trump's America, and the ways immigration is depicted as an overwhelming disease, with devastating effects on attitudes towards ethnic minorities.[38]

The language of a loneliness epidemic fulfils the same function. Loneliness becomes an outbreak, a plague, a scourge, and an infestation. Loneliness invites panic, revulsion, and knee-jerk responses which do not encourage us to consider what it means, why it is framed as a problem, and when it might be a force for good. It also, by invoking biological inevitability, ignores the ways in which loneliness is a product of culture and circumstances and not an inevitable part of the human condition. Thus, a steady stream of media reports on loneliness in the elderly actually creates fear of loneliness in the elderly. Old age becomes something to be anxious about, rather than a state of which one can be proud (though, to be fair, the lack of provision for most elderly people would be enough to generate anxiety).

Because it is an epidemic, because it is pathologized, loneliness is framed as a problem to be fixed by biomedicine. There is no more telling example of this medicalization than the news, in January 2019, that neuroscientists were developing a 'loneliness pill'. The 'race was on', claimed the tabloids and the broadsheets alike. And why not? 'If there are medications for social pains like depression and anxiety, why not loneliness?' asked Laura Entlis in *The Guardian*.[39] Stephanie Cacioppo, Director of the Brain Dynamics Lab at the University of Chicago Pritzker School of Medicine, was also married to the late John Cacioppo, and their individual and collaborative work on the social neuroscience of loneliness has been influential.

The way the media took up and ran with this story—which is more complex than the headlines suggest—is indicative of the medicalization of loneliness. The published clinical findings show that Cacioppo and her team have developed extensive analyses of the interventions that work in lonely people, including building opportunities for social contact, social skills, and mentoring. An 'appropriate pharmacologic treatment' was being explored in 2015 to reduce the emotional discomfort associated with reconnecting with people; it would work in much the same way as antidepressants, but without related side-effects that include tiredness and nausea.[40] This intervention would 'reduce the alarm system in the minds of lonely individuals' in order that they might 'reconnect, rather than withdraw from others'.

So it is not loneliness that would be targeted by a 'loneliness pill', but its accompanying distressing emotional symptoms, which is an important distinction (though those symptoms in themselves can cause social withdrawal, leading to loneliness). Cacioppo's approach is firmly rooted in a neurocentric approach to loneliness as an emotional state, of course, which has significant differences from the argument being developed in this book. My claim is that understandings of the brain as the centre of emotions (and loneliness as an emotional state) are not inevitable but products of history. Moreover, there are physical, embodied experiences of loneliness that suggest bodily, rather than mental responses (or at least a two-way interaction between mind and body, if not the dissolution of that Cartesian division).[41]

And, loneliness is not always bad; it can be beneficial, and creative. Loneliness can be an asset; a moment that is sought and claimed and defended, as a means for spiritual or secular reflection. Loneliness can provide a pathway to understanding something about the self and about others. It is not positive, however, when it is unwanted, unsought, prolonged; when the emotions it invokes are only negative. Like any emotional state, moreover, loneliness signals something about how we want to be in the world, the relationships and attachments that we want to have, the needs that cry out to be tended to, even if (for whatever reasons) those needs are not communicated or heard. We need to distinguish between positive and negative loneliness, then, between solitariness or 'oneliness' that is sought in order to reach a particular emotional and spiritual clarity, and loneliness that is a destructive, existential sense of lack. An engaged, effective response to loneliness must lie in a historically informed understanding of the difference.

APPENDIX

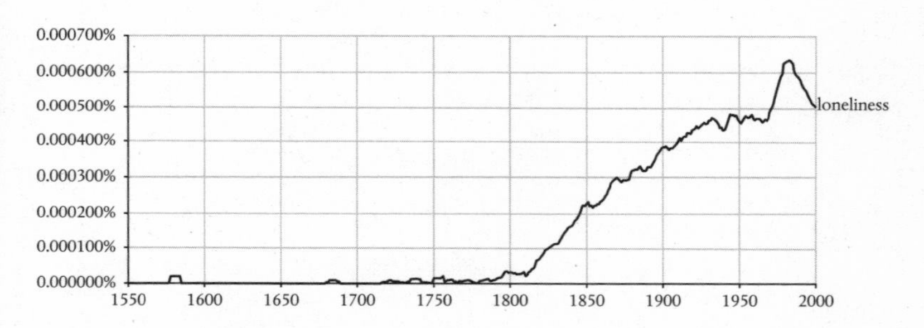

Figure 10. Use of the term 'loneliness' in English printed works between 1550 and 2000.

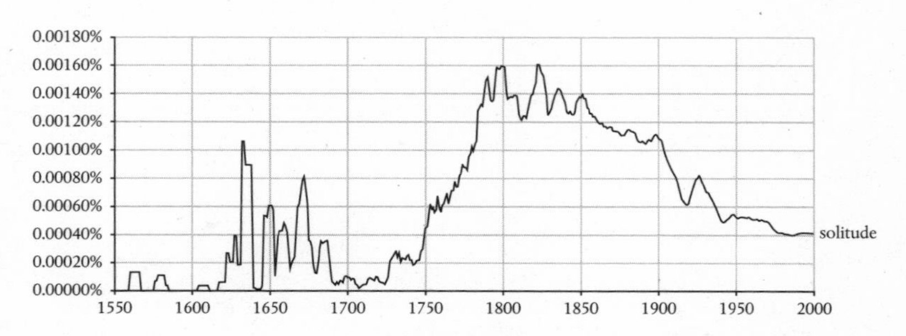

Figure 11. Use of the term 'solitude' in English printed works between 1550 and 2000.

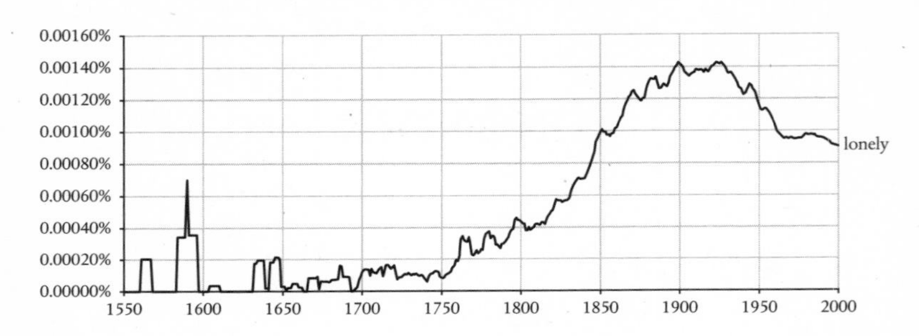

Figure 12. Use of the term 'lonely' in English printed works between 1550 and 2000.

NOTES

Introduction

1. http://www.beatlesebooks.com/eleanor-rigby, accessed 11 May 2018.
2. K.D.M. Snell, 'The rise of living alone and loneliness in history', *Social History*, 42 (2017), pp. 2–28.
3. I. Kar-Purkayastha, 'An epidemic of loneliness', *The Lancet*, 376 (2010), pp. 2114–15; E. White, 'The loneliness epidemic', *Daily Mail*, 28 July 2011.
4. J. Bingham, 'Britain: The loneliness capital of Europe', *Daily Telegraph*, 18 June 2014.
5. The following is an indicative sample, all accessed 12 May 2018: 'Loneliness a key concern for thousands of children', NSPCC, 18 June 2017: https://www.nspcc.org.uk/what-we-do/news-opinion/loneliness-key-concern-thousands-children; S. Marsh, 'Teenagers on loneliness: "We want to talk to our parents. We need their guidance"', *The Guardian*, 8 April 2017: https://www.theguardian.com/society/2017/apr/08/teenagers-loneliness-social-media-isolation-parents-attention; A. Packham, 'More than 90% of mums feel lonely after having children and many don't confide in their partner', *Huffington Post*, 7 March 2017: https://www.huffingtonpost.co.uk/entry/mums-feel-lonely-after-birth_uk_58bec088e4b09ab537d6bdf9; L. Hodgkinson, 'Living alone after divorce can feel like liberation. But trust me, it turns into aching loneliness', *Daily Mail*, 4 July 2012: http://www.dailymail.co.uk/femail/article-2168926/Living-divorce-feel-like-liberation-But-trust-turns-aching-loneliness.html; R. Vitelli, 'Grief, loneliness and losing a spouse', *Psychology Today*, 16 March 2015: https://www.psychologytoday.com/us/blog/media-spotlight/201503/grief-loneliness-and-losing-spouse.
6. BBC News, 17 January 2018: http://www.bbc.co.uk/news/uk-42708507, accessed 1 May 2018.
7. https://www.jocoxloneliness.org, accessed 12 May 2018.
8. https://www.bbc.co.uk/news/uk-politics-46057548, accessed 1 April 2019.

9. https://www.jocoxloneliness.org, accessed 1 December 2017.
10. https://www.theguardian.com/uk-news/2016/nov/23/thomas-mair-slow-burning-hatred-led-to-jo-cox-murder, accessed 1 June 2018.
11. https://www.reuters.com/article/us-britain-eu-murder-idUSKBN13I190.
12. G. Monbiot, 'Neoliberalism is creating loneliness: That's what's wrenching society apart', *The Guardian*, 12 October 2016: https://www.theguardian.com/commentisfree/2016/oct/12/neoliberalism-creating-loneliness-wrenching-society-apart, accessed 1 July 2017.
13. L.C. Hawkley and J.T. Cacioppo, 'Loneliness and pathways to disease', *Brain, Behaviour and Immunity*, 17 (2003), pp. 98–105.
14. https://www.nhs.uk/news/mental-health/loneliness-increases-risk-of-premature-death, accessed 3 June 2018.
15. L. Andersson, 'Loneliness research and interventions: A review of the literature', *Ageing & Mental Health*, 2 (1998), pp. 264–74, 265.
16. https://public.psych.iastate.edu/ccutrona/uclalone.htm, accessed 4 June 2018.
17. K.D.M. Snell, 'The rise of living alone'.
18. D.E. Christie, 'The work of loneliness: Solitude, emptiness and compassion', *Anglican Theological Review*, 88 (2006), pp. 25–46.
19. O. Laing, *The lonely city: Adventures in the art of being alone* (New York: Macmillan, 2016).
20. P. Ekman, 'Are there basic emotions?', *Psychological Review*, 99 (1992), pp. 550–3.
21. R. Plutchik and H. Kellerman, *Biological foundations of emotion* (Orlando, FL: Academic Press, 1986); R. Plutchik, 'A general psychoevolutionary theory of emotion', *Theories of Emotion*, 1 (1980), pp. 197–219.
22. The Centre for the History of Emotions at Queen Mary University of London, which I co-founded with Thomas Dixon, Colin Jones, Rhodri Hayward, and Elena Carrera, was the first such centre in the UK. It has given rise to a new generation of historians of emotion as well as a vast and interdisciplinary literature on the subject.
23. J.J. Gross, *Handbook of emotion regulation* (New York: Guilford Press, 2007); J. Plamper, *The history of emotions: An introduction* (Oxford: Oxford University Press, 2015); B. Rosenwein and R. Cristiani, *What is the history of emotions?* (Cambridge, UK; Malden, MA: Polity Press, 2018).
24. L.F. Barrett, *How emotions are made: The secret life of the brain* (London: Macmillan, 2017).

25. D. Konstan, *The emotions of the ancient Greeks* (Toronto; London: University of Toronto Press, 2006).
26. F. Bound Alberti, *This mortal coil: The human body in history and culture* (Oxford: Oxford University Press, 2016).
27. P.T. James, 'Obesity: The worldwide epidemic', *Clinics in Dermatology*, 22 (2004), pp. 276–80.
28. C.E. Moustakas, *Loneliness* (Englewood Cliffs, NJ: Prentice Hall, 1961), preface.
29. G. Monbiot, 'Neoliberalism: The ideology at the root of all our problems', *The Guardian*, 15 April 2016: https://www.theguardian.com/books/2016/apr/15/neoliberalism-ideology-problem-george-monbiot.
30. ACEVO, *Coming in from the cold: Why we need to talk about loneliness among our young people* (London, 2015).
31. J.M. Szczuka, M. Jessica, and N.C. Krämer, 'Not only the lonely—how men explicitly and implicitly evaluate the attractiveness of sex robots in comparison to the attractiveness of women, and personal characteristics influencing this evaluation', *Multimodal Technologies and Interaction*, 1 (2017), p. 3.
32. S.E. Caplan, 'Relations among loneliness, social anxiety, and problematic internet use', *CyberPsychology & Behaviour*, 10 (2007), pp. 234–42.
33. C. Rubenstein, P. Shaver, and L. Anne Peplau, 'Loneliness', *Human Nature*, 2 (1979), pp. 58–65.
34. S.R. Alterovitz and G.A. Mendelsohn, 'Relationship goals of middle-aged, young-old, and old-old internet daters: An analysis of online personal ads', *Journal of Ageing Studies*, 27 (2013), pp. 159–65.
35. J.D. DeLamater and M. Sill, 'Sexual desire in later life', *Journal of Sex Research*, 42 (2005), pp. 138–49.
36. S. Matt, *Homesickness: An American history* (Oxford: Oxford University Press, 2011).
37. R.L. Allen and H. Oshagan, 'The UCLA Loneliness Scale', *Personality and Individual Differences*, 19 (1995), pp. 185–95.
38. Tom Ambrose, *Heroes and exiles: Gay icons through the ages* (London: New Holland, 2010).
39. L.A. Jackson et al., 'Gender and the internet: Women communicating and men searching', *Sex Roles*, 44 (2001), pp. 363–79.
40. T. Scharf, 'Social exclusion of older people in deprived urban communities of England', *European Journal of Ageing*, 2 (2005), pp. 76–87.
41. Bound Alberti, *This mortal coil.*

42. V.A. Lykes and M. Kemmelmeier, 'What predicts loneliness? Cultural difference between individualistic and collectivistic societies in Europe', *Journal of Cross-Cultural Psychology*, 45 (2014), pp. 468–90.
43. H. Barakat, 'The Arab family and the challenge of social transformation', in H. Moghissi (ed.), *Women and Islam: Critical concepts in sociology, vol. II: Social conditions, obstacles and prospects* (Abingdon: Routledge, 2005), pp. 145–65. Thank you to Abigail Alberti for help in translation.
44. Evidence given in an ESRC Strategic Think Piece on Loneliness headed up by Pamela Qualter, to which I contributed, 2018.

Chapter 1

1. F. Bound [Alberti], 'Writing the self? Love and the letter in England, c. 1660–c. 1760', *Literature and History*, 11 (2002), pp. 1–19.
2. H. Lee, *Virginia Woolf* (New York: Knopf, 1997).
3. Bound [Alberti], 'Writing the self?'
4. A. Worsley, 'Ophelia's loneliness', *ELH*, 82 (2015), pp. 521–51.
5. F. Kaba et al., 'Solitary confinement and risk of self-harm among jail inmates', *American Journal of Public Health*, 104 (2014), pp. 442–7. See: http://www.wilson.com/en-us/volleyball/balls/outdoor-volleyball/cast-away-volleyball, accessed 31 January 2018.
6. S. Johnson, *A dictionary of the English language* (London: W. Strahan, 1755).
7. M. Raillard, 'Courting wisdom: Silence, solitude and friendship in eighteenth-century Spain', *Vanderbilt e-journal of Luso-Hispanic Studies*, 10 (2016), pp. 80–9.
8. G. Campbell, *The hermit in the garden: From imperial Rome to ornamental gnome* (Oxford: Oxford University Press, 2013); B. Taylor, *Mary Wollstonecraft and the feminist imagination* (Cambridge: Cambridge University Press, 2003).
9. C.R. Long and J.R. Averill, 'Solitude: An exploration of benefits of being alone', *Journal for the Theory of Social Behaviour*, 33 (2003), pp. 21–44.
10. One of Bigg's shoes survives at the Ashmolean Museum in Oxford: http://britisharchaeology.ashmus.ox.ac.uk/highlights/dinton-hermits-shoes.html, accessed 16 October 2018.
11. F. Bound Alberti, *This mortal coil: The human body in history and culture* (Oxford: Oxford University Press, 2016).
12. L. Gowing, *Common bodies: Women, sex and reproduction in seventeenth-century England* (New Haven, CT: Yale University Press, 2003).

13. B. Taylor, *Mary Wollstonecraft and the feminist imagination* (Cambridge: Cambridge University Press, 2003), p. 212.
14. L. Lipking, *Abandoned women and poetic tradition* (Chicago, IL: University of Chicago Press, 1988); Bound [Alberti], 'Writing the self'.
15. F. Bound Alberti, *Matters of the heart: History, medicine, emotion* (Oxford: Oxford University Press, 2010).
16. R. Burton, *The anatomy of melancholy, 1621* (Philadelphia, PA: J.W. Moore, 1857), p. iv.
17. D.E. Shuttleton, 'The medical consultation letters of Dr William Cullen', *Journal of the Royal College of Physicians of Edinburgh*, 45 (2015), pp. 188–9.
18. M. Louis-Courvoisier and S. Pilloud, 'Consulting by letter in the eighteenth century: Mediating the patient's view?', in W. de Blécourt and C. Usborne (eds), *Cultural approaches to the history of medicine* (London: Palgrave Macmillan, 2004), pp. 71–8.
19. W. Buchan, *Domestic medicine: Or, the family physician* (Edinburgh: Balfour, Auld and Smellie, 1769).
20. Taylor, *Mary Wollstonecraft*.
21. Cullen Project (1777 and 1779), http://www.cullenproject.ac.uk, docs ID 4087 and 4509.
22. J. de Jong-Gierveld, 'A review of loneliness: Concept and definitions, determinants and consequences', *Reviews in Clinical Gerontology*, 8 (1998), pp. 73–80.
23. J. Mullan, *Sentiment and sociability: The language of feeling in the eighteenth century* (Oxford: Clarendon, 1988).
24. W.M. Reddy, *The navigation of feeling: Framework for a history of emotions* (Cambridge: Cambridge University Press, 2001).
25. G.J. Barker-Benfield, *The culture of sensibility: Sex and society in eighteenth-century Britain* (Chicago, IL; London: University of Chicago Press, 1992).
26. L. Klein, 'Politeness and the interpretation of the British eighteenth century', *The Historical Journal*, 45 (2002), pp. 869–98.
27. J. Addison, *Selections from the Spectator*, edited by J.H. Lobban (Cambridge: Cambridge University Press, 1952), p. 173.
28. L.P. Agnew, *Outward, visible propriety: Stoic philosophy and eighteenth-century British rhetorics* (Columbia, SC: University of South Carolina Press, 2008); A. Pope, *An essay on man: Epistle III* (London: Printed for J. Wilford, 1733).
29. G.S. Rousseau, 'Nerves, spirits and fibres: Towards defining the origins of sensibility', *Studies in Eighteenth-Century Culture*, 3 (1976), pp. 137–57.

30. I am conscious that the concept of the 'individual' is itself problematic and historically contingent, and I am interested in the ways that other historians might negotiate this concept in relation not only to 'loneliness' but also to connected states like 'sociability', 'belonging', and the 'self'. Yet the version of individualism being articulated here as the result of social forces from the eighteenth to the twenty-first centuries echoes other historical work, such as Canadian philosopher Charles Taylor's discussion of the 'inward turn' perceived to be central to rational, secular versions of personal identity in the modern age. C. Taylor, *Sources of the self: Making of the modern identity* (Cambridge: Cambridge University Press, 1992).
31. K.D.M. Snell, 'Agenda for the historical study of loneliness and lone living', *Open Psychology Journal*, 8 (2015), pp. 61–70 and 'The rise of living alone and loneliness in history', *Social History*, 42 (2017), pp. 2–28.
32. R. Stivers, *Shades of loneliness: Pathologies of a technological society* (Lanham, MD; Oxford: Rowman & Littlefield, 2004), p. 11.
33. O. Laing, *The lonely city: Adventures in the art of being alone* (London: Canongate, 2017).
34. G. Beer, *Darwin's plots: Evolutionary narrative in Darwin, George Eliot and nineteenth-century fiction* (Cambridge: Cambridge University Press, 2000).
35. H.C. Sheth et al., 'Anxiety disorders in ancient Indian literature', *Indian Journal of Psychiatry*, 52 (2010), pp. 289–91; M.-G. Lallemand, 'On the proper use of curiosity: Madeleine de Scudéry's Célinte', in L. Cottegnies et al. (eds), *Women and curiosity in early modern England and France* (Leiden; Boston, MA: Brill, 2016), pp. 107–22.
36. R. Gooding, 'Pamela, Shamela and the politics of the Pamela vogue', *Eighteenth-Century Fiction*, 7 (1995), pp. 109–30.
37. A. Borunda, 'Mechanical metaphor and the emotive in Charles Dickens' *Hard Times*', *The Victorian*, 3 (2015), pp. 2–10.
38. I.R. Morus, '"The nervous system of Britain": Space, time and the electric telegraph in the Victorian age', *British Journal for the History of Science*, 33 (2000), pp. 455–75.
39. L. Spira and A.K. Richards, 'On being lonely, socially isolated and single: A multi-perspective approach', *Psychoanalysis and Psychotherapy*, 20 (2003), pp. 3–21; S. Freud, *The problem of anxiety*, 1916–1917 (New York: Norton, 1936), pp. 392–411.

40. M. Seeman, 'On the meaning of alienation', *American Sociological Review*, 24 (1959), pp. 783–91; E. Durkheim, *The elementary forms of the religious life*, K.E. Fields, trans. (New York: Free Press, 1996).
41. W. Schirmer and D. Michailakis, 'The lost *Gemeinschaft*: How people working with the elderly explain loneliness', *Journal of Ageing Studies*, 33 (2015), pp. 1–10.
42. L.P. Hemming, *Heidegger's atheism: The refusal of a theological voice* (Notre Dame, IN: University of Notre Dame Press, 2002); M. Heidegger, *Basic problems of phenomenology*, S.M. Campbell, trans. (New York: Bloomsbury, 2013); L. Svendsen, *A philosophy of loneliness*, K. Pierce, trans. (London: Reaktion, 2017).
43. J.-P. Sartre, *No exit* (New York: Caedmon, 1968).
44. M. Weber, *The protestant ethic and the spirit of capitalism*, T. Parsons, trans. (London: HarperCollins, 1991).
45. C.T. Burris et al., '"What a friend..." Loneliness as a motivator of intrinsic religion', *Journal for the Scientific Study of Religion*, (1994), pp. 326–34, 326.
46. C. Taylor, *A secular age* (Cambridge, MA; London: Belknap, 2007).
47. J. Brewer, *The pleasures of the imagination: English culture in the eighteenth century* (London: Harper Collins, 1997); R.J. Harnish and K.R. Bridges, 'Mall haul videos: Self-presentational motives and the role of self-monitoring', *Psychology & Marketing*, 33 (2016), pp. 113–24.
48. J.T. Cacioppo et al., 'Alone in the crowd: The structure and spread of loneliness in a large social network', *Journal of Personality and Social Psychology*, 97 (2009), pp. 977–91.

Chapter 2

1. S. Plath, *The unabridged journals of Sylvia Plath, 1950–1962*, edited by K.V. Kukil (New York: Anchor, 2000), p. 31. I am grateful to Faber and Faber, Harper Collins, and Penguin for permission to cite from Sylvia Plath's work in this chapter.
2. S. Plath, *Letters of Sylvia Plath, volume I: 1940–1956*, edited by P.K. Steinberg and K.V. Kukil (London: Faber & Faber, 2017) and *Letters of Sylvia Plath, volume 2: 1956–1963* (London: Faber and Faber, 2018).
3. O. Blair, 'Sylvia Plath's daughter criticises feminist activists who blamed her death on father Ted Hughes', *The Independent*, 4 October 2015:

https://www.independent.co.uk/news/people/sylvia-plaths-daughter-criticises-feminist-activists-who-blamed-her-death-on-father-ted-hughes-a6679051.html, accessed 4 October 2018 and D. Kean, 'Unseen Sylvia Plath letters claim domestic abuse by Ted Hughes', *The Guardian*, 11 April 2007: https://www.theguardian.com/books/2017/apr/11/unseen-sylvia-plath-letters-claim-domestic-abuse-by-ted-hughes, accessed 4 October 2018.

4. A. Wilson, *Mad girl's love song: Sylvia Plath and life before Ted* (London: Simon and Schuster, 2013), p. 313.
5. Wilson, *Mad girl's love song*.
6. For a discussion of the early relationship of Otto Plath and Aurelia Schober, see Wilson, *Mad girl's love song*, chapter 1.
7. http://www.bbc.co.uk/programmes/articles/2yzhfv4DvqVp5nZyxBD8G23/who-feels-lonely-the-results-of-the-world-s-largest-loneliness-study, accessed 18 October 2018.
8. Plath, *Unabridged journals*, p. 33.
9. Plath, *Letters*, p. 14.
10. 8 September 1947 in Plath, *Letters*, p. 107.
11. 'I AM A SMITH GIRL NOW': 28 September 1950 in Plath, *Letters*, p. 180. Capitalization in original.
12. 24 September 1950 in *Letters*, pp. 173–4.
13. 2 October 1950 in *Letters*, p. 185.
14. E.F. Perese and M. Wolf, 'Combating loneliness among persons with severe mental illness: Social network interventions' characteristics, effectiveness and applicability', *Issues in Mental Health Nursing*, 26 (2005), pp. 591–609.
15. 14 November 1950 in *Letters*, p. 223.
16. 7 January 1951 in *Letters*, p. 255.
17. 29 January 1951 in *Letters*, p. 268.
18. S. Plath, *Letters*, volume 2, letter to Aurelia, 10 December 1956, p. 27.
19. 19 November 1950 in *Letters*, p. 227.
20. 12 January 1951 in *Letters*, p. 259.
21. 10 December 1950 in *Letters*, p. 244.
22. 7 January 1951 in *Letters*, p. 254.
23. 7 January 1951 in *Letters*, p. 255.
24. 12 January 1951 in *Letters*, p. 258.
25. 13 January 1951 in *Letters*, p. 260.
26. For instance, letter to Marcia B. Stern, 8 July 1952 in *Letters*, p. 464.

27. J.T. Cacioppo, J.H. Fowler, and N.A. Christakis, 'Alone in the crowd: The structure and spread of loneliness in a large social network', *Journal of Personality and Social Psychology*, 97 (2009), pp. 977–91.
28. Plath, *Unabridged journals*, p. 29.
29. M.J. Bernstein and H.M. Claypool, 'Social exclusion and pain sensitivity: Why exclusion sometimes hurts and sometimes numbs', *Personality and Social Psychology Bulletin*, 38 (2012), pp. 185–96.
30. Plath, *Unabridged journals*, p. 30.
31. Plath, *Unabridged journals*, p. 26.
32. Plath, *Unabridged journals*, p. 33.
33. Plath, *Unabridged journals*, p. 149.
34. C. Millard, 'Making the cut: The production of "self-harm" in post-1945 Anglo-Saxon psychiatry', *History of the Human Sciences*, 26 (2013), pp. 126–50.
35. A. Stravynski and R. Boyer, 'Loneliness in relation to suicide ideation and parasuicide: A population-wide study', *Suicide and Life-Threatening Behavior*, 31 (2001), pp. 32–40.
36. Plath, *Unabridged journals*, pp. 150–1.
37. Plath, *Unabridged journals*, p. 150.
38. S. Plath, *Letters home: Correspondence, 1950–1963*, edited with a commentary by Aurelia Schober Plath (London: Faber and Faber, 1999), p. 124; discussion in Wilson, *Mad girl's love song*, p. 264.
39. See the discussion of Kenneth Tillotson, Plath's psychiatrist in Wilson, *Mad girl's love song*, p. 265.
40. Wilson, *Mad girl's love song*, pp. 285–6.
41. Personal conversation with Chris Millard, 2017.
42. 28 December 1953 in *Letters*, p. 654.
43. Plath, *Unabridged journals*, pp. 186–7.
44. O. Sletta et al., 'Peer relations, loneliness, and self-perceptions in school-aged children', *British Journal of Educational Psychology*, 66 (1996), pp. 431–45.
45. Wilson, *Mad girl's love song*, p. 287.
46. 25 December 1953 in *Letters*, p. 652.
47. 28 December 1953 in *Letters*, p. 657.
48. Wilson, *Mad girl's love song*, p. 291.
49. Wilson, *Mad girl's love song*, p. 302.
50. A small number of copies of Plath's thesis were subsequently published posthumously, as she became better known as a writer. The references here derive from a copy held at the British Library: Sylvia Plath, *The*

magic mirror: A study of the double in two of Dostoevsky's novels (Llanwddyn, Powys: Embers Handpress, 1989).

51. Plath, *The magic mirror*, p. 12.
52. Plath, *The magic mirror*, p. 13.
53. Plath, *Unabridged journals*, p. 30.
54. Plath, *Unabridged journals*, p. 147.
55. H. Sweeting and P. West, 'Being different: Correlates of the experience of teasing and bullying at age 11', *Research Papers in Education*, 16 (2001), pp. 225–46.
56. Plath, *Unabridged journals*, p. 187.
57. Plath, *Unabridged journals*, p. 199.
58. Wilson, *Mad girl's love song*, p. 300.
59. 24 February 1956 in *Letters*, p. 113.
60. Plath, *Unabridged journals*, p. 21.
61. Plath, *Unabridged journals*, p. 25.
62. Plath, *Unabridged journals*, p. 211.
63. 4 May 1956 in *Letters*, p. 1185.
64. A. Van Gennep, *The rites of passage* (Abingdon: Routledge, 2013).
65. 9 October 1956 in *Letters*, p. 1293.
66. Plath, *Unabridged journals*, p. 51.
67. C. Waddell, 'Creativity and mental illness: Is there a link?', *The Canadian Journal of Psychiatry*, 43 (1998), pp. 166–72.

Chapter 3

1. L.A. Baker and R.E. Emery, 'When every relationship is above average: Perceptions and expectations of divorce at the time of marriage', *Law and human behavior*, 17 (1993), p. 439.
2. *The symposium of Plato*, translated by B. Jowett (1968), available online at: http://classics.mit.edu/Plato/symposium.html, accessed 15 February 2018.
3. Aristophanes in *The symposium of Plato*.
4. Aristophanes in *The symposium of Plato*.
5. C. Darwin, *On the origin of species by means of natural selection, or the preservation of favoured races in the struggle for life* (London: John Murray, 1859). On the continued discussion of evolutionary biology and psychology and what it means for modern dating patterns, see: C. Ryan and C. Jethá, *Sex at dawn: The prehistoric origins of modern sexuality* (New York: Harper, 2010).

6. G. Claeys, 'The "survival of the fittest" and the origins of Social Darwinism', *Journal of the History of Ideas*, 61 (2000), pp. 223–40, 223.
7. J. Speake, *The Oxford dictionary of proverbs* (Oxford: Oxford University Press, 2015), p. 104; J. Lyly, *The anatomy of wit: editio princeps, 1579: Euphues and his England*, ed. E. Arber (London: Edward Arber, 1868); J.E. Mahon, 'All's fair in love and war? Machiavelli and Ang Lee's "Ride with the Devil"', in R. Apr, A. Barkman, and N. King (eds), *The philosophy of Ang Lee* (Lexington, KY: University Press of Kentucky, 2013), pp. 265–90.
8. *Letter to a young lady* in Samuel Taylor Coleridge, *Letters, conversations and recollections of S.T. Coleridge*, vol. 2 (London: Edward Moxon, Dover Street, 1836), pp. 89–90.
9. *Letter to a Young Lady*, p. 91.
10. D. Vaisey, *The diary of Thomas Turner, 1754–1765* (East Hoathly: CTR Publishing, 1994), p. 229. See the discussion of Thomas Turner's diary, and the context in which he spoke about his wife in this manner, in Chapter 4 of this book.
11. *Letter to a young lady*, p. 93.
12. *Letter to a young lady*, p. 90.
13. F. Bound [Alberti], 'An "uncivill" culture: Marital violence and domestic politics in York, c. 1660–c.1760', in M. Hallett and J. Rendall (eds), *Eighteenth-century York: Culture, space and society* (York: Borthwick Institute, 2003).
14. F. Bound Alberti, *Matters of the heart: History, medicine, emotion* (Oxford: Oxford University Press, 2010).
15. M.R. Watson, '"Wuthering Heights" and the critics', *The Trollopian*, 3 (1949), pp. 243–63.
16. D. Punter and G. Byron, *The gothic*, vol. 10 (Oxford: Blackwell Publishing, 2004).
17. J. Bhattacharyya, *Emily Brontë's Wuthering Heights* (New Delhi: Atlantic Publishers & Dist, 2006), p. 67.
18. S.R. Gorsky, '"I'll cry myself sick": Illness in *Wuthering Heights*', *Literature and Medicine*, 18 (1999), pp. 173–91.
19. S. R. Gorsky, *Femininity to feminism: Women and literature in the nineteenth century* (New York; Toronto: Macmillan, 1992), p. 44.
20. For a discussion of the nineteenth-century origins of the Byronic hero, see A. Stein, *The Byronic hero in film, fiction and television* (Carbondale, IL: Southern Illinois University Press, 2009), pp. 10–11.

21. S. Wooton, *Byronic heroes in nineteenth-century women's writing and screen adaptation* (Houndmills, Basingstoke: Palgrave Macmillan, 2016).
22. Cited in Stein, *The Byronic hero*, p. 27.
23. A. Ben-Ze'ev and R. Goussinsky, *In the name of love: Romantic ideology and its victims* (Oxford; New York: Oxford University Press, 2008).
24. L. Kokkola, 'Sparkling vampires: Valorizing self-harming behavior in Stephenie Meyer's *Twilight* series', *Bookbird: A Journal of International Children's Literature*, 49 (2011), pp. 33–46; J. Taylor, 'Romance and the female gaze obscuring gendered violence in the *Twilight* saga', *Feminist Media Studies*, 14 (2014), pp. 388–402.
25. S. Meyer, *Eclipse* (Boston, MA: Little, Brown, 2007), e.g. pp. 50, 123, 519.
26. Meyer, *Eclipse*, p. 265.
27. Meyer, *Eclipse*, p. 265.
28. Meyer, *Eclipse*, p. 517.
29. A. McRobbie, 'Notes on post-feminism and popular culture: Bridget Jones and the new gender regime', in A. Harris (ed.), *All about the girl: Culture, power and identity* (Abingdon: Routledge, 2004), pp. 3–14.
30. A. Ford, *The soulmate secret* (HarperCollins e-books, 2014); C. Ozawa-de Silva, 'Too lonely to die alone: Internet suicide pacts and existential suffering in Japan', *Culture, Medicine, and Psychiatry*, 324 (2008), pp. 516–51; L. TerKeurst, *Uninvited: Living loved when you feel less than, left out, and lonely* (Nashville, TN: Nelson Books, 2016).
31. V. Walkerdine, 'Some day my prince will come: Young girls and the preparation for adolescent sexuality', in A. McRobbie and M. Nava (eds), *Gender and generation: Youth questions* (London: Palgrave Macmillan, 1984), pp. 162–84.
32. C. Rubenstein, P. Shaver, and L.A. Peplau, 'Loneliness', *Human Nature* 2 (1979), pp. 58–65.
33. M. Pinquart, 'Loneliness in married, widowed, divorced and never-married adults', *Journal of Social and Personal Relationships*, 20 (2003), pp. 31–53; K.L. Olson and E.H. Wong, 'Loneliness in marriage', *Family Therapy*, 28 (2001), p. 105.
34. A dated but still relevant study is P. Parmelee and C. Werner, 'Lonely losers: Stereotypes of single dwellers', *Personality and Social Psychology Bulletin*, 4 (1978), pp. 292–5.
35. K. Lahad, '"Am I asking for too much?": The selective single woman as a new social problem', *Women's Studies International Forum*, 40 (2013), pp. 23–32.

36. C. Shipman, 'The anomalous position of the unmarried woman', *The American Review*, 190 (1909), pp. 338–46.
37. C. Hakim, 'Erotic capital', *European Sociological Review*, 26 (2010), pp. 499–518.
38. http://www.bbc.co.uk/news/blogs-trending-43881931, accessed 25 May 2018; J. Katz and V. Tirone, 'From the agency line to the picket line: Neoliberal ideals, sexual realities, and arguments about abortion in the US', *Sex Roles*, 73 (2015), pp. 311–18.
39. M. Griffiths, 'Excessive Internet use: Implications for sexual behavior', *CyberPsychology & Behavior*, 3 (2000), pp. 537–52.
40. J. Ward, 'Swiping, matching, chatting: Self-presentation and self-disclosure on mobile dating apps', *Human IT: Journal for Information Technology Studies as a Human Science*, 13 (2016), pp. 81–95.

Chapter 4

1. The Age UK advert can be found at: https://www.youtube.com/watch?v=FALlh-a1uEg, accessed 18 September 2018.
2. J. Pritchard, '"I REALLY CRIED": Gogglebox widow June Bernicoff reveals heartbreaking moment she watched the show without husband Leon for the first time after his sudden death', *The Sun*, 10 September 2018: https://www.thesun.co.uk/tvandshowbiz/7218092/june-bernicoff-leon-gogglebox-tears-empty-chair, accessed 18 September 2018.
3. M. Hegge and C. Fischer, 'Grief responses of senior and elderly widows: Practice implications', *Journal of Gerontological Nursing*, 26 (2000), pp. 35–43.
4. A. Barbato and H.J. Irwin, 'Major therapeutic systems and the bereaved client', *Australian Psychologist*, 27 (1992), pp. 22–7.
5. X. Zhou et al., 'Counteracting loneliness: On the restorative function of nostalgia', *Psychological Science*, 19 (2008), pp. 1023–9.
6. Zhou et al., 'Counteracting loneliness', p. 1023.
7. http://www.opentohope.com/lonely-not-powerful-enough-word-to-describe-widowhood, accessed 12 October 2017.
8. D.K. van den Hoonaard, *The widowed self: The older woman's journey through widowhood* (Waterloo, Ont.: Wilfrid Laurier University Press, 2000).
9. S. Cavallo and L. Warner, *Widowhood in medieval and early modern Europe* (Harlow, UK; New York: Longman, 1999).

10. Van den Hoonaard, *The widowed self*, p. 38.
11. P. de Larivey, *The widow (La veuve)*, translated by Catherine E. Campbell (Ottawa: Dovehouse Editions, 1992).
12. See the widow of Zarephath, 1 Kings 17.10–24 and the discussion in R.A. Anselment, 'Katherine Austen and the widow's might', *Journal for Early Modern Cultural Studies*, 5 (2005), 5–25.
13. S. Mendelson and P. Crawford, *Women in early modern England, 1550–1720* (Oxford: Oxford University Press, 1998).
14. T. Fuller, *The holy and the profane states* (Boston, MA, 1864), pp. 52–3, discussed in M. Macdonald, *Mystical bedlam: Madness, anxiety and healing in seventeenth-century England* (Cambridge: Cambridge University Press, 1984), p. 77.
15. Anselment, 'Katherine Austen', p. 8.
16. Anselment, 'Katherine Austen', p. 18.
17. D. Vaisey, *The diary of Thomas Turner, 1754–1765* (East Hoathly: CTR Publishing, 1994), p. xviii. All quotations are taken from this edition.
18. Vaisey, *Diary*, xxi.
19. Vaisey, *Diary*, 30 August 1755, p. 13.
20. Vaisey, *Diary*, 10 February 1756, p. 28.
21. Vaisey, *Diary*, 22 February 1756, p. 31.
22. Vaisey, *Diary*, 24 June 1758, p. 155.
23. Vaisey, *Diary*, 5 April 1759, p. 180.
24. Vaisey, *Diary*, 3 October 1760, p. 212.
25. Vaisey, *Diary*, 28 May 1760, p. 205.
26. Vaisey, *Diary*, p. 213.
27. E. Gibson, *Trust in God, the best remedy against fears of all kinds: designed by way of spiritual comfort, to such unhappy persons as are subject to MELANCHOLY FEARS, and to others who are at any time under anxiety and dejection of mind upon just and reasonable fears of some approaching evil*, sixth edition (London: E. Owen, 1752).
28. Gibson, *Trust in God*, p. 8.
29. Vaisey, *Diary*, p. 228.
30. Vaisey, *Diary*, 27 June 1761, p. 229.
31. N. Rowe, *The royal convert: A tragedy* (London: Jacob Tonson, 1714), p. 35.
32. F. Bound [Alberti], 'Writing the self? Love and the letter in England, c. 1660–c. 1760', *Literature & History*, 1 (2002), pp. 1–19.
33. Vaisey, *Diary*, 14 June 1761, p. 227.
34. Vaisey, *Diary*, 27 June 1761, p. 230.

35. Vaisey, *Diary*, 1 July 1761, p. 230.
36. R. Sparić et al., 'Hysterectomy throughout history', *Acta chirurgica Iugoslavica*, 58 (2011), pp. 9–14.
37. F. Bound [Alberti], 'An "angry and malicious mind": Narratives of slander at the Church Courts of York, c.1660–c.1760', *History Workshop Journal*, 56 (2003), pp. 59–77.
38. Vaisey, *Diary*, 1 July 1761, pp. 230–1.
39. Vaisey, *Diary*, 17 January 1762, p. 243.
40. Vaisey, *Diary*, 16 October 1762, p. 259.
41. Vaisey, *Diary*, 17 September 1762, p. 258.
42. This is the final entry in Turner's *Diary*, p. 323.
43. F. Bound [Alberti], 'An "uncivill" culture: Marital violence and domestic politics in York, c. 1660–c. 1760', in M. Hallett and J. Rendall (eds), *Eighteenth-century York: Culture, space and society* (York: Borthwick Institute, 2003).
44. Vaisey, 'Introduction', in *Diary*, p. xx.
45. M. Pavlíková, 'Despair and alienation of modern man in society', *European Journal of Science and Theology*, 11 (2015), pp. 191–200.
46. S. Solicari, 'Selling sentiment: The commodification of emotion in Victorian visual culture', *Interdisciplinary Studies in the Long Nineteenth Century*, 4 (2007), pp. 1–21.
47. C. Huff, 'Private domains: Queen Victoria and Women's Diaries', *Auto/Biography Studies*, 1 (1988), pp. 46–52.
48. C. Erickson, *Her little majesty: The life of Queen Victoria* (London: Robson Books, 1997), p. 56.
49. D. Marshall, *The life and times of Queen Victoria* (London: Weidenfeld & Nicolson, 1992), p. 27.
50. C. Hibbert, *Queen Victoria: A personal history* (London: Harper Collins, 2000), p. 123.
51. See H. Rappaport, *Magnificent obsession: Victoria, Albert and the death that changed the monarchy* (London: Windmill, 2012).
52. Hibbert, *Queen Victoria*, chapters 14–36.
53. Hibbert, *Queen Victoria*, p. 299.
54. H. Matthew and K. Reynolds (2004-09-23), Victoria (1819–1901), queen of the United Kingdom of Great Britain and Ireland, and empress of India. *Oxford Dictionary of National Biography*, retrieved 20 March 2018 from http://www.oxforddnb.com/view/10.1093/ref:odnb/9780198614128.001.0001/odnb-9780198614128-e-36652.

55. See also Y.M. Ward, *Censoring Queen Victoria: How two gentlemen edited a queen and created an icon* (London: One World, 2014); Y.M. Ward, *Unsuitable for publication: Editing Queen Victoria* (Collingwood, Vic.: Black Inc, 2013).
56. Queen Victoria's journal, RA VIC/MAIN/WVJ, 4 December 1861. All entries referred to, retrieved 11 February 2018, can be found at: http://www.queenvictoriasjournals.org.
57. Queen Victoria's journal, RA VIC/MAIN/WVJ, 5 December 1861.
58. Rappaport, *Magnificent obsession*, p. 80.
59. Cited in Rappaport, *Magnificent obsession*, p. 81.
60. Cited in Rappaport, *Magnificent obsession*, p. 82.
61. Queen Victoria's journal, RA VIC/MAIN/WVJ, 1 January 1862.
62. J. Baird, *Victoria the queen: An intimate biography of the woman who ruled an empire* (New York: Random House, 2016), p. 221.
63. Queen Victoria's journal, RA VIC/MAIN/WVJ, 2 January 1862.
64. Queen Victoria's journal, RA VIC/MAIN/WVJ, 6 January 1862.
65. Queen Victoria's journal, RA VIC/MAIN/WVJ, 7 January 1862.
66. Queen Victoria's journal, RA VIC/MAIN/WVJ, 20 January 1862.
67. Queen Victoria's journal, 8; RA VIC/MAIN/WVJ, 15 January 1862.
68. Queen Victoria's journal, RA VIC/MAIN/WVJ, 10 February 1862.
69. Queen Victoria's journal, RA VIC/MAIN/WVJ, 18 January 1862.
70. Queen Victoria's journal, RA VIC/MAIN/WVJ, 23 January 1862.
71. Queen Victoria's journal, RA VIC/MAIN/WVJ, 1 February 1862; 3 February 1862.
72. D. Russell, L.A. Peplau, and M.L. Ferguson, 'Developing a measure of loneliness', *Journal of Personality Assessment*, 42 (1978), pp. 290–4; C. Vega et al., 'Symptoms of anxiety and depression in childhood absence epilepsy', *Epilepsia*, 52 (2011), pp. 70–4; S. Ueda and Y. Okawa, 'The subjective dimension of functioning and disability: What is it and what is it for?', *Disability and Rehabilitation*, 25 (2003), pp. 596–601.
73. Queen Victoria's journal, RA VIC/MAIN/WVJ, 15 January 1862.
74. Queen Victoria's journal, RA VIC/MAIN/WVJ, 21 January 1862.
75. 'All the [parliamentary] speeches so full of unbounded admiration & appreciation of Albert', Victoria recorded in her journal on 7 February; '& full of sympathy for my immense misery!'
76. Queen Victoria's journal, RA VIC/MAIN/WVJ, 23 January 1862.
77. Queen Victoria's journal, RA VIC/MAIN/WVJ, 27 January 1862.
78. Queen Victoria's journal, RA VIC/MAIN/WVJ, 2 February 1862.
79. Queen Victoria's journal, RA VIC/MAIN/WVJ, 29 January 1862.

80. Queen Victoria's journal, RA VIC/MAIN/WVJ, 31 December 1864.
81. Queen Victoria's journal, RA VIC/MAIN/WVJ, 24 February 1866.
82. Queen Victoria's journal, RA VIC/MAIN/WVJ, 11 July 1868.
83. First published in 1890; see: http://www.kiplingsociety.co.uk/rg_widowatwindsor1.htm.
84. C. Dickens, *Great expectations* (London: Chapman and Hall, 1861).
85. D. Lutz, *Relics of death in Victorian literature and culture* (Cambridge: Cambridge University Press, 2015).
86. K. Brittain et al., 'An investigation into the patterns of loneliness and loss in the oldest old: Newcastle 85+ study', *Ageing & Society*, 37 (2017), pp. 39–62.
87. B.L. Zhong, S.L. Chen, and Y. Conwell, 'Effects of transient versus chronic loneliness on cognitive function in older adults: Findings from the Chinese Longitudinal Healthy Longevity Survey', *The American Journal of Geriatric Psychiatry*, 24 (2016), pp. 389–98.
88. S.S. Alterovitz and G.A. Mendelsohn, 'Relationship goals of middle-aged, young-old, and old-old internet daters: An analysis of online personal ads', *Journal of Aging Studies*, 27 (2013), pp. 159–65.

Chapter 5

1. R. Grenoble, 'Distracted driver dies after posting on Facebook about the song "Happy", taking selfies', *Huffington Post*, 28 April 2014: https://www.huffingtonpost.co.uk/entry/driver-dies-happy-song-facebook-_n_5223175?guccounter=1&guce_referrer_us=aHR0cHM6Ly93d3cuZ29vZ2xlLmNvbS8&guce_referrer_cs=EvR1NVWv5yUzi-ttXvYO5g, accessed 28 September 2018.
2. C.A. Kahn et al., 'Distracted driving, a major preventable cause of motor vehicle collisions: "Just hang up and drive"', *Western Journal of Emergency Medicine*, 16 (2015), pp. 1033–6.
3. A. Nassehi et al., 'Surveying the relationship of Internet addiction with dependence on cell phone, depression, anxiety, and stress in collegians (Case study: Bam University of Medical Sciences)', *International Journal of Advanced Biotechnology and Research*, 7 (2016), pp. 2267–74.
4. C.T. Barry et al., 'Adolescent social media use and mental health from adolescent and parent perspectives', *Journal of Adolescence*, 61 (2017), pp. 1840–8.
5. Barry et al., 'Adolescent social media use', p. 1840.

6. T. Ryan and S. Xenos, 'Who uses Facebook? An investigation into the relationship between the Big Five, shyness, narcissism, loneliness and Facebook usage', *Computers in Human Behavior*, 27 (2011), pp. 1658–64.
7. J. Kim, R. LaRose, and W. Peng, 'Loneliness as the cause and the effect of problematic Internet use: The relationship between Internet use and psychological well-being', *CyberPsychology & Behavior*, 12 (2009), pp. 451–5.
8. D.M. Boyd and N.B. Ellison, 'Social network sites: Definition, history and scholarship', *Journal of Computer-Mediated Communication*, 13 (2008), pp. 210–30.
9. R.N. Bolton et al., 'Understanding Generation Y and their use of social media: A review and research agenda', *Journal of Service Management*, 24.3 (2013), pp. 245–67.
10. Bolton et al., 'Understanding Generation Y', p. 249.
11. P. Valkenburg and A.P. Schouten, 'Friend networking sites and their relationship to adolescents' well-being and social self-esteem', *Cyberpsychology & Behavior*, 9 (2006), pp. 584–90 (p. 585).
12. S. Bennett, K. Maton, and L. Kervin. 'The "digital natives" debate: A critical review of the evidence', *British Journal of Educational Technology*, 39 (2008), pp. 775–86.
13. S.D. Vogt, 'The digital underworld: Combating crime on the dark web in the modern era', *Santa Clara Journal of International Law*, 15 (2017), p. 104; D. Clay, V.L. Vignoles, and H. Dittmar, 'Body image and self-esteem among adolescent girls: Testing the influence of sociocultural factors', *Journal of Research on Adolescence*, 15 (2005), pp. 451–77; J. Carter, 'Patriarchy and violence against women and girls', *The Lancet*, 385 (2015), pp. e40–1.
14. https://www.ons.gov.uk/peoplepopulationandcommunity/wellbeing/articles/lonelinesswhatcharacteristicsandcircumstancesareassociatedwithfeelinglonely/2018-04-10, accessed 1 June 2018.
15. http://www.bbc.co.uk/programmes/articles/2yzhfv4DvqVp5nZyxBD8G23/who-feels-lonely-the-results-of-the-world-s-largest-loneliness-study, accessed 2 October 2018.
16. A.M. Manago and L. Vaughn, 'Social media, friendship, and happiness in the millennial generation', in M. Demir (ed.), *Friendship and happiness across the life-span and cultures* (Dordrecht: Springer, 2015), pp. 187–206: https://www.multivu.com/players/English/8294451-cigna-us-loneliness-survey/docs/IndexReport_1524069371598-173525450.pdf, accessed 6 June 2018.

17. W.Y. Chou, A. Prestin, and S. Kunath, 'Obesity in social media: A mixed methods analysis', *Translational Behavioral Medicine*, 12 (2014), pp. 314–23; J.P. Harman et al., 'Liar, liar: Internet faking but not frequency of use affects social skills, self-esteem, social anxiety, and aggression', *CyberPsychology & Behavior*, 8 (2005), pp. 1–6.
18. M. Corstjens and A. Umblijs, 'The power of evil: The damage of negative social media strongly outweigh positive contributions', *Journal of Advertising Research*, 52 (2012), pp. 433–49.
19. C. Beaton, 'Why millennials are lonely', *Forbes Magazine*, 9 February 2017: https://www.forbes.com/sites/carolinebeaton/2017/02/09/why-millennials-are-lonely/#24e5e5407c35, accessed 1 June 2018.
20. A. Muise, E. Christofides, and D. Desmarais, 'More information than you ever wanted: Does Facebook bring out the green-eyed monster of jealousy?', *CyberPsychology & Behavior*, 12 (2009), pp. 441–4.
21. Ryan and Xenos, 'Who uses Facebook?', p. 1842.
22. M. Pittman and B. Reich, 'Social media and loneliness: Why an Instagram picture may be worth more than a thousand Twitter words', *Computers in Human Behaviour*, 62 (2016), pp. 155–67.
23. R. Zhu et al., 'Does online community participation foster risky financial behaviour?', *Journal of Marketing Research*, 49 (2012), pp. 394–407.
24. H. Dittmar, 'How do "body perfect" ideals in the media have a negative impact on body image and behaviors? Factors and processes related to self and identity', *Journal of Social and Clinical Psychology*, 28 (2009), pp. 1–8; G.S. O'Keeffe and K. Clarke-Pearson. 'The impact of social media on children, adolescents, and families', *Pediatrics*, 127 (2011), pp. 800–4.
25. M.H. Immordino-Yang, J.A. Christodoulou, and V. Singh, V. 'Rest is not idleness: Implications of the brain's default mode for human development and education, *Perspectives on Psychological Science*, 7 (2012), pp. 352–64.
26. M.A. Carskadon, 'Sleep in adolescents: The perfect storm', *Pediatric Clinics*, 58 (2011), pp. 637–47.
27. J. Lewis and A. West, '"Friending": London-based undergraduates' accounts of Facebook', *New Media & Society*, 11 (2009), pp. 1209–29.
28. M.Z. Yao and Z.J. Zhong, 'Loneliness, social contacts and Internet addiction: A cross-lagged panel study', *Computers in Human Behavior*, 30 (2014), pp. 164–70; L.A. Jelenchick, J.C. Eickhoff, and M.A. Moreno, '"Facebook depression?" Social networking site use and depression in

older adolescents', *Journal of Adolescent Health*, 52 (2013), pp. 128–30; Ryan and Xenos, 'Who uses Facebook?', pp. 1658–64.

29. P. Seargeant and C. Tagg (eds), *The language of social media: Identity and community on the internet* (Basingstoke: Palgrave Macmillan, 2014), p. 5.
30. A.D. Kramer, J.E. Guillory, and J.T. Hancock, 'Experimental evidence of massive-scale emotional contagion through social networks', *Proceedings of the National Academy of Sciences*, 111 (2014), pp. 8788–90.
31. L. Mehlum, 'The internet, suicide, and suicide prevention', *Crisis: The Journal of Crisis Intervention and Suicide Prevention*, 21 (2000), p. 186.
32. G. Rosen, 'Psychopathology in the social process: I. A study of the persecution of witches in Europe as a contribution to the understanding of mass delusions and psychic epidemics', *Journal of Health and Human Behavior*, 1 (1960), pp. 200–11; G. Le Bon, *The crowd* (London: Routledge, 2017); W.R. Doherty, 'The emotional contagion scale: A measure of individual differences', *Journal of Nonverbal Behavior*, 21 (1997), pp. 131–54.
33. J.T. Cacioppo, J.H. Fowler, and N.A. Christakis, 'Alone in the crowd: The structure and spread of loneliness in a large social network', *Journal of Personality and Social Psychology*, 97 (2009), p. 977.
34. L.A. Frakow, 'Women and the telephone: The gendering of a communications technology', in C. Kramarae (ed.), *Technology and women's voices: Keeping in touch* (Routledge & Kegan Paul: New York and London, 1988), pp. 179–99, 179.
35. J. Tacchi, K.R. Kitner, and K. Crawford, 'Meaningful mobility: Gender, development and mobile phones', *Feminist Media Studies*, 12 (2012), pp. 528–37.
36. Cited in C.S. Fischer, *America calling: A social history of the telephone to 1940* (Berkeley, CA: University of California Press, 1992), p. 1.
37. Fischer, *America calling*, p. 247.
38. D.G. Krutka and J.P. Carpenter, 'Why social media must have a place in schools', *Kappa Delta Pi Record*, 52 (2016), pp. 6–10; J.K. Hammick and J.L. Moon, 'Do shy people feel less communication apprehension online? The effects of virtual reality on the relationship between personality characteristics and communication outcomes', *Computers in Human Behavior*, 33 (2014), pp. 302–10; M. Indian and R. Grieve, 'When Facebook is easier than face-to-face: Social support derived from Facebook in socially anxious individuals', *Personality and Individual Differences*, 59 (2014), pp. 102–6; C.L. Ventola, 'Social media and health care professionals: Benefits, risks, and best practices', *Pharmacy and*

Therapeutics, 39 (2014), pp. 491–9; V. Burholt et al., 'A social model of loneliness: The roles of disability, social resources, and cognitive impairment', *The Gerontologist*, 57 (2016), pp. 1020–30.
39. K.M. Sheldon, N. Abad, and C. Hinsch, 'A two-process view of Facebook use and relatedness need-satisfaction: Disconnection drives use, and connection rewards it', *Journal of Personality and Social Psychology*, 100 (2011), pp. 766–75.
40. J.E. Katz, R.E. Rice, and P. Aspden, 'The Internet, 1995–2000: Access, civic involvement, and social interaction', *American Behavioural Scientist*, 45 (2001), pp. 405–19.
41. J.L. Clark, S.B. Algoe, and M.C. Green, 'Social network sites and well-being: The role of social connection', *Current Directions in Psychological Science*, 21 (2017), pp. 32–7.
42. Clark, Algoe, and Green, 'Social network sites'.
43. B. Anderson, *Imagined communities: Reflections on the origin and spread of nationalism* (London: Verso, 1991).
44. M.C. Benigni, K. Joseph, and K.M. Carley, 'Online extremism and the communities that sustain it: Detecting the ISIS supporting community on Twitter', *PLoS ONE*, 12 (2017), e0181405: https://doi.org/10.1371/journal.pone.0181405, accessed 2 October 2018.
45. H. Rheingold, *Virtual community: Finding connection in a computerised world* (London: Secker and Warburg, 1994), introduction.
46. https://www.reddit.com/r/The_Donald, accessed 2 October 2018.
47. Rheingold, *Virtual community*; B. Wellman, *Networks in the global village: Life in contemporary communities* (Boulder, CO: Westview Press, 1999).
48. J. Ronson, *So you've been publicly shamed* (New York: Riverhead Books, 2015).
49. J. van Dijck, *The culture of creativity: A critical history of social media* (Thousand Oaks, CA: Sage Publications, 2014), p. 14.
50. Van Dijck, *The culture of creativity*, p. 11.
51. Laing, *The lonely city*.
52. M. Ratto and M. Boler (eds), *DIY citizenship: Critical making and social media* (Cambridge, MA: MIT Press, 2014), introduction.
53. Van Dijck, *The culture of creativity*, pp. 112, 144.
54. R. Yuqing et al., 'Building member attachment in online communities: Applying theories of group identity and interpersonal bonds', *MIS Quarterly*, 36 (2012), pp. 841–64, 843.
55. R. Yuqing et al., 'Building member attachment', p. 843.

56. *Oxford English Dictionary* online, accessed 3 June 2018.
57. 'Report on the investigation into Russian interference in the 2016 Presidential election', by Special Counsel Robert S. Mueller, vol. III, p. 4: 'Executive summary to volume I and volume II. RUSSIAN "ACTIVE MEASURES" SOCIAL MEDIA CAMPAIGN', pp. 24–6, U.S. Operations Through Facebook.
58. F. Comunello and G. Anzera, 'Will the revolution be tweeted? A conceptual framework for understanding the social media and the Arab Spring', *Islam and Christian–Muslim Relations*, 23 (2012), pp. 1–18.
59. S. Frennert and B. Östlund, 'Seven matters of concern of social robots and older people', *International Journal of Social Robotics*, 6 (2014), pp. 299–310; K. Devlin, *Turned on: Science, sex and robots* (London: Bloomsbury Sigma, 2018); I. Torjesen, 'Society must consider risks of sex robots, report warns', *BMJ: British Medical Journal*, 358 (2017), http://dx.doi.org/10.1136/bmj.j3267.
60. M. Tiggemann and I. Barbato, '"You look great!": The effect of viewing appearance-related Instagram comments on women's body image', *Body Image*, 27 (2018), pp. 61–6; T.M. Dumas et al., 'Lying or longing for likes? Narcissism, peer belonging, loneliness and normative versus deceptive like-seeking on Instagram in emerging adulthood', *Computers in Human Behaviour*, 71 (2017), pp. 1–10.
61. P. Gale, *Your network is your net worth: Unlock the hidden power of connections for wealth, success and happiness in the digital age* (London: Simon and Schuster, 2013).
62. Y. Ren, R. Kraut, and S. Kiesler, 'Applying common identity and bond theory to design of online communities', *Organization Studies*, 28 (2007), pp. 377–408.
63. K.J. Miller et al., 'Effectiveness and feasibility of virtual reality and gaming system use at home by older adults for enabling physical activity to improve health-related domains: A systematic review', *Age and Ageing*, 43 (2013), pp. 188–95; A. Gallace, *In touch with the future: The sense of touch from cognitive neuroscience to virtual reality* (Oxford: Oxford University Press, 2014).

Chapter 6

1. T.J. Holwerda et al., 'Feelings of loneliness, but not social isolation, predict dementia onset: Results from the Amsterdam Study of the Elderly (AMSTEL)', *Journal of Neurology, Neurosurgery and Psychiatry*, 85 (2012),

pp. 135–42; R.S. Wilson et al., 'Loneliness and risk of Alzheimer disease', *Archives of General Psychiatry*, 64 (2007), pp. 234–40; W. Moyle et al., 'Dementia and loneliness: An Australian perspective', *Journal of Clinical Nursing*, 20 (2011), pp. 1445–53.

2. K. Holmén and H. Furukawa, 'Loneliness, health and social network among elderly people: A follow-up study', *Archives of Gerontology and Geriatrics*, 35 (2002), pp. 261–74.
3. Personal conversation with Karen Bloor, York University, 2018.
4. C. Harrefors, S. Sävenstedt, and K. Axelsson, 'Elderly people's perceptions of how they want to be cared for: An interview study with healthy elderly couples in northern Sweden', *Scandinavian Journal of Caring Sciences*, 23 (2009), pp. 353–60.
5. F. Shaw, 'Is the ageing population the problem it is made out to be?', *Foresight*, 4 (2002), pp. 4–11.
6. E. Shanas et al., *Old people in three industrialised societies* (London: Routledge, 2017), p. 2.
7. A. Rokach et al., 'Cancer patients, their caregivers and coping with loneliness', *Psychology, Health & Medicine*, 18 (2013), pp. 135–44; A. Rokach, 'Loneliness in cancer and multiple sclerosis patients', *Psychological Reports*, 94 (2004), pp. 637–48.
8. D. Mintz, 'What's in a word: The distancing function of language in medicine', *Journal of Medical Humanities*, 13 (1992), pp. 223–33; M. Rosedale, 'Survivor loneliness of women following breast cancer', *Oncology Nursing Forum*, 36 (2009), pp. 175–83.
9. https://www.nhs.uk/Livewell/women60-plus/Pages/Loneliness-in-older-people.aspx, accessed 8 March 2018.
10. https://www.nhs.uk/Livewell/women60-plus/Pages/Loneliness-in-older-people.aspx, accessed 8 March 2018.
11. N.R. Nicholson, 'A review of social isolation: An important but under-assessed condition in older adults', *Journal of Primary Prevention*, 33 (2012), pp. 137–52.
12. K. Windle, J. Francis, and C. Coomber, 'Preventing loneliness and social isolation: Interventions and outcomes', *Social Care Institute for Excellence*, 39 (2011); S. Kinsella and F. Murray, 'Older people and social isolation: A review of the evidence', *Wirral Council Business and Public Health Intelligence Team* (2015), pp. 1–16.
13. Cited in M. Glauber and M.D. Day, 'The unmet need for care: Vulnerability among older adults', *Carsey Research*, 98 (Spring 2016):

https://carsey.unh.edu/publication/vulnerability-older-adults, accessed 8 June 2018.

14. K. Walters, S. Iliffe, and M Orrell, 'An exploration of help-seeking behaviour in older people with unmet needs', *Family Practice*, 18 (2001), pp. 277–82.
15. Walters, Iliffe, and Orrell, 'An exploration of help-seeking behaviour'.
16. Commission for Social Care Inspection, *Cutting the cake fairly: CSCI review of eligibility criteria for social care* (London: CSCI, 2008), discussed in A. Vlachantoni et al., 'Measuring unmet need for social care amongst older people', *Population Trends*, 145 (2011), pp. 60–76.
17. Vlachantoni et al., 'Measuring unmet need'.
18. Vlachantoni et al., 'Measuring unmet need'.
19. B. Simmonds, *Ageing and the crisis in health and social care* (London: Polity, forthcoming).
20. J.M. Montepare and M.E. Lachman, '"You're only as old as you feel": Self-perceptions of age, fears of ageing, and life satisfaction from adolescence to old age', *Psychology and Ageing*, 4 (1989), pp. 73–8.
21. H. Yallop, *Age and identity in eighteenth-century England* (London: Routledge, 2016); P. Laslett, *A fresh map of life: The emergence of the Third Age* (Cambridge, MA: Harvard University Press, 1991); P. Thane, *Old age in English history: Past experiences, present issues* (Oxford: Oxford University Press, 2000).
22. Yallop, *Age and identity*.
23. J. Carper, *Stop aging now! The ultimate plan for staying young and reversing the aging process* (London: HarperCollins, 1995).
24. Thane, *Old age in English history*, p. 299.
25. Thane, *Old age in English history*, p. 300.
26. See, for instance, C.F. Karlsen, *The devil in the shape of a woman: Witchcraft in colonial New England* (New York: Vintage, 1989).
27. F. Bound Alberti, *This mortal coil: The human body in history and culture* (Oxford: Oxford University Press, 2016), introduction.
28. A. Vickery, 'Mutton dressed as lamb? Fashioning age in Georgian England', *Journal of British Studies*, 52 (2013), pp. 858–86.
29. For an introduction to the biography, see A. Janssens, 'The rise and decline of the male breadwinner family? An overview of the debate', *International Review of Social History*, 42 (1997), pp. 1–23.
30. P. Sharpe, *Adapting to capitalism: Working women in the English economy, 1700–1850* (Basingstoke: Macmillan, 2000).

31. L.A. Botelho, *Old age and the English poor law, 1500–1700* (Woodbridge: Boydell Press, 2004), p. 137.
32. L.H. Lees, *The solidarities of strangers: The English poor laws and the people, 1700–1948* (Cambridge: Cambridge University Press, 1998), p. 116.
33. Yallop, *Age and identity*, introduction.
34. For a dated but still useful discussion, see J. Roebuck, 'When does old age begin? The evolution of the English definition', *Journal of Social History*, 12 (1979), pp. 416–28.
35. S.L. Gatto and S.H. Tak, 'Computer, internet, and e-mail use among older adults: Benefits and barriers', *Educational Gerontology*, 22 (2008), pp. 800–11.
36. G.M. Jones, 'Elderly people and domestic crime: Reflections on ageism, sexism, victimology', *The British Journal of Criminology*, 27 (1987), pp. 191–201.
37. J. de Jong-Gierveld, F. Kamphuis, and P. Dykstra, 'Old and lonely?', *Comprehensive Gerentology*, 1 (1987), pp. 13–17.
38. Shanas et al., *Old people*, p. 3.
39. C. Victor, S. Scambler, and J. Bond, 'Social exclusion and social isolation', in C. Victor, S. Scambler, and J. Bond (eds), *The social world of older people: Understanding loneliness and social isolation in later life* (Maidenhead: Open University Press, 2009), pp. 168–200.
40. See my blog post: http://the-history-girls.blogspot.com/2018/08/the-lifeline-of-libraries-in-age-of.html, accessed 3 April 2019.
41. J. Kempton and S. Tomlin, *Ageing alone: Loneliness and the 'oldest old'* (London: CentreForum, 2014), p. 7.
42. https://www.huffingtonpost.co.uk/fran-whittakerwood/the-rise-of-the-silver-su_b_16255428.html?guccounter=1, accessed 30 May 2018.
43. H. Song et al., 'Does Facebook make you lonely? A meta analysis', *Computers in Human Behavior*, 36 (2014), pp. 446–52.

Chapter 7

1. The poem reads backwards and forwards, with a different meaning depending on how it is read. See: https://brianbilston.com/2016/03/23/refugees, accessed 1 June 2018.
2. https://ec.europa.eu/echo/refugee-crisis, accessed 4 April 2019.
3. A. Nickerson et al., 'Emotion dysregulation mediates the relationship between trauma exposure, post-migration living difficulties and

psychological outcomes in traumatized refugees', *Journal of Affective Disorders*, 173 (2015), pp. 185–92.

4. The following citations are taken from the *Oxford English Dictionary Online*, 'homelessness', accessed 1 October 2017.
5. L. Woodbridge, 'The neglected soldier as vagrant, revenger, tyrant slayer in early modern England', in A.L. Beier and P.R. Ocobock (eds), *Cast out: Vagrancy and homelessness in global and historical perspective* (Athens, OH: Ohio University Press, 2008), pp. 64–87.
6. J. Taylor, *The eighth wonder of the world, or Coriats escape from his supposed drowning* (London: Nicholas Okes, 1613), n.p.
7. http://www.legislation.gov.uk/ukpga/1977/48/contents/enacted.
8. J. Henley, 'The homelessness crisis in England: A perfect storm', *The Guardian*, 25 June 2018: https://www.theguardian.com/society/2014/jun/25/homelessness-crisis-england-perfect-storm, accessed 29 May 2018.
9. S. Madden, *Themistocles, the lover of his country, a tragedy* (London: R. King, 1729), p. 2.
10. Henley, 'The homelessness crisis'.
11. F.S. Wiggins, *The monthly repository and library of entertaining knowledge*, vol. 1 (New York: Francis Wiggins, 1831), p. 27.
12. https://www.crisis.org.uk/ending-homelessness/homelessness-knowledge-hub, accessed 29 May 2018.
13. T.S. Dowse, *The brain and the nerves: Their ailments and their exhaustion* (London; Paris; Madrid: Baillière, Tindal and Cox, 1884), p. 134. See also M. Gijswijt-Hofstra and R. Porter, *Cultures of neurasthenia from Beard to the First World War* (Amsterdam: Rodopi, 2001).
14. 'Homelessness in Canada: Past, Present, Future', keynote address at Growing Home: Housing and Homelessness in Canada University of Calgary, 18 February 2009.
15. A. Rokach, 'Loneliness of the marginalized', *Open Journal of Depression*, 3 (2014), pp. 147–53.
16. A. Bloom, 'Review essay: Toward a history of homelessness', *Journal of Urban History*, 31 (2005), pp. 907–17.
17. Rokach, 'Loneliness of the marginalized', p. 148.
18. J. Sandford, *Cathy come home* (London: Marion Boyars, 2002); K. Loach, *Cathy come home* (BBC Television, 16 November 1966).
19. A. Rokach, 'Private lives in public places: Loneliness of the homeless', *Social Indicators Research*, 72 (2005), pp. 99–114.

20. http://www.legislation.gov.uk/ukpga/1977/48/contents/enacted, accessed 4 April 2019; D. Paget, '"Cathy come home" and "accuracy" in British Television Drama', *New Theatre Quarterly*, 15 (1999), pp. 75–90.
21. Rokach, 'Private lives in public places', p. 103.
22. A. Tomas and H. Dittmar, 'The experience of homeless women: An exploration of housing histories and the meaning of home', *Housing Studies*, 10 (1995), pp. 493–515.
23. N. Myers, 'Environmental refugees: A growing phenomenon of the 21st century', *Philosophical Transactions of the Royal Society B: Biological Sciences*, 357 (2002), pp. 609–13.
24. T. Piacentini, 'Refugee solidarity in the everyday', *Soundings: A Journal of Politics and Culture*, 64 (2016), pp. 57–61.
25. P.J.M. Strijk, B. van Meijel, and C.J. Gamel, 'Health and social needs of traumatized refugees and asylum seekers: An exploratory study', *Perspectives in Psychiatric Care*, 47 (2011), pp. 48–55.
26. Strijk, van Meijel, and Gamel, 'Health and social needs'.
27. Strijk, van Meijel, and Gamel, 'Health and social needs'.
28. J. Strong et al., 'Health status and health needs of older refugees from Syria in Lebanon', *Conflict and Health*, 9 (2015), pp. 8–10: https://doi.org/10.1186/s13031-014-0029-y.
29. E. Gruffydd and J. Randle, 'Alzheimer's disease and the psychosocial burden for caregivers', *Community Practitioner*, 79 (2006), pp. 15–18.
30. G.C. Wenger, 'Elderly carers: The need for appropriate intervention', *Ageing & Society*, 10 (1990), pp. 197–219.
31. Strong et al., 'Health status and health needs', p. 8.

Chapter 8

1. https://schloss-post.com/objects-of-solitude, accessed 1 July 2017.
2. C. Buse, D. Martin, and S. Nettleton, 'Conceptualising "materialities of care": Making visible mundane material culture in health and social care contexts', *Sociology of Health and Illness*, 40 (2018), pp. 243–55, 244.
3. A. Pechurina, *Material cultures, migrations, and identities: What the eye cannot see* (Dordrecht: Springer, 2016).
4. S.H. Dudley, *Materialising exile: Material culture and embodied experience among Karenni refugees in Thailand* (New York; Oxford: Berghahn Books, 2010).

5. M. Epp, '"The dumpling in my soup was lonely just like me": Food in the memories of Mennonite women refugees', *Women's History Review*, 25 (2016), pp. 365–81.
6. J.T. Cacioppo and W. Patrick, *Loneliness: Human nature and the need for social connection* (New York: W.W. Norton & Company, 2008).
7. http://www.contemporaryartsociety.org/news/friday-dispatch-news/daria-martin-hunger-artist-maureen-paley-london, accessed 1 February 2019.
8. F. Bound Alberti, *This mortal coil: The human body in history and culture* (Oxford: Oxford University Press, 2016).
9. M.A. Bauer et al., 'Cuing consumerism: Situational materialism undermines personal and social well-being', *Psychological Science*, 23 (2012), pp. 517–23.
10. T. Kasser et al., 'Materialistic values: Their causes and consequences', *Psychology and Consumer Culture: The Struggle for a Good Life in a Materialistic World*, 1 (2004), pp. 11–28.
11. L. Van Boven, M.C. Campbell, and T. Gilovich, 'Stigmatizing materialism: On stereotypes and impressions of materialistic and experiential pursuits', *Personality and Social Psychology Bulletin*, 36 (2010), pp. 551–63.
12. R. Pieters, 'Bidirectional dynamics of materialism and loneliness: Not just a vicious cycle', *Journal of Consumer Research*, 40 (2013), pp. 615–31.
13. R.M. Ryan and E.L. Deci, 'Self-determination theory and the facilitation of intrinsic motivation, social development and well-being', *American Psychologist*, 555 (2000), pp. 68–78.
14. A. Pope, *Essay on man* (Princeton, NJ: Princeton University Press, 2016), with introduction by Tom Jones, pp. lxxvii, 61, 72.
15. For example, N. Epley et al., 'Creating social connection through inferential reproduction: Loneliness and perceived agency in gadgets, gods, and greyhounds', *Psychological Science*, 19 (2008), pp. 114–20.
16. L.A. Keefer et al., 'Attachment to objects as compensation for close others' perceived unreliability', *Journal of Experimental Social Psychology*, 48 (2012), pp. 912–17.
17. R.W. Belk, G. Güliz, and S. Askegaard, 'The fire of desire: A multisited inquiry into consumer passion', *Journal of Consumer Research*, 30 (2003), pp. 326–51.
18. Belk, Güliz, and Askegaard, 'The fire of desire'.
19. Y.K. Kim, J. Kang, and M. Kim, 'The relationships among family and social interaction, loneliness, mall shopping motivation, and

mall spending of older consumers', *Psychology & Marketing*, 22 (2005), pp. 995–1015.

20. R.L. Rubenstein, 'The significance of personal objects to older people', *Journal of Ageing Studies*, 1 (1987), pp. 225–38.
21. Rubenstein, 'The significance of personal objects', p. 229.
22. Rubenstein, 'The significance of personal objects', p. 236.
23. J. Fast, *Body language* (New York: M. Evans, 1970, repr. 2002), pp. 7–8.
24. Fast, *Body language*, p. 7.
25. Queen Victoria's journal, RA VIC/MAIN/WVJ, 3 June 1862.
26. Cited in H. Rappaport, *Magnificent obsession: Victoria, Albert and the death that changed monarchy* (London: Windmill Books, 2012), p. 136.
27. Rappaport, *Magnificent obsession*, pp. 136–7.
28. Rappaport, *Magnificent obsession*, p. 184.
29. Queen Victoria's journal, RA VIC/MAIN/WVJ, 22 February 1864.
30. Cited in H. Rappaport, *Magnificent obsession*, p. 184.
31. F. Bound [Alberti], 'An "uncivill" culture: Marital violence and domestic politics in York, c. 1660–c. 1760', in M. Hallett and J. Rendall (eds), *Eighteenth-century York: Culture, space and society* (York: Borthwick Institute, 2003).
32. S. Downes, S. Holloway, and S. Randles, *Feeling things: Objects and emotions through history* (Oxford: Oxford University Press, 2018).
33. O. Riis and L. Woodhead, *A sociology of religious emotion* (Oxford: Oxford University Press, 2010).
34. Riis and Woodhead, *A sociology of religious emotion*, p. 61.
35. M.R. Banks and W.A. Banks, 'The effects of animal-assisted therapy on loneliness in an elderly population in long-term facilities', *The Journals of Gerontology*, 57 (2002), pp. 428–32.
36. M.R. Banks et al., 'Animal-assisted therapy and loneliness in nursing homes: Use of robotic versus living dogs', *Journal of the American Medical Directors Association*, 9 (2008), pp. 173–7.
37. J. Heathcote, 'Paws for thought: Involving animals in care', *Nursing and Residential Care*, 12 (2010), pp. 145–8.
38. F. Bound Alberti, *This mortal coil*.
39. As a bizarre aside, the slogan was based on the final words of convicted killer, Gary Gilmore, just before a firing squad executed him in Utah in 1977: 'Let's do it'. See Jeremy W. Peters, 'The birth of "Just do it" and other magic words', *New York Times*, 19 August 2009: https://www.nytimes.com/2009/08/20/business/media/20adco.html, accessed 8 June 2018.

40. J.T. Cacioppo and W. Patrick, *Loneliness: Human nature and the need for social connection* (New York: W.W. Norton, 2009): http://www.nytimes.com/2012/12/09/opinion/sunday/the-chill-of-loneliness.html?_r=1, accessed 9 March 2018.
41. Bound Alberti, *This mortal coil*, introduction.
42. L. Blair, 'Loneliness isn't inevitable: A guide to making new friends as an adult', *The Guardian*, 30 April 2018: https://www.theguardian.com/lifeandstyle/2018/apr/30/how-to-make-new-friends-adult-lonely-leap-of-faith, accessed 8 April 2019.
43. T. Duffey, 'Saying goodbye', *Journal of Creativity in Mental Health*, 1 (2005), pp. 287–95.
44. A. Beetz et al., 'Psychosocial and psychophysiological effects of human–animal interactions: The possible role of oxytocin', *Frontiers in Psychology*, 3 (2012), p. 234.
45. S. Sussman, *Substance and behavioural addictions: Concepts, causes and cures* (Cambridge: Cambridge University Press, 2017), p. 4.
46. J.T. Cacioppo and L.C. Hawkley, 'Loneliness', in M.R. Leary and R.H. Hoyle (eds), *Handbook of individual differences in social behavior* (New York: Guilford Press, 2009), pp. 227–40, abstract.
47. https://www.mind.org.uk/information-support/tips-for-everyday-living/loneliness/#.WvQenyPMzVo, accessed 9 May 2017.
48. F. Fromm-Reichmann, 'Loneliness', *Psychiatry: Journal for the Study of Interpersonal Processes*, 22 (1959), pp. 1–15, discussed in W.G. Bennis et al., *Interpersonal dynamics: Essays and readings on human interaction* (London: Dorsey Press; Irwin-Dorsey International, 1973), p. 131.
49. J.A. Bargh and I. Shalev, 'The substitutability of physical and social warmth in daily life', *Emotion*, 12 (2012), pp. 154–62.
50. B. Bruce and W.S. Agras, 'Binge eating in females: A population-based investigation', *International Journal of Eating Disorders*, 12 (1992), pp. 365–73.
51. J.F. Schumaker et al., 'Experience of loneliness by obese individuals', *Psychological Reports*, 57 (1985), pp. 1147–54.
52. T.P. Chithambo and S.J. Huey, 'Black/white differences in perceived weight and attractiveness among overweight women', *Journal of Obesity*, 2013: https://doi.org/10.1155/2013/320326; K.J. Flynn and M. Fitzgibbon, 'Body images and obesity risk among black females: A review of the literature', *Annals of Behavioral Medicine*, 20 (1998), pp. 13–24.

53. T. Matthews et al., 'Sleeping with one eye open: Loneliness and sleep quality in young adults', *Psychological Medicine*, 47 (2017), pp. 2177–86.
54. I.S. Whitaker et al., 'Hirudo medicinalis: Ancient origins of, and trends in the use of medicinal leeches throughout history', *British Journal of Oral and Maxillofacial Surgery*, 42 (2004), pp. 133–7; J.M. Hyson, 'Leech therapy: A history', *Journal of the History of Dentistry*, 53 (2005), pp. 25–7.
55. C. Sengoopta, *The most secret quintessence of life: Sex, glands, and hormones, 1850–1950* (Chicago, IL: University of Chicago Press, 2006).
56. https://www.ageuk.org.uk/doncaster/our-services/circles-for-independence-in-later-life and https://www.ageuk.org.uk/services/in-your-area/men-in-sheds, accessed 8 April 2019; F. Bound Alberti, 'Loneliness is a modern illness of the body, not just the mind', *The Guardian*, 1 November 2018: https://www.theguardian.com/commentisfree/2018/nov/01/loneliness-illness-body-mind-epidemic, accessed 8 April 2019.
57. L. Bickerdike et al., 'Social prescribing: Less rhetoric and more reality. A systematic review of the evidence', *British Medical Journal Open*, 7 (2017), e013384.
58. J.L. Hillman, *Clinical perspectives on elderly sexuality* (New York; London: Springer, 2011), introduction.
59. F. Bound Alberti, 'From the big five to emotional clusters: In search of meaning in the history of emotions', submitted to *Emotion Review*, 2019.
60. B. Pease and A. Pease, *The definitive book of body language: The hidden meaning behind people's gestures and expressions* (London: Orion, 2005).
61. W.L. Gardner et al., 'On the outside looking in: Loneliness and social monitoring', *Personality and Social Psychology Bulletin*, 31 (2005), pp. 1549–60.
62. K. Thomas, 'Introduction', in J. Bremmer and H. Roodenburg (eds), *A cultural history of gesture: From antiquity to the present day* (Utrecht: Polity Press, 1991), pp. 1–14, 2.
63. A. Forbes, 'Caring for older people: Loneliness', *British Medical Journal*, 313 (1996), pp. 352–4, 353.
64. Thanks to Sarah Nettleton for sharing her and her colleagues' work, especially C. Bus, D. Martin, and S. Nettleton, 'Conceptualising "materialities of care": Making visible mundane material culture in health and social care contexts', *Sociology of Health and Illness*, 40 (2018), pp. 243–55.
65. For example, J. Davidson, M.M. Smith, and L. Bondi (eds), *Emotional geographies* (Farnham: Ashgate, 2012).

66. M. MacDonald, *Mystical bedlam: Madness, anxiety and healing in seventeenth-century England* (Cambridge: Cambridge University Press, 1981).
67. F. Bound [Alberti], 'An "uncivill" culture'.
68. F. Murphy, 'Loneliness: A challenge for nurses caring for older people', *Nursing Older People*, 18 (2006), pp. 22–5.
69. M.M.S. Lima and A.P. Vieira, 'Ballroom dance as therapy for the elderly in Brazil', *American Journal of Dance Therapy*, 29 (2007), pp. 129–42.

Chapter 9

1. V. Woolf, *A writer's diary* (London: Hogarth Press, 1954), 10 September 1928.
2. O. Laing, *The lonely city: Adventures in the art of being alone* (London: Canongate, 2017).
3. L. Nocblin, 'Edward Hopper and the imagery of alienation', *Art Journal*, 41 (1981), pp. 136–41.
4. W. Deresiewicz, 'The end of solitude', *The Chronicle of Higher Education*, 55 (2009), 6.
5. F. Kermode, *Romantic image* (London: Routledge, 2002).
6. See G. Russell and C. Tuite (eds), *Romantic sociability: Social networks and literary culture in Britain, 1770–1840* (Cambridge: Cambridge University Press, 2006), p. 4.
7. W. Blake, *Jerusalem* (1804), foreword by Geoffrey Keynes (London: William Blake Trust, 1953).
8. R.L. Brett and A.R. Jones (eds), *Wordsworth and Coleridge: Lyrical ballads* (London; New York: Routledge, 2005), introduction.
9. S. Pile, 'Emotions and affect in recent human geography', *Transactions of the Institute of British Geographers*, 35 (2010), pp. 5–20.
10. S. de Vries et al., 'Streetscape greenery and health: Stress, social cohesion and physical activity as mediators', *Social Science & Medicine*, 94 (2013), pp. 26–33.
11. V. Janković, *Confronting the climate: British airs and the making of environmental medicine* (New York: Palgrave Macmillan, 2010).
12. S. McEathron, 'Wordsworth, lyrical ballads, and the problem of peasant poetry', *Nineteenth Century Literature*, 54 (1999), pp. 1–26.
13. M. Wollstonecraft Shelley, *Frankenstein, or the Modern Prometheus* (1818 edition, Wisehouse Classics Kindle edition).
14. Shelley, *Frankenstein*, p. 59.

15. On wandering women, see A. Keane, *Women writers and the English nation in the 1790s: Romantic belongings* (Cambridge: Cambridge University Press, 2000).
16. http://the-history-girls.blogspot.com/2017/12/the-heart-of-westminster-abbey-poets.html, accessed 1 June 2018.
17. J.C. Kaufman (ed.), *Creativity and mental illness* (Cambridge: Cambridge University Press, 2014).
18. S. Cain, *Quiet: The power of introverts in a world that can't stop talking* (New York: Crown, 2012).
19. On the life and works of Virginia Woolf, see: H. Lee, *Virginia Woolf* (New York: A.A. Knopf, 1997).
20. Lee, *Virginia Woolf*, pp. 127, 754.
21. A.V. Woolf, *A room of one's own* (Harmondsworth: Penguin, 1973).
22. Woolf, *A writer's diary*, 10 September 1929.
23. Woolf, *A writer's diary*, 10 August 1940.
24. Woolf, *A writer's diary*, 26 September 1920.
25. V. Woolf, *To the lighthouse* (Oxford: Oxford University Press, 2006), p. 101.
26. B. Mijuskovic, 'Loneliness and time-consciousness', *Philosophy Today*, 22 (1978), pp. 276–86.
27. On daydreaming and temporal loneliness, see: R.A. Mar, M.F. Mason, and A. Litvack, 'How daydreaming relates to life satisfaction, loneliness, and social support: The importance of gender and daydream content', *Consciousness and Cognition*, 21 (2012), pp. 401–7.
28. Woolf, *A room of one's own* (London: Penguin, 2000), p. 66.
29. Woolf, *A writer's diary*, 11 October 1929.
30. The phrase is most commonly associated with Nietzsche's *Thus spoke Zarathustra: A book for all and none* (1883–91), though it was used in an earlier work.
31. R.M. Rilke, *Rilke and Andreas-Salomé: A love story in letters*, trans. E. Snow and M. Winkler (New York; London: W.W. Norton, 2008), p. 248.
32. M. Sarton, *Journal of a solitude* (London: The Women's Press, 1994), p. 23.
33. M. Sarton, *At seventy: A journal* (South Yarmouth, MA: Curley, 1984).
34. Sarton, *Journal of a solitude*, 18 September, p. 6.
35. K. Kuyper and T. Fokkema, 'Loneliness among older lesbian, gay, and bisexual adults: The role of minority stress', *Archives of Sexual Behavior*, 39 (2010), pp. 1171–80.

36. M. Sullivan and J.S. Wodarski, 'Social alienation in gay youth', *Journal of Human Behaviour in the Social Environment*, 5 (2002), pp. 1–17.
37. M. Bucholtz, '"Why be normal?": Language and identity practices in a community of nerd girls', *Language in Society*, 28 (1999), pp. 203–23.
38. J. Alexander, 'Beyond identity: Queer values and community', *International Journal of Sexuality and Gender Studies*, 4 (1999), pp. 293–314.
39. M.-L. Bernadac, *Louise Bourgeois: Destruction of the father reconstruction of the father: Writings and interviews 1923–1997* (London: Violette Editions, 1998), p. 132.
40. K. Ball, 'Who'd fuck an ableist?', *Disability Studies Quarterly*, 15 (2002), pp. 166–72.
41. L. Chittaro, and A. Vianello, 'Evaluation of a mobile mindfulness app distributed through on-line stores: A 4-week study', *International Journal of Human-Computer Studies*, 86 (2016), pp. 63–80; P. O'Morain, *Mindfulness for worriers: Overcome everyday stress and anxiety* (London: Yellow Kite, 2015).

Conclusion

1. F. Braudel, *On history*, trans. S. Matthews (Chicago, IL; London: University of Chicago Press; Weidenfeld and Nicolson, 1982).
2. R. Rorty, *The linguistic turn: Essays in philosophical method* (Chicago, IL: University of Chicago Press, 1992); N.Z. Davies, *Fiction in the archives: Pardon tales and their tellers in sixteenth-century France* (Stanford, CA: Stanford University Press, 1987); D. Sabean, *Power in the blood: Popular culture and village discourse in early modern Germany* (Cambridge: Cambridge University Press, 1984); R. Darnton, *The great cat massacre and other episodes in French cultural history* (New York: Basic Books, 1999).
3. For a useful introduction to the big theories in emotion history, see J. Plamper, 'The history of emotions: An interview with William Reddy, Barbara Rosenwein, and Peter Stearns', *History and Theory*, 49 (2010), pp. 237–65.
4. P.N. Stearns and C.Z. Stearns, 'Emotionology: Clarifying the history of emotions and emotional standards', *The American Historical Review*, 90 (1985), pp. 813–36; B. Rosenwein, *Emotional communities in the early middle ages* (Ithaca, NY: Cornell University Press, 2006); W.M. Reddy, *The navigation of feeling: A framework for the history of emotions* (Cambridge: Cambridge University Press, 2001).
5. S. Ahmed, *The cultural politics of emotion* (New York: Routledge, 2004), p. 9.

6. https://www.nhs.uk/conditions/cognitive-behavioural-therapy-cbt, accessed 1 June 2018.
7. G.F. Koob, 'The dark side of emotion: The addiction perspective', *European Journal of Pharmacology*, 15 (2015), pp. 73–87.
8. P. Bourdieu, *Outline of a theory of practice*, trans. Richard Nice (Cambridge: Cambridge University Press, 1977), introduction.
9. Bourdieu, *Outline of a theory of practice*, Part 1, The objective limits of objectivism.
10. G. Claeys, 'The "survival of the fittest" and the origins of Social Darwinism', *Journal of the History of Ideas*, 61 (2000), pp. 223–40.
11. R. Wright, *The moral animal: Why we are, the way we are: The new science of evolutionary psychology* (London: Vintage, 2010).
12. R. Dawkins, *The selfish gene* (Oxford: Oxford University Press, 1989); W.R. Goldschmidt, *The bridge to humanity: How affect hunger trumps the selfish gene* (New York: Oxford University Press, 2006).
13. I.T. Berend, *An economic history of twentieth-century Europe: Economic regimes from laissez-faire to globalization* (Cambridge: Cambridge University Press, 2016).
14. Feminist work on the construction of biology as a discipline provides a necessary relief from the constant narratives of exploitation (of nature, of the 'other', and of women and minorities) that have been inherent in the construction of the sciences. It also offers the possibility of more collaborative and pluralist approaches. See V. Shiva, 'Democratizing biology: Reinventing biology from a feminist, ecological and third world perspective', in L. Birke and R. Hubbard (eds), *Reinventing biology: Respect for life and the creation of knowledge* (Bloomington, IN: Indiana University Press, 1995), pp. 50–73.
15. A. Lovejoy, *The great chain of being: A study of the history of an idea* (Cambridge, MA: Harvard University Press, 1970).
16. G. Monbiot, 'Neoliberalism is creating loneliness: That's what's wrenching society apart', *The Guardian*, 12 October 2016: https://www.theguardian.com/commentisfree/2016/oct/12/neoliberalism-creating-loneliness-wrenching-society-apart, accessed 1 December 2017.
17. D. Leshem, *The origins of neoliberalism: Modelling the economy from Jesus to Foucault* (Abingdon: Routledge, 2017).
18. B. Skyrms, *Evolution of the social contract* (Cambridge: Cambridge University Press, 2014).
19. Claeys, 'The "survival of the fittest"'.

20. See M. Hawkins, *Social Darwinism and European and American thought, 1860–1945: Nature as model and nature as threat* (Cambridge: Cambridge University Press, 1997) and the discussion in Claeys, 'The "survival of the fittest"', p. 228.
21. https://venturebeat.com/2018/03/12/tim-berners-lee-we-need-a-legal-or-regulatory-framework-to-save-the-web-from-dominant-tech-platforms, accessed 1 June 2018.
22. https://www.bbc.co.uk/news/health-45861468, accessed 16 October 2018.
23. V. La Placa, A. McNaught, and A. Knight, 'Discourse on wellbeing in research and practice', *International Journal of Wellbeing*, 7 (2013), pp. 116–25.
24. M. Harris and K.C. Richards, 'The physiological and psychological effects of slow-stroke back massage and hand massage on relaxation in older people', *Journal of Clinical Nursing*, 19 (2010), pp. 917–26.
25. B.S. Cronfalk, P. Strang, B.M. Ternestedt et al., 'The existential experiences of receiving soft tissue massage in palliative home care: An intervention', *Support Care Cancer*, 17 (2009), pp. 1203–11, 1208.
26. https://www.spitz.org.uk, accessed 10 September 2018.
27. N. Osborne, 'How opera can stop war', *The Guardian*, 1 October 2005: https://www.theguardian.com/music/2004/oct/01/classicalmusicandopera2, accessed 16 October 2018.
28. M.M.S. Lima and A.P. Vieriea, 'Ballroom dance as therapy for the elderly in Brazil', *American Journal of Dance Therapy*, 29 (2007), pp. 129–42.
29. J. Troisi and S. Gabriel, 'Chicken soup really is good for the soul: "Comfort food" fulfils the need to belong', *Psychological Science*, 22 (2011), pp. 747–53.
30. https://menssheds.org.uk, accessed 16 October 2018.
31. I. Siraj-Blatchford, 'Learning in the home and at school: How working class children "succeed against the odds"', *British Educational Research Journal*, 36 (2010), pp. 463–82.
32. B. Rubenking et al., 'Defining new viewing behaviours: What makes and motivates TV binge-watching?', *International Journal of Digital Television*, 9 (2008), pp. 69–85; J. Blankenship and J. Hayes-Conroy, 'The flâneur, the hot-rodder, and the slow food activist: Archetypes of capitalist coasting', *ACME: An International E-Journal for Critical Geographies*, 16 (2017), pp. 185–209.

33. C. Niedzwiedz et al., 'The relationship between wealth and loneliness among older people across Europe: Is social participation protective?', *Preventive Medicine*, 91 (2016), pp. 24–31.
34. J. Pearson, *Painfully rich: J. Paul Getty and his heirs* (London: Macmillan, 1995).
35. Niedzwiedz et al., 'The relationship between wealth and loneliness'.
36. S. Chokkanathan and A.E. Lee, 'Elder mistreatment in urban India: A community based study', *Journal of Elder Abuse & Neglect*, 17 (2006), pp. 45–61.
37. C. J. Davis, 'Contagion as metaphor', *American Literary History*, 14 (2002), pp. 828–36.
38. M. Brown et al., 'Is the cure a wall? Behavioural immune system responses to a disease metaphor for immigration', *Evolutionary Psychological Science*, 17 (2019), pp. 1–14.
39. L. Entlis, 'Scientists are working on a pill for loneliness', *The Guardian*, 26 January 2019: https://www.theguardian.com/us-news/2019/jan/26/pill-for-loneliness-psychology-science-medicine, accessed 1 March 2019.
40. S. Cacioppo et al., 'Loneliness: Clinical import and interventions', *Perspectives on Psychological Science*, 10 (2015), pp. 238–49.
41. F. Bound Alberti, *This mortal coil: The human body in history and culture* (Oxford: Oxford University Press, 2016), chapter 1.

PICTURE ACKNOWLEDGEMENTS

1 Wellcome Collection
2 Archivio G.B.B./Contrasto/eyevine
3 mptvimages.com
4 Wellcome Collection
5 n/a (public domain)
6 © Age UK, used with permission
7 Photo by Matt Collamer on Unsplash
8 iStock.com/AndreyPopov
9 MS Thr 564 (55). Houghton Library, Harvard University
10 Source: Google Books Ngram Viewer (http://books.google.com/ngrams)
11 Source: Google Books Ngram Viewer (http://books.google.com/ngrams)
12 Source: Google Books Ngram Viewer (http://books.google.com/ngrams)

SOURCE ACKNOWLEDGEMENTS

Eclipse by Stephenie Meyer, copyright © 2007, 2009, reprinted by permission of Little, Brown and Co., an imprint of Hachette Book Group, Inc.

Excerpt from *A Writer's Diary* by Virginia Woolf. Copyright © 1954 by Leonard Woolf, renewed by Quentil Bell and Angelica Garnett. Reprinted by permission of Houghton Mifflin Harcourt Publishing Company. All rights reserved. All additional material by Virginia Woolf reproduced by permission of the Society of Authors as the Literary Representative of the Estate of Virginia Woolf.

The Unabridged Journals of Sylvia Plath, reproduced by permission of Penguin Random House LLC and Faber and Faber UK; *Letters of Sylvia Plath*, reproduced by permission of Harper-Collins US and Faber and Faber UK; extract from Sylvia Plath's 'Daddy', reproduced by permission of Harper-Collins US

Louise Bourgeois, diary entry, August 8, 1987 © The Easton Foundation/ VAGA at ARS, NY; reprinted in M.-L. Bernadac, *Louise Bourgeois: Destruction of the Father/Reconstruction of the Father: Writings and Interviews 1923–1997* (London: Violette Editions, 1998), p. 132.

FURTHER READING

Allen, R.L. and H. Oshagan, 'The UCLA Loneliness Scale', *Personality and Individual Differences*, 19 (1995), pp. 185–95.

Andersson, L., 'Loneliness research and interventions: A review of the literature', *Aging & Mental Health*, 2 (1998), pp. 264–74, 265.

Barrett, L.F., *How emotions are made: The secret life of the brain* (London: Macmillan, 2017).

Birke, L. and R. Hubbard, *Reinventing biology: Respect for life and the creation of knowledge* (Bloomington, IN: Indiana University Press, 1995).

Bound Alberti, F., *This mortal coil: The human body in history and culture* (Oxford: Oxford University Press, 2016).

Bound Alberti, F., '"This modern epidemic": Loneliness as both an "emotion cluster" and a neglected subject in the history of emotions', *Emotion Review*, 10 (2018), pp. 242–54.

Brittain, K., A. Kingston, K. Davies, J. Collerton, L. Robinson, T. Kirkwood, J. Bond, and C. Jagger, 'An investigation into the patterns of loneliness and loss in the oldest old: Newcastle 85+ study', *Ageing & Society*, 37 (2017), pp. 39–62.

Buse, C., D. Martin, and S. Nettleton, 'Conceptualising "materialities of care": Making visible mundane material culture in health and social care contexts', *Sociology of Health and Illness*, 40 (2018), pp. 243–55, 244.

Cacioppo, J.T., J.H. Fowler, and N.A. Christakis, 'Alone in the crowd: The structure and spread of loneliness in a large social network', *Journal of Personality and Social Psychology*, 97 (2009), pp. 977–91.

De Jong, Gierveld, 'A review of loneliness: Concept and definitions, determinants and consequences', *Reviews in Clinical Gerontology*, 8 (1998), pp. 73–80.

Durkheim, E., *The elementary forms of the religious life*, translated by K.E. Fields (New York: Free Press, 1996).

Eickhoff, J.C. and M.A. Moreno, '"Facebook depression?" Social networking site use and depression in older adolescents', *Journal of Adolescent Health*, 52 (2013), pp. 128–30.

Epp, M., '"The dumpling in my soup was lonely just like me": Food in the memories of Mennonite women refugees', *Women's History Review*, 25 (2016), pp. 365–81.

Forbes, A., 'Caring for older people: Loneliness', *British Medical Journal*, 313 (1996), pp. 352–4.

Goldschmidt, W.R., *The bridge to humanity: How affect hunger trumps the selfish gene* (New York: Oxford University Press, 2006).

Hazan, C. and P. Shaver, 'Romantic love conceptualized as an attachment process', *Journal of Personality and Social Psychology*, 52 (1987), pp. 511–24.

Kar-Purkayastha, I., 'An epidemic of loneliness', *The Lancet*, 376 (2010), pp. 2114–15.

Konstan, D., *The emotions of the ancient Greeks* (Toronto; London: University of Toronto Press, 2006).

Lutz, D., *Relics of death in Victorian literature and culture* (Cambridge: Cambridge University Press, 2015).

Matt, S., *Homesickness: An American history* (Oxford: Oxford University Press, 2011).

Monbiot, G., 'Neoliberalism is creating loneliness: That's what's wrenching society apart', *The Guardian*, 12 October 2016.

Muise, A., E. Christofides, and D. Desmarais, 'More information than you ever wanted: Does Facebook bring out the green-eyed monster of jealousy?', *CyberPsychology & Behavior*, 12 (2009), pp. 441–4.

Plath, S., *The unabridged journals of Sylvia Plath, 1950–1962*, edited by K.V. Kukil (New York: Anchor, 2000).

Plath, S., *Letters of Sylvia Plath, Volume I: 1940–1956*, edited by P.K. Steinberg and K.V. Kukil (London: Faber & Faber, 2017).

Rheingold, H., *Virtual community: Finding connection in a computerised world* (London: Secker and Warburg, 1994).

Rokach, A., 'Loneliness in cancer and multiple sclerosis patients', *Psychological Reports*, 94 (2004), pp. 637–48.

Rokach, A., 'Private lives in public places: Loneliness of the homeless', *Social Indicators Research*, 72 (2005), pp. 99–114.

Rose, H. and S. Rose, *Alas poor Darwin: Arguments against evolutionary psychology* (New York: Harmony Books, 2000).

Rosenwein, B. and R. Cristiani, *What is the history of emotions?* (Cambridge; Malden, MA: Polity Press, 2018).

Sarton, S., *Journal of a solitude* (New York: Norton, 1973).

Schirmer, W. and D. Michailakis, 'The lost Gemeinschaft: How people working with the elderly explain loneliness', *Journal of Ageing Studies*, 33 (2015), pp. 1–10.

Seeman, M., 'On the meaning of alienation', *American Sociological Review*, 24 (1959), pp. 783–91.

Snell, K.D.M., 'The rise of living alone and loneliness in history', *Social History*, 42 (2017), pp. 2–28.

Stivers, R., *Shades of loneliness: Pathologies of a technological society* (Lanham, MD; Oxford: Rowman & Littlefield, 2004).

Strijk, P.J.M., B. van Meijel, and C.J. Gamel, 'Health and social needs of traumatized refugees and asylum seekers: An exploratory study', *Perspectives in Psychiatric Care*, 47 (2011), pp. 48–55.

Svendsen, L., *A philosophy of loneliness*, translated by K. Pierce (London: Reaktion, 2017).

Vaisey, D., *The diary of Thomas Turner, 1754–1765* (East Hoathly: CTR Publishing, 1994).

Van den Hoonard, D.K., *The widowed self: The older woman's journey through widowhood* (Waterloo, Ont.: Wilfrid Laurier University Press, 2000).

Vlachantoni, A., R. Shaw, R. Willis, M. Evandrou, J. Falkingham, and R. Luff, 'Measuring unmet need for social care amongst older people', *Population Trends*, 145 (2011), pp. 60–76.

Zappavigna, M., *Discourse of Twitter and social media: How we use language to create affiliation on the web* (London: Bloomsbury Academic, 2013).

INDEX OF NAMES

For the benefit of digital users, indexed terms that span two pages (e.g., 52–53) may, on occasion, appear on only one of those pages.

INDEX OF SUBJECTS

For the benefit of digital users, indexed terms that span two pages (e.g., 52–53) may, on occasion, appear on only one of those pages.